D0908743

ALSO BY MIRIAM EHRENBERG AND OTTO EHRENBERG:

The Psychotherapy Maze
Optimum Brain Power

The
Sexual
Dynamics
of Family
Life

A Fireside Book
Published by Simon & Schuster, Inc.
New York   London   Toronto   Sydney   Tokyo

THE INTIMATE CIRCLE

MIRIAM EHRENBERG, Ph.D.,
&
OTTO EHRENBERG, Ph.D.

Copyright © 1988 by Miriam Ehrenberg, Ph.D., and Otto Ehrenberg, Ph.D.

Simon and Schuster/Fireside Books, Published by Simon & Schuster, Inc. Simon & Schuster Building Rockefeller Center 1230 Avenue of the Americas New York, New York 10020

SIMON AND SCHUSTER, FIRESIDE and colophons are registered trademarks of Simon & Schuster, Inc.

Designed by Barbara Marks Manufactured in the United States of America
1   3   5   7   9   10   8   6   4   2
1   3   5   7   9   10   8   6   4   2 Pbk.
Library of Congress Cataloging in Publication Data

Ehrenberg, Miriam.
   The intimate circle.

   "A Fireside book."
   Includes index.
   1. Sex instruction—United States.   2. Parent and child—United States.   3. Sex (Psychology) 4. Sexual ethics—United States.   I. Ehrenberg, Otto. II. Title.
HQ57.E35   1987   306.7   87-28663
              ISBN: 0-671-64455-6
                    0-671-62854-2 Pbk.

Grateful acknowledgment is made for permission to reprint the excerpt from *Something Happened* by Joseph Heller. Copyright © 1966, 1974 by Scapegoat Productions, Inc. Published 1974 by Alfred A. Knopf, Inc., and Random House, Inc.

ACKNOWLEDGMENTS

We want to thank the many people we interviewed for this book, who graciously shared their time and family experiences with us. Some have given us permission to use their names, and so we can individually say thank you to Lynn Caine, Julius Fast, Gloria Jones, Erik Lee Preminger, Alicia Travers, and Mary Travers. We also want to thank Steve Ashkinazy, clinical director of the Institute for Gay and Lesbian Youth, and Stu Gross, founder of the Gay Fathers Forum, for giving us the benefit of their experiences working with the gay community. Claire Berman, past president of the Stepfamily Association of America, provided helpful comments about stepfamilies. Some people we did not interview went out of their way to round up interviewees for us, and we would like to thank Jane Greer, Sallye Washington Jiles, Jane Kronick, Linda Nessel, Sharon Nolting, and Elizabeth Phillips for their efforts.

Our thanks also go to Barbara Gess for her belief in this project and to Deborah Bergman for her thoughtful editing. As always, our sister and attorney, Vivienne W. Nearing, provided us with expert legal counsel. Thanks, Vi.

To our daughters,
Erica and Ingrid,
and to our cousin/brother,
Walter Philip Ehrenberg,
whose love of family stretches around the globe

CONTENTS

Contents

ON THE IMPORTANCE OF SEXUAL FEELINGS IN THE FAMILY AND AN INVITATION TO INTERVIEW YOURSELF

Though few people acknowledge it, there are, within every family, constant sexual currents. These occur not only between husbands and wives but also between mothers and sons, fathers and daughters, mothers and daughters, fathers and sons, sisters and brothers.

Despite the so-called sexual revolution of recent years, very little has been said about the role of sexuality in the family, even though healthy personality development depends on recognizing and affirming sexual feelings. This does not mean acting sexual at home; it does mean respecting each other's basic sexual nature. Repressing sexual feelings is hard on everyone and makes it difficult later on for children to fall in love and create happy families of their own.

Many parents see sex as an isolated aspect of life, not very relevant before children enter puberty. They think that too much fuss is made about sex. Nothing could be further from the truth. Family attitudes towards sexuality are deeply embedded in everyday activities and shape the child's basic personality and growth. The way a parent holds children, responds to their self-explorations, or answers their questions affects how children feel about their natural impulses, how comfortable they are with their bodies, and ultimately how confident they feel about themselves when they are grown—not only as lovers but as people.

When people come to us for psychotherapy or family counseling they, like their parents, rarely see sex as an issue. Instead they come with such problems as feelings of inadequacy, inability to express their feelings spontaneously, or difficulty forming lasting relationships. These problems, though, often relate to sexual attitudes in the home. People who were brought up feeling guilty and ashamed of their sexuality do not feel positive about themselves and cannot relate comfortably to people in other areas as well.

To bring up healthy, well-adjusted children, parents need to be aware of the role family sexuality plays in personality development and of the messages they themselves send out about sex. Our purpose in writing this book is to help parents examine their real feelings about sexuality. Once we have this understanding, we can express our feelings honestly to ourselves and make informed choices about how to manage them in the family. Unfortunately, there is often a big gap between what people *think* about sex and how they *feel* about sex. When parents are unable to sort out their own feelings, children are caught up in the conflict and left to muddle through on their own.

Parents have good reason to be worried about their children's sexual behavior. In addition to moral compunctions, parents have very real fears about the potential for heartache, and about the possibility of pregnancy or infection with sexually transmitted diseases. Until recently, some solutions to all these problems, though not perfect, were available: psychotherapy to deal with the emotional scars, adoption or abortion to deal with unwanted babies, drugs to deal with venereal diseases. Of late, the dangers associated with sex have escalated. First came herpes, still without a cure, and just when we got used to coping with that fear, it was overshadowed by AIDS, which is life threatening.

Because of these new risks, the parents' role as sex educators has become much more demanding. We don't want our children to grow up the way many of us did, feeling sex is bad, but we do not want our youngsters behaving promiscuously either. For safety's sake we want our children to be cautious, but we do not want them to be too anxious about sex. We are pleased when our children turn into young men and women, but we worry that they are not mature enough to handle sex. On top of it all, many parents are so uncomfortable themselves about sex, especially as it relates to the family, that they cannot talk to their offspring about it.

To aid in clarifying the various sexual feelings that exist in families, we have pulled together the experiences of many different people to whom we've spoken, in order to show you how they deal with family sexuality and to give you insights into what works and what does not. Our practice with psychotherapy clients was a jumping-off point for this book, but the problems they face in this area are common to practically everyone. Some of the material in this book is drawn from case histories, but most of it comes from the life experiences of a broad spectrum of people representing different backgrounds and attitudes.

The people we interviewed were pleased to share their experiences because they, like us, want to find ways to help work out the sexual issues of families. We are very grateful to them because the account of their experiences so enriches this book. Occasionally we interviewed more than one member of a family to provide a rounded perspective. We requested permission to identify some respondents by name because we felt their experiences would have special significance to readers, and we are pleased that these people felt free enough to let us do so. Others have been given fictitious names to preserve their privacy. Most people we approached were exceptionally cooperative and our conversations turned out to be mutually beneficial. We accumulated valuable illustrations for this book, and our interviewees learned a lot about themselves. Virtually none of the respondents grew up in homes where sex was accepted as a wholesome part of life to be nurtured. Hardly anyone, as is to be expected under these circumstances, feels completely at ease about sex. Most of the people we talked to found, to their surprise, that they were less comfortable about sex and less permissive in their attitudes than they believed themselves to be.

Because the interview process opened up a lot of areas for thought and provided a new focus for many of the people we spoke to, we decided to include as an appendix the interview guide we used for the book. If you would like to interview yourself, you may find it most helpful to do so just after reading Chapter 1. That way you will be able to analyze the attitudes towards sexuality in your family and have that as a framework as you go through the rest of the book. It's a good idea for both parents in a family to do the interview separately and, after they finish the book, to get together and discuss their feelings about how sexual issues are handled in their home.

Miriam Ehrenberg, Ph.D.
Otto Ehrenberg, Ph.D.
New York, N.Y.

ONE

OLD SEXUAL GHOSTS
AND THE NEW
DOUBLE STANDARD

In many respects, ours is a sexually liberated society. Almost everyone agrees that sex is an important part of life, that people have sexual needs and feelings which should not be repressed, and that it is healthy both physically and emotionally to be open in expressing one's sexuality. Even though the AIDS epidemic has caused a reconsideration of our sexual mores, the issue for most people is how to have safe sex rather than whether or not to have sex. Hardly anyone gives a second look at people who buy *Penthouse,* or couples who rent an X movie for the VCR. TV panel shows let us listen in to a group of singles talking about alternate life-styles, or of gays talking about difficulties in adopting children, and Dr. Ruth answers questions about how to have good sex. People live openly together without getting married and college students share unisex bathrooms. Yet despite all this new freedom and openness, most people are still very uncomfortable about allusions to sexual feelings in the family setting. A moment's reflection will make this quite evident: how many homes do you know of in which children chat with their parents about sex without stammering and blushing, if indeed they talk about it at all? The fact remains that despite all the changes that have been occurring in sexual behavior, nothing very much has changed at home, where attitudes are formed and feelings molded.

In the family, the birthplace of sexual feelings, children are not learning from their parents how to accept and integrate sexuality into their lives. Rather, sex is bombarding the family from the outside, creating more tension within. The new sexual mores that allow greater freedom to both men and women represent not so much an organic change emanating from genuine feelings about sexuality so much as they do unassimilated social attitudes. We now have a new double standard; it is no longer a different code of sexual behavior for men and women, but a different code of behavior for inside and outside the home.

WHY PARENTS KEEP SEX OUT OF THE FAMILY

Although the family comes into being through the sexual union of husband and wife, the basic sexuality of family life makes people uncomfortable. But why is this so?

To begin with, mothers and fathers are no different from other people, having grown up with the same hang-ups as everyone else, and having learned early on that sex is supposed to be OK but really isn't. Consider, for example, the patterning of family attitudes described by Mary Travers, of the singing group Peter, Paul and Mary. Her mother was orphaned at an early age and raised by a grandmother who, according to Mary, "would have made Whistler's mother look like a lady of the evening." This great-grandmother not only molded the sexual attitudes of Mary's mother, but influenced the way in which the mother, in turn, would communicate sexual attitudes to Mary:

⊰ My great-grandmother never told my mother anything. My mother married when she was very young—seventeen and a half—and the only reason she knew she was pregnant was she fainted in the street one day and someone suggested to her that she should see a lady doctor. Truly my mother knew zip starting out. With me she was open and direct the way repressed people are direct. They know intellectually "This is what I should say" and they say it, but they're not comfortable with it. She wasn't told comfortably, but one hopes from one generation to another things get better. ⊱

The problem in talking to children, communicating attitudes, and answering their questions is, as Mary indicates, that "parents go back to the kid in themselves and the answer this kid in you gives depends on your upbringing." As will become evident when we listen to what her daughter has to say a little later, Mary Travers was more successful than most mothers in breaking away from the restrictive attitudes with which she had been raised. But her achievement does not represent the norm. In most homes, the cycle perpetuates itself: the family unit, instead of encouraging an acceptance of sexuality, remains the medium through which guilt and anxiety are first instilled. As long as sex has the connotation of something shameful, preserving "the sanctity of the home" means, in effect, keeping it sex free. Just as one leaves one's dirty galoshes at the front door, so family members are supposed to keep their sexuality on the other side of the threshold.

This is easier said than done as the home environment is particularly conducive to the expression of sexuality. Home is where strong feelings flow and engage the total sexual self. Home is also where one is supposed to let down one's hair, throw off one's clothes, relax, and be oneself. All those manifestations of sexuality that make people uptight—nudity, wet bodies, exploratory play, masturbation—are more apt to occur in the family setting than elsewhere.

Much of parents' concerns about the sexuality of children grows out of a broader concern about their children's development. All parents want their children to do well, to be liked, to be popular. Sexuality in children worries parents because they are afraid it may keep their children from gaining social approval, ruin their reputations, or threaten the parents' image. Some parents are concerned that sexuality in children will divert them from other pursuits. Parents are also worried about disease, pregnancy, homosexuality, and painful emotional consequences and find sexuality hard to tolerate as it raises their anxiety level about their children. As Mary Travers reflected, we do not trust our children to be able to handle situations that we ourselves have survived:

≈§ One of the things about parents, we all trust our own selves. When we wanted to do something and did it, we either felt guilt about it or didn't feel guilty about it or jettisoned the guilt, or whatever, but it was all right because we survived it. But somehow we don't give our children credit for the ability to survive something that we have been able to survive. Somehow we feel we have produced some kind of weak thing that is going to be shattered by something

22

that didn't shatter us. I don't understand why we do that. It may be part of that protective shield, the nurturing shield that deliberately forgets what is survivable. ঌ

Still other factors contribute to making parents uncomfortable with sexuality in the home. For one thing, the sexuality of children can threaten parents' authority and their perceived roles. Many families maintain their stability through clear-cut role divisions and parents do not want children crossing the line from child to adult behavior or usurping parental prerogatives. In similar fashion, parents may have difficulty granting their children what they were themselves denied. Parents who were reared in sexually repressive environments find it evokes their feelings of deprivation to see children experiencing pleasures that they were forbidden. Eliza, a working mother of two teenagers, told us that after she married and visited her parents for the weekend, they would "accept" her sleeping in the same room with her husband but not behavior that suggested enjoyment of sex:

ঌ We slept at my parents' beach house after we were married and they accepted it, but they did not like us taking a shower together. Mom said, "We don't like that. It makes us very uncomfortable." And I said, "This is what we do. We're married now," but she said it made them uncomfortable and it was their house. After that I told her, "If that's the way it's going to be, well then we can't come out here. This is the way we treat our married life." ঌ

Not only can the emerging sexuality of children activate parental feelings of envy and rivalry, but it can also dredge up despair about aging. Fathers are less apt to feel bad about their waning potency or mothers about their fading attractiveness if their growing children are discouraged from expressing sexuality at home.

Perhaps the biggest stumbling block to acknowledging sexuality in the family stems from the confusion of sexuality with sex. Appreciating and respecting the sexuality of a family member is a far cry from engaging in sexual acts with a family member, but people are so afraid of the possibility of incest that they reject healthy sexual feelings as well. The thought of incest arouses instant horror in most people's minds, yet the horrible thing about incest is not the sexual feelings and fantasies family members evoke in one another but the sexual acts one forces on another. Most acts of incest do not grow out of love for the other person but out of a need to satisfy oneself sexually without regard to the other person. Children who stand in unequal power positions relative to their parents and older siblings are used in exploitative fashion to provide sexual gratification to the latter. Even though incest does not occur in most homes, fears about incest can make it difficult for family members to accept each other's sexuality. Acknowledging sexual feelings between parents and children, however, makes it possible to bring them under control and allows family members to enjoy one another without being threatened. Dr. Mary Calderone, a pioneer in the field of sex education, and her collaborator Eric Johnson note in *The Family Book About Sexuality* that "many parents . . . feel sexually turned on by their own children . . . and these feelings are usually disturbing to the mother or father. Children, too, can have sexual feelings towards their parents. It is helpful for both parents and children to know that such feelings are common and, if they are managed reasonably, are nothing to be ashamed of."[*]

More positively, awareness and appreciation of one another's sexuality enhances family life. Julius Fast, who has written several books about sex, most recently *Sexual Chemistry*, described to us the warm glow that comes with the ability to acknowledge family sexual feelings:

⋖§ I know that when my girls were born I definitely felt a sexual bond—a sexual feeling. I can understand how any father would have sexual feelings towards a daughter. I just know it's something we cover up. I experienced a sexual feeling from the time they were little girls, but it was

---

[*] Mary S. Calderone and Eric W. Johnson, *The Family Book About Sexuality* (New York: Bantam Books, 1983), p. 150.

something I acknowledged to myself, and I said it's there and it's kind of nice. When my son was born I felt the same kind of sexuality toward him, a tremendous love, and you almost felt you could embrace the kid sexually. But I think that's a normal feeling that fathers get and just push down. It may have been more intense with the girls—more sexual with the girls. I can easily understand an Oedipal arrangement—how a kid can fall in love with a mother. I know there had come a time when my wife said to the girls, "No, you're not going to marry Daddy. I've got him, and you've got to find someone for yourself." My son said, "I'm going to marry Mommy when I grow up," and I said to him, "You're not going to marry Mommy. She's mine." So I think there are sexual feelings in the family and you just deal with them. Now my granddaughter is going to marry me. I think there's a sexual component, always, that society has taught us to push out, but if for some reason you can allow yourself to feel it, then you know it's there. And it's a lovely feeling. It's just a matter of control. And you control it, you sort of cherish it, and it turns into paternal love. It's control in the sense that you don't allow it to get to the point where it might disturb the kid. Perhaps what I call sexuality is parental love, but I certainly think that some of it is a sexual element—and it's a nice warm thing. ❧

Few parents, however, are so adept at dealing with their sexual feelings. Probably more typical is Jack, a biogeneticist who has an eighteen-year-old daughter, Melissa, from a first marriage and a two-year-old daughter, Amy, from his present marriage. Jack considers himself liberated about sexual issues but nevertheless has a hard time accepting the sexuality of his older daughter and is even too uncomfortable to have any conversations with her about sex:

❧ I'm trying to accept her growing up and I'm really very proud of her, but underneath it all, way, way, way back there somewhere, behind the young woman, there's the adolescent, there's the child, all the way back there's the close intimacy with the young child, and the cuddling and the holding and the coming into bed for a visit in the morning and all that it had behind it, and if you weren't careful, maybe a little sexual overtone to it. And all through her upbringing, lurking in the background, there could be sexuality stimulated. As she got older, maybe I became afraid of my own sexual feelings and I stopped talking to her about sex. Somehow I think there are limits to what a father and daughter should talk about in this area. When it gets down to physical sexuality, that's not an appropriate subject to talk about. Maybe after all I'm turning out to be very Victorian. ଈ∾

If anything, Jack is more reticent now with Amy than he was before with Melissa, who he feared was overstimulated by him:

∾§ When Melissa was around three or four, I took baths with her. That was a mistake. It is too stimulating for children of the opposite sex to take baths with their parents. It's over-stimulating for a daughter and a father to be naked together in the bathtub. It was one of those things of the sixties. A lot of those things were wonderful, but that wasn't one of the better ideas. I now feel it is inappropriate to be naked at all with your children of the opposite sex. A month or two ago, I was drying myself and then covered myself up with the towel when Amy just came into the bathroom, out of nowhere, and her hand just absolutely shot up under the towel and grabbed me. Suddenly she had just become aware of something. I was completely nonplussed, but I didn't say a word. I just put my trousers on. ଈ∾

Jack's present wife Betsy, a copy editor with a magazine, feels very differently. In her opinion, Amy is not getting enough input from her father and he is keeping himself artificially removed:

∾§ I think I'm freer with Amy physically. There's a lot of hugging and kissing and touching and rubbing. She does it with me, and I with her. She kisses on the lips and I kiss her on the lips. Jack told me that wasn't such a good thing to do and he didn't like to do it, and it should always be on the cheek. I told him I thought that was silly. A child wants to kiss you on the mouth, so what? Go ahead and do it. I think he may be more behind in responding than I am because he doesn't want to foul her up. Because when his older daughter was a little girl they would take showers together and bathe together, and she was very unhappy with her father for quite a while. So now he's trying to be more conservative with Amy, but I don't see it. He doesn't let her see him naked at all. Never. She saw him the other day and noticed that he had a bulge under the towel, and so she squeezed it. He tried not to react. She must know at this point that she and I undress together but when it's she and Daddy only she undresses. I think she must notice that. Oh yes, I like to play with her and nibble her ear, and it makes her laugh. He thinks it's too sexual, but I do it anyway. I think he's not sure what's appropriate and inappropriate and I think he wants to cool it. It feels right to me and I've always been very affectionate, and she likes to giggle and I like to make her giggle. I can't see how hugging and kissing is going to screw somebody up. ❧

THE FAMILY AS HOMEROOM FOR SEX EDUCATION

Because of these discomforts with sexuality in the family, many parents try to avoid dealing with it, at least until puberty. They prefer to think that sexualization does not start until this point, and that sex education is unnecessary beforehand. Some parents maintain this fiction right up to their children's marriage. We still occasionally hear about parents whose first acknowledgement of sex comes the night before the wedding, when they unobtrusively put a book about sex on their child's night table. One mother who tried to make believe that sex did not exist was, surprisingly, Gypsy Rose Lee. Although she worked for many years as a stripper and took her son on the road with her, as far as their family life went sex was virtually nonexistent. In his book *Gypsy and Me*, Erik Lee Preminger describes how his mother's asexual attitude permeated their relationship.* In conversation he told us about how his mother avoided talking to him even about the basic "facts of life":

&§ She never talked with me about sex. When I was, I guess, eleven years old, some of the kids at camp started teasing me because I didn't know anything about ejaculation or anything like that. I didn't know what they were talking about. The kids suggested that I go and ask my mother about it when I got home. And so I did, and I said, "Mother," I always called her Mother, "what are the facts of life?" And she said, "Oh, birth, death, marriage, things like that, dear." She was very uncomfortable, hard as it is to believe, about sex. §&

Although we may not like it, children are born as sexual beings, and parents, whether or not they are aware of it, are constantly providing lessons in sex education. The way parents respond to a child's innate sexuality and allow it to unfold is the core of a child's sex education. *This response does more to mold that child's mature sexual behavior than all the information or misinformation parents may provide.*

The process of shaping a child's sexuality starts at day one. When a child is born, the first thing announced about this new person is its sex—"It's a girl," "It's a boy"—and from that moment on, sexuality continues to play a central role in a child's life. Just as babies are born with functioning respiratory and digestive systems, they also are born with functioning sexual-response systems and the capacity for sexual pleasure. Girl babies start producing fluid in the vagina that is a precursor of the lubricating fluid of mature women. Boy babies start having erections in utero, again the precursor of many more to come. In fact, one of the signs that a baby is healthy is that its sexual organs are sensitive to touch and provide gratification. Human beings are born with a capacity for erotic feelings. The child's comfort with and acceptance of his or her own body will be greatly influenced

---

* Erik Lee Preminger, *Gypsy and Me* (Boston: Little, Brown & Company, 1984).

by the way the parents respond to the baby's natural expression of its sexuality.

Infants and small children not only derive their sense of security from being held and feeling their parents' skin against their own, but the tender caresses also help the baby enjoy its own body and set the stage for the expression of erotic love later in life. Parents also shape the infant's attitude to its own body by the way they react to the baby's self-exploratory behavior: they may either encourage or unknowingly interfere with the development of a natural, unselfconscious sexuality. Parents who are delighted when a baby discovers its toes often experience embarrassment when a baby discovers its genitals and begin to send out negative messages about self-exploration. A baby can't feel good about its body, however, if that baby is not allowed to experience how good *all* of its body feels.

While the baby is being given an education about its body, it is also learning about its gender. Parents give a baby many cues that mold its gender identity aside from the still-traditional pink and blue blankets. Even before babies can understand language, they are taught through tone of voice, touch, and gesture that they are little boys or little girls, reinforcing whatever gender-based predispositions exist. Research indicates that parents behave quite differently towards baby girls and baby boys: girls are treated more tenderly than boys, picked up more often, and held longer. Also, parents tend to encourage boy babies in independent movements and to be overprotective towards girl babies. As they become older, boys will be given toy trucks and blocks to play with while girls will be given stuffed animals and dolls. And as they learn to talk, boys are told what "big boys" they are while girls are told that they are "lovely little girls." By the age of three, gender identity is already firmly implanted, and the differences in gender identity grow stronger as children mature. All the people they meet—other children, teachers, parents of their friends, not to speak of their own family members—provide role models for them of what women are like and men are like and the sex-related behaviors expected of each. Children also learn that departing from the standard sexual scripts leads to social disapproval and rejection: to be different or "queer" is to be a social outcast.

Another way the child obtains its sex education is by observing how the parents interact with each other. It sees the role behaviors of Mommy and Daddy and how Mommy and Daddy feel about sex. The child may be completely ignorant of the facts about reproduction and still assimilate a full complement of attitudes and feelings about sex from the parents—that it is loving and it is fun, or that it is furtive and somewhat frightening. These attitudes are communicated by a glance, by a touch, by a withdrawal or a cringing movement. The importance of the parents' relationship as a model for children is illustrated by the situation of Katrina, a twenty-one-year-old college senior whom we saw in psychotherapy. As far back as Katrina can remember, her parents had a very bad relationship. She cannot recall them ever being physically affectionate, holding hands or hugging, but instead remembers them arguing behind closed doors and ultimately ending up in separate bedrooms. Although her parents were asexual with each other, Katrina's father went so far as to introduce her to his women friends and make it clear that he was sexually involved with them. Afraid of being sexually rejected like her mother, Katrina started coming on to boys, spending time at their apartments while her girlfriends covered for her. She soon became sexually active even with boys she did not particularly like, because she needed their acceptance. Now, after therapy, she has been able to extricate herself from such situations and feels that her behavior had a lot to do with her parents' bad example. She resents her mother's compliance with her father's behavior as much as she resents her father, and feels they both failed to provide her with proper models.

The spontaneous sex education that is built into family life is very different and much more effective than the "formal" sex education that parents provide their children when they sit them down to tell them about the facts of life. This information can be important, but it is only a small part of the more global education that is transmitted on a daily basis, and it tends to be relayed after the fact. Many parents told us that when they finally got around to "having a talk" with their children, the response was "Gee, Ma, I know that." Doris, a friend of ours and mother of three sons now in their twenties, told us about the time she took her middle son aside, telling him, "I want to talk to you about sex." He answered, "Sure, Mom. What do you want to know?"

One reason many parents are reluctant to discuss sex with their children is their fear that sex information will act as a stimulus for them to have sex. A recent survey of American teenagers, conducted by *Rolling Stone*, suggests quite the opposite: parental openness and positive attitudes to sex help children withstand the pressures to have sex that often emanate from their peers and dates.* Parents who cut children off from sexual information and discussions miss the opportunity to provide their sons and daughters with guidelines and to set prudent limits. The lack of parent-child communication contributes to the huge gap, documented by the *Rolling Stone* survey, between what children think is right and what they think their parents think is right.

Another reason parents hold back information is that it embarrasses them to talk about sex. Even when providing routine sex-information, they often find it hard to do so in a relaxed, informal way. Because of this, many child-development experts counsel parents to provide their children with reading matter as a substitute for direct conversation. In his book *How to Father*, a classic in child-raising, Dr. Fitzhugh Dodson stresses the importance of helping a child develop positive attitudes towards sexuality that incorporate the connection between sexuality, love, and the family. "One of the best ways to do this," he says, "is to read a book to him which will give him an overall view of the sexual process and its place in family living." Dr. Dodson does suggest that the parent answer any questions the child might raise, but in case the same questions crop up again and

* Robert Coles and Geoffrey Stokes, *Sex and the American Teenager* (New York: A Rolling Stone Press Book, Harper Colophon Books, Harper & Row Publishers, 1985).

again, Dr. Dodson says, "it is a good idea to read these books to your child several times."* We agree that it is a good idea to supplement with printed materials the sex education of children, but we feel that relying on books as a primary medium will give the child the impression that sex is too awesome for parents to handle on their own. The best way to communicate information about sex is to tell it like it is, using the same matter-of-fact approach that any other area is handled with. We don't rely on special books to teach children about the weather, about illness, or about God, but discuss these topics on a day-to-day basis. Similarly, it is better to talk about sex in an informal way rather than relegating it to a special reading period. Just as we don't wait for children to ask us how bread is made or where the sun goes at night, we do not have to wait to be asked how babies are made. Parents often worry that their children are not ready for this information, but it is usually parents who are not ready to deal with it.

Larry, a colleague of ours in private practice, described how he makes it a point to talk with his five kids about sex in the context of ordinary conversations, whenever it is relevant:

≈§ I think my approach to my children is a response to my own life experience around sexuality. I was considered by my parents sexually precocious, but I found out that I was less sexually precocious than they were sexually retarded. I have always discussed those sexual matters that come up in conversation between myself and my wife, friends, colleagues, without any attempt at exclusion of the children. It takes place in front of them. Sometimes you want to formalize it, but the best sex information that my kids get is not in those careful conversations, but in an easy exchange like when something comes up on TV, or they ask a question about something that happened at school. The other day I was talking to my wife and my youngest daughter was

---

* Fitzhugh Dodson, *How to Father* (New York: New American Library, 1975), pp. 103 and 105.

sitting at the table and I said something about, "I just saw this guy and it's a shame, he's struggling with impotence, he thinks." And my daughter asked, "What makes people impotent?" I explained, "That's what happens when you try to do something you don't really want to do. Many people think they want to have sex, but their bodies have other ideas and often our bodies tell us more how we feel than our ideas do." ఇ≈

Another father who integrated the process of sex education into the everyday events of his family life is Julius Fast. As he described it:

≈§ I don't think there should be any one time that you sit down and tell them the facts of life. I think that from the time the child is little you feed them the facts of life and they ask questions in concurrence with their age. I'm always reminded of the story of the kid who asks his mother where babies come from. And she gets into a tizzy with the sperm and the egg, and he says, "But Georgie comes from Chicago, and Sally comes from New York, and where do babies come from?" You have to know what the kid is asking in order to answer in accordance with what the kid is able to understand and then it should be an ongoing process. Whenever they want to know, you tell them. When my kids would ask how babies are made, I would tell them how babies were made and then I would always add, "You know you do it because it is nice. Sometimes for babies, and sometimes for fun." So there was that feeling. ఇ≈

An important aspect of sex education that parents often forget to mention when they do talk about sex is the pleasurable side of sex. Informing children about reproduction is not equivalent to educating them about sex, and does little to promote an affirmative attitude towards sex. Parents who talk about the birds and the bees often neglect to talk about penises and vaginas, while those who call a sexual organ by its name invariably neglect to talk to their children about how nice sex feels. If parents do talk about intercourse, they generally convey a mechanical, impersonal description of the reproductive act but not that people have sex for pleasure. Bradford, a soft-spoken and reserved securities analyst now in his thirties, recalled for us how uncomfortable both he and his father were when he asked his father to tell him what intercourse was like. As happens in so many families, his father failed both to educate Bradford in depth and to convey a positive feeling about sex to his son:

◄§ I asked my father about it, so he told me. He sat on my bed. I was uncomfortable because he was sitting on my leg, unknowingly. I didn't tell him because I didn't want to interrupt him, because it was such an overwhelming thing he was telling me. I couldn't understand how the sperm came out, 'cause he never told me. He told me how it was done, but he left out the part that it felt good. I remember where I was sitting exactly to this day. He said that a man inserts his penis into a woman's vagina and the sperm comes out. But I didn't really understand. He didn't describe it in terms of emotion or feelings, so it was purely the mechanics of it—a brief discussion. I kept asking, "How does the sperm come out?" and he said, "It just does." It wasn't a satisfactory answer. I felt bewildered, amazed, funny. It was a mystery to me because I still didn't understand how it worked. I knew how you went about doing it, but I didn't know you had to get an erection, I didn't know about foreplay, I didn't know about orgasm. I knew I could explain how to play bridge in two minutes, but that doesn't make you know how to play bridge, and that was the way my father taught me. My friends had told me that it feels good, but that's the part he left out, you see, so that's why I had to make the leap for myself. §►

The basic communication in most homes is still that sex is a disreputable activity to be engaged in furtively. Even when the intellectual message may be that sex is a normal, healthy part of life, the underlying emotional message usually is that sex is something to be ashamed of.

We in the United States probably send out more mixed messages about sex than anywhere else in the world. Some countries, particularly those in the Middle East, have very rigid sexual codes, and other countries, particularly those in Scandinavia, are generally relaxed about their sexuality. But in the United States we speak out of both sides of our mouth at once: on the one hand society encourages sexuality and openness, but on the other, at home, we treat sex as something dirty. Thus, micro-bikinis are great, but nudity at home is frowned upon. Explicit sex may be depicted in the movies, but teens under seventeen, and in some communities anyone under twenty-one, cannot gain admittance. Contraceptives may be purchased at the drugstore but may still not be advertised on many TV stations because children might see the ads at home. Sex is "in," but it is still so poorly dealt with in the family that children and teenagers in this country are practically ignorant about reproduction and sexual ethics. The United States leads nearly all the developed countries in the world in the rate of teenage pregnancies. Among white adolescents the rate is double that of their British, Canadian, or French peers and six times that of the Dutch. For black teenagers the rate is even higher. According to Faye Wattleton, president of the Planned Parenthood Federation, "While European societies have chosen to recognize sexual development as a natural part of human development, we have chosen to repress it. At the same time, we behave as if we're not repressing it."* Rather than recognize the natural erotic component that is inherent in every healthy child, many parents mistakenly believe that their offspring become interested in sex only after they learn about birth control and reproductive health.

PUTTING THE PIECES TOGETHER AGAIN

It is not difficult to figure out where the split in family sexual attitudes comes from and why it is so hard for many parents to accept emotionally what they verbalize intellectually, namely that sexuality is a healthy aspect of

* As quoted in *Time*, December 9, 1985, p. 82.

life. Much of the problem can be attributed to our religious tradition and its dichotomy between the body and soul, which holds the life of the flesh to be impure and the mortification of the flesh to be the route to spiritual salvation. In this context, sex is seen as a necessary evil to be tolerated in order to perpetuate the species. Only recently have liberal segments of some religious traditions, namely the Jewish and Protestant, come to view sex as a gift from God that one should use joyously and responsibly to bring about fulfillment and intimacy. The Catholic tradition continues to sanction sex solely within marriage, holding extramarital sex and "artificial" contraception to be sinful, and the evangelical new right wing of Protestantism is obsessed with sexuality as a manifestation of all that is evil, condemning in one breath abortion, pornography, homosexuality, planned parenthood, sex education, and equal rights for women.

Quite a few of the people we spoke to described the stultifying effects of their religious traditions on sexual attitudes in the home. Among them was Gloria Jones, an editor at a publishing house, the mother of two children, and the widow of James Jones, the novelist. Gloria was raised as a Catholic and her husband Jim as a Christian Scientist. According to Gloria, they both felt the heavy arm of the church reaching down to them:

◄§ I had fear. Fear. It was an attitude that came through my mother. I was sent to Catholic convent school, so they didn't have to say too much after that. You seemed to know that sex was a big mortal sin. I didn't know what sin was yet, but the big sin was, you were not supposed to do it. It was adultery, obviously. It was an attitude . . . because I don't think anyone ever said, "Thou shalt not have sex." I would never discuss sex with my mother. My mother was very strict about the church . . . Jim's mother was a Christian Scientist. He wrote about this and the hypocrisy, the misery, and the unhappiness in the family, and he would certainly not live that way as he had his fill of that. Hypocrisy can ruin people's lives and it does . . . Jim thought [exposure to sexual information] was all right if it didn't upset the kids. Then it was fine. ❧

While Freud has been credited with making people aware of the detrimental effects of parental sexual repression, in many ways he too has kept families from accepting their sexuality. In fact, the one disciple of his who had a truly sex-affirmative view, Wilhelm Reich, was ostracized from the psychoanalytic community. As a product of his times Freud not only had difficulty integrating sexuality into his own life, but he viewed the expression of sexuality in others from the Victorian perspective in which body and mind were seen as different entities, with the one morally inferior to the other. While he believed that sex was a driving force in life, he also felt it should be sublimated into more creative and "higher" forms of human endeavor. Similarly, while he believed that all children are sexual, he labeled their sexual interest as "polymorphous perversity." Freud regarded sex as a raging force that had to be controlled rather than as an inseparable aspect of one's total being. Exploratory bodily play of infants and physical bonding with the mother were understood by Freud in terms of sexual lust, and women's search for sexually gratifying relationships and fulfilling experiences outside the home were understood as penis envy. By interpreting such complex behaviors as mechanistic, instinctual responses, Freud helped perpetuate the harmful old Judeo-Christian distinction between spirituality and sexuality and actually hindered parents from integrating sexuality into the life of the family.

Modern sexologists have not helped matters much either, maintaining the same body-mind split, though with a new twist. In trying to free people to enjoy their bodies and indulge the flesh, they overlooked the vital role of attitudes and emotions. Kinsey's studies on sexual behavior provided statistics on what people were doing but did not inquire into their feelings. Similarly, Masters and Johnson's studies of the human sexual response equated people's physiological reactions to masturbatory stimulation in a laboratory setting with the way they interact during sexual intercourse. The numerous books on sexual techniques also instruct people in various methods and positions of intercourse and masturbation, while ignoring feelings towards the sexual partner. Only recently have sexologists started to turn their attention to the role of feelings in the sex act. Ironically, the new sexual permissiveness facilitated by sex researchers has encouraged a turning away from sexuality, that is, away from the integration of one's sexual feelings with one's sexual behavior. We are now faced with the curious phenomenon of young adults who, though educated on how to achieve bigger and better orgasms, have so little intrinsic interest in sex that they place it way down on their hierarchy of activities. This new generation is so busy jogging, learning how to prepare sushi, and building careers that it doesn't find time for sex. Magazine articles no longer instruct couples on how to have good sex but on how to schedule it into their appointment calendars.

So far society has not helped us find a comfortable place for sex in our lives. It remains for parents to foster healthy sexuality in their children by creating a family atmosphere where sexual feelings are respected as a vital aspect of life through which one enhances caring relationships.

TWO

THE WAYS
OF ALL FLESH:
FOUR SEXUAL TYPES

We have found that there are basically four ways parents relate to sexuality at home, and we call these patterns Sex Repressive, Sex Avoidant, Sex Obsessive, and Sex Expressive. Because everyone is a unique individual, no one pattern can totally describe a person's feelings and attitudes. Mothers and fathers do not necessarily share wholly identical views but usually their attitudes coincide. Some families, however, may have a Sex Repressive father and a Sex Avoidant mother, others a Sex Obsessive father and a Sex Expressive mother or any other combination of types.

The four sexual patterns manifest themselves over a wide range of family issues, including attitudes to sex education, parental sexuality, interactions between parents and children, and the way children themselves express their own sexuality. And these sets of attitudes generally also affect a wide spectrum of nonsexual behaviors, including social conduct, attitude towards authority, and religious observance. The four patterns can be expressed in various ways, and have different consequences for every family.

The interviews on the following pages will illustrate the way the four patterns work and how they affect the lives of children and their parents. Whenever possible we have offered the perspectives of mothers, fathers, and siblings from the same household.

SEX REPRESSIVE PARENTS

Sex Repressive parents feel that sex is inherently immoral and take an active role in squelching sexuality in their children. They set rigid rules about language used in the home, friends who may or may not visit, dress codes, and more. They also tend to raise their children according to the old gender-role stereotypes. Because of their traditional attitude Sex Repressive parents are likely to maintain a double standard about sex and allow sons more leeway than daughters. Sexual activity in boys, while not approved, is tolerated, whereas sexual activity in girls, when it occurs, is punished. Either way, the message these parents send out is that sex is dirty and evil.

Sex Repressive parents tend to be firmly convinced that they are in the right, and they harbor little doubt about sexual morality. Sex Repressive parents were once the norm; they are now fewer in number, but their ranks are on the upswing again. The recent trend towards conservatism has brought with it a reassertion of old sexual standards, and many Sex Repressive parents find that the political climate makes their point of view more acceptable. Further, the upsurge in teenage pregnancies, the alarming news about sexually transmitted diseases such as herpes and chlamydia, and the more recent AIDS epidemic have brought out a new wave of Sex Repressive parents. Mingled with very realistic fears for the well-being of their children is the feeling that the problems now associated with sex represent almost a form of divine retribution for immoral behavior. Many Sex Repressive parents do not want their children becoming sexually involved because they are anxious about possible consequences, but they also feel that pregnancy and disease are the punishment one must pay for deviating from the moral code.

Isabelle, who is in her early forties, has three daughters, aged fourteen, sixteen, and seventeen. Both she and her husband work for a local radio station, he as an administrator, she as a broadcaster. Isabelle grew up in the sixties and adopted some of the progressive attitudes of that era, including the conviction that women should pursue careers as well as become homemakers, but she basically retained the Sex Repressive attitudes of her own parents. She is very strict with her daughters, closely supervises their dates, and feels that sex has no place in the lives of girls under twenty-one and unmarried:

≤§ I am, quite frankly, horrified at the way many young people carry on today. They have sex at the drop of a hat. And they think this is a sophisticated way of life. They see sex in the movies, in the advertising, on the newsstands, and feel it is smart to have sex, but they are much too young and irresponsible. Sex belongs in a relationship of two mature people who love each other, but children today engage in sex as casually as they chew gum. Except that nobody would pass a piece of gum around from mouth to mouth—yet these young people pass their bodies around from one person to another. I recognize that young people want to date and form relationships, but that does not mean that these relationships have to be sexual. They have a whole lifetime ahead of them and sex can wait until they are ready for it. Most girls today do not even want to have sex, but they feel pressured into it by society. They are exposed to so much sex, and now there are birth control clinics right in the high school. Adults who should be teaching them restraint and responsibility are instead teaching them to go out there and become sexually active, and you can see what the consequences are. We never had the diseases before that we have today. People are even forgetting to worry about herpes because they are more afraid of AIDS.

I resent very much being told that I am old-fashioned and out of touch with the times. I feel I am a thoroughly modern parent and more attuned than most to the needs of children. I am not going to stand by helplessly and let my girls become teenage mothers or let their friends decide for them what is right and what is wrong. I have told them straight out that sex is not a game, that it is a serious matter, and that it is like matches. You do not play with it because you can get badly burned. When you have a husband and a home and do not have to worry about getting pregnant is the time you are ready to have sex. And when you have a decent relationship with a decent man, you do not have to worry about becoming infected. Diseases come from improper and unclean living. If you live the way God and nature intended you to, you will not get herpes or AIDS. The way to stop these diseases is not to pour more and more government money into research, but for people to stop living like animals and start living like respectable human beings. ॐ

Other parents also worry about the dangers sexual activity poses for their children, including the emotional pains that many children will suffer, but Sex Repressive parents are alone in the belief that their children should forgo sex entirely. They are not inclined to educate their children as to how to deal with birth control and how to prevent infections, because at heart they do not want their children to be sexual under any circumstances. They also cannot instruct their children on how to deal with sexual feelings in a girl-boy relationship because they do not believe sex has any place in those relationships.

While Sex Repressive parents feel comforted by their position, life for their children is anything but easy. Lynn Caine, who has written about family issues, most notably in *Widow* and *What Did I Do Wrong?*, described for us the difficulties of growing up in a classic Sex Repressive family. According to Lynn, an antisexual attitude permeated the home. Both her mother and father gave her negative messages about sex, making her feel that sex was dirty and that she was a bad person because she was going through the natural sexual development of adolescence. As a girl and the oldest of three siblings, Lynn bore the brunt of her parents' repressive attitudes. Her father, in particular, was verbally abusive and suspicious of her:

◦§ My parents' attitudes were traditional, read rigid. My father was terrified that I was going to get pregnant, so he followed me and he waited up for me. He talked about it in the most destructive way—that there are good girls and bad girls, and if I wore too much makeup, for example, I was a bad girl. My father was obviously going to have problems with me. I had a lot of boyfriends, I went out a lot, I was precocious, I did stay out late, I went dancing. I was a "bad" girl, but I certainly was a virgin, and he accused me of not being one.

Sex was not discussed in my house. It really wasn't. In those days we just picked it up. I heard older girls in school using a terrible expression—blood pads—for Kotex, not calculated to make you feel too terrific about sex. My mother did not tell me anything about menstruation; I didn't know my mother had periods. I remember one time when I was very little, my mother was nursing my sister who was three years younger and I was sent out of the room. My mother was embarrassed. I learned that the human breast was something to be ashamed of, that the body was not to be uncovered. I do remember having gotten my period at an early age—ten and a half—and not knowing what it was, thinking I had diarrhea and being scared. I went to my mother, and all she told me was, "Now you can have babies. Now you're a woman." Ten and a half years old! I made no connection with it whatsoever and I didn't feel much like a woman. The only thing she told me then was, "Don't take gym." My mother, by the way, used cutesy-poo names for genitalia, and if anybody said anything dirty she would giggle. From my father I got dirty-bad, from my mother dirty-bad-silly. I really got nothing except that sex was dirty, and that my father was scared that I was going to get knocked up. ঌ

The repressive attitudes of Lynn's parents and their predictions of dire consequences, based on nothing more than her natural growth into adolescence, took their toll on her. It was only through the affirmation of her second husband, Martin, that Lynn came to develop positive feelings about her own sexuality:

ঌ I think I was aware fairly early about sexual feelings because of my passionate nature. Essentially I think I would have grown up as I did, but I was probably more promiscuous than I would have been if I hadn't had that kind of background. I used alcohol to get high and get sexually involved because alcohol relaxes. And as a consequence I went so far as to marry somebody I shouldn't have married first time around because I was so grateful anybody asked me to marry them. I felt I was damaged goods. I can't document this, but I think that my inability to become pregnant until I was in my thirties had to do with that. It was psychological sterility, because as you know I did become pregnant. But I was told right up until I had a child that my tubes were blocked. I thought I would never get pregnant. If I had gotten pregnant, I would have disgraced my father because only bad girls get pregnant.

By the time Martin came around, I knew everything they told me was a lie, that it was good for a woman to be sexual. . . . As I got older I understood what sex was about and knew that what they had told me came out of fear. Men do marry women who are sexual—two of them married me. Sex does not make you dirty. &

What happens to the children of Sex Repressive parents? Some, as we saw with Isabelle, are able to incorporate fully the Sex Repressive values of their parents and turn away from sex, continuing the cycle of tradition when they establish their own families. They are in the minority, however. Research* shows that children who grow up in homes that can be characterized as Sex Repressive are more likely to become sexually active than their peers and, unfortunately, less likely to use birth control. Unable to accept the categorical "no" of their parents, many teens in Sex Repressive homes engage in sex furtively, too guilty to seek advice from their parents or adult authorities, and too uninformed about sex to understand the risks involved. Even though these teens disobey parental strictures about sex, they feel, at heart, ashamed of their sexuality and often tend not to find pleasure in their forbidden activities.

In other Sex Repressive homes, children reject their parents' values as well as their rules. Some try but never quite free themselves entirely from their lingering discomforts about sex. Betsy, for example, found herself questioning her parents' attitudes towards sexuality from an early age and discreetly defied them, but she still thinks of sex as an illicit activity, even with her husband. This makes her even more determined, however, that her daughter should grow up in a sexually expressive manner and without the guilts she still harbors from her own Sex Repressive upbringing:

* Coles and Stokes, *Sex and the American Teenager.*

◄§ They never talked about sex in my house. There was a book about the wonderful story of how you were born, and when it was time for me to learn about sex, my mother read me part of that book but just before she got to the part about how to make babies she said that she'd tell me that another year. I don't think we ever got back to it. My friends told me the story—that you have to stroke a boy's penis until it gets stiff like cardboard and then he puts it in a little hole, and I said, "Ugh, that's terrible."

I remember walking into the bathroom, in on my father once. I didn't know what a penis was, and I said, "Oh Mommy, Daddy has a tail!" First they laughed, and then my father did something that was not so good: he spanked me. I didn't understand. If it was funny, why did he hit me? When I was about twelve or thirteen, when everybody was asleep and I was in bed, I would take off my pajamas because the sheets felt so good. Once my mother came in and found that I didn't have any pajamas on. She ripped off the covers, spanked me, and made me put my pajamas back on.

My first sexual contact, or should I say physical contact, was when I was twelve years old, and I certainly never told my parents. I never talked to my parents about anything sexual in my life because I was afraid of being hit. I wouldn't even share that "I think he likes me or he doesn't." I never had that kind of mother-daughter talk.

I think my parents' sex attitude affected my attitude, because I think it's dirty. I love dirty sex, I love dirty movies and magazines and stories, and the more so-called taboo, the better. It has to have that for me. Getting married took out the illicit fun, but I can do a little thing in my mind because I'm black and I'm married to a white man. To this day I hope in my mind that the sexual part of my relationship does not enter into my father's head and that he pretends we found our daughter under a bush. When my husband takes my hand and my parents are there I have to say "stop it" to myself because I have trouble holding hands with him if my parents are there. ᢒᴥ

Not infrequently, when the family is very rigid in its attitudes, the children become confused about their own feelings. In trying to conform to the demands of the parents, they often end up in inappropriate relationships. This is what happened to Faith, a publicist, now in her early forties. Although she came of age in the swinging sixties, her parents' attitudes towards sexuality were still molded by a strict Victorian morality that ultimately produced a counter-reaction in Faith:

&§ I was not allowed to wear make up until I was sixteen, to date until I was eighteen. I have to tell you a vivid memory that describes everything. I had a date who kissed me outside the door of the apartment just as my parents got off the elevator and saw me, and I was banned from going out for the next month. I was a virgin when I got married because of my parents' attitudes. To them, sex was bad—it was something you did not do until you got married. It was not right. It affected me, and I'm in therapy because of it. I don't have any sexual hang-ups now, but I'm sure my relationships have to do with how I grew up. I've been married and divorced twice, and I have lived with different men. After I got divorced the first time and had a good apartment and a good job and was on my own, I had to do and try everything. I was in and out of bed every other day, because I felt a sudden sense of freedom and that's how I handled it. §∞

The aim of Sex Repressive parents is very specific: to curb sexual behavior and keep their children, especially their daughters, away from sexual entanglements before they are married. The impact of Sex Repressive parents, however, goes way beyond this goal: they instill a sense of shame in children about their innate sexuality which alienates children from their parents and interferes with their later capacity to form satisfying relationships with the opposite sex. The antisexual climate that permeates Sex Repressive homes makes it difficult for family members to approach one another in a spontaneous way, because they are so fearful that sexuality may somehow intrude. Children in these circumstances grow up feeling bad about the sexual stirrings which are an essential part of their nature, and resentful towards their parents for disapproving of this very basic aspect of their being. Many of the people we see in our psychotherapy practice come to work out this conflict with their parents, or its lingering aftereffects, and to make peace with their own sexuality. In the chapters that follow we will see how a Sex Repressive atmosphere disturbs the relationships between mothers, fathers, and siblings, and keeps them from full acceptance and enjoyment of themselves and one another.

SEX AVOIDANT PARENTS

Sex Avoidant parents are intellectually accepting of the concept of sex as a healthy part of life but emotionally unable to go along with this idea. They have, for the most part, grown up in Sex Repressive homes, and remain conflicted between the attitude imbued in them by their parents that sex is something dirty and their own sense that sex is an integral part of life, a sentiment fostered by the social permissiveness of the sixties, the time at which most Sex Avoidant parents came of age. They feel pulled in these two different directions and try to solve their dilemma by avoiding the issue as much as possible. In bringing up their own children, Sex Avoidant parents deal with sexual issues by not dealing with sexual issues. They avoid talk about sex at home, brush aside questions, and generally do not provide any information unless they feel it is absolutely necessary or they are directly confronted by their children. When faced with sexual behavior in the home they tend to ignore it. These parents often think of themselves as liberated because they do not put undue restrictions on their children or say negative things about sex, but the message they provide is that sex is too threatening to talk about.

A fairly typical Sex Avoidant parent is Virginia's mother, Eunice. The two lived alone together after Eunice divorced her husband when Virginia was twelve years old. As described by Virginia, Eunice is a very intelligent woman with an exceedingly sharp and questioning mind. Although Eunice never finished college, she is very well-read and has always seemed to be ahead of her time: she made clothes of denim before jeans were fashionable, ate health food when others thought it was for kooks only, and walked in peace marches when it was still considered unpatriotic. Eunice took pains to help Virginia develop a broad outlook and to be analytical in her thinking—discussing newspaper editorials with her, dissecting the motivations of characters in the movies they saw, and looking deeply into every aspect of life—except sex. Eunice never put any restrictions on Virginia, and Virginia led a free life sexually, including having her boyfriends sleep over in her room. With all that, nary a word about sex was ever spoken:

⋅§ My mother never told me anything about sex. It was a totally avoided topic. In retrospect it is very odd because she was always so concerned about my being awake and aware, and feeding me information, lecturing me about the state of the world, trying to get me to think. It is hard for me to know where I ever learned about sex. I guess just by osmosis or probably from novels more than anything else. My mother belonged to several book clubs and I used to devour all the novels. I guess in a way they were my pornography, although never explicit enough for me to really understand what was happening. Somehow or other I put it all together but I never asked my mother a thing. I just sensed I wasn't supposed to. I remember a conversation sitting on the campus steps with my boyfriend and he was talking about chickens fornicating. And I was surprised. I said, "Chickens don't fornicate. They lay eggs." And he laughed at me and then told me about how chickens and roosters do it. His name was Lance, and he was the first boy I ever slept with. He would come home with me on weekends from school, and at first I would visit him in the attic room where he slept, but then after a while he would come and visit me in my room and stay there for the night. My mother never said "boo." She had to know what was going on, but she acted completely nonchalant. In one way she was so cool and ahead of her time about sex, but in another way she was totally repressed. §⋅

Even when Sex Avoidant parents realize that they are "hung-up" about sex, they tend to minimize how avoidant they have really been. Sherry, a bank vice president, is a fairly typical Sex Avoidant mother in this regard. She describes herself and her husband as "traditional and unliberated" and feels she was probably not sufficiently open with her two children, Blake and Sara, about sexual issues when they were younger; however, she still feels that she discussed all the questions that her children raised:

⋖§ I remember vaguely conversations in the house, more with Blake than with Sara, about sex and the birth of children, and I think we simply answered the questions as they came. We probably didn't go out of our way to discuss sex but we simply didn't hide from the questions, and we obviously had read through some books and had some around on how to deal with sexual questions. The kids would probably give you an entirely different picture if you talked to them—an entirely different perspective. We didn't discuss sex a lot. It was not something that was openly discussed in the family. It was not conversation at dinner, but I have just a vague feeling of sitting around the room with Blake and of his asking questions and answering them, starting with the traditional birds-and-bees kinds of things, and leading up to humans, but I don't remember any particular discussions about the subject. Maybe there was too little. We probably answered the questions about where babies come from and probably didn't discuss sex at all. Neither child ever asked. I'm trying to think back to my own childhood where that awareness came from. I remember asking questions of my own mother and her being uncomfortable about the answers, and my learning more about sex from other children, and maybe that was true for Blake and Sara as well. ξ∾

When we talked to Sherry's son we found out, as she anticipated, that her children do have "an entirely different picture." According to Blake, a young, successful architect, his mother never spoke to him about sex at all, and it wasn't until he was fourteen that his father felt it necessary to have a man-to-man talk with him, one of the most uncomfortable one-way conversations of his life:

⁓§ My parents provided no information about sex whatsoever. They directly and in a premeditated way provided no information. They are by nature not terribly demonstrative sexually. I have seen them hug and kiss each other hello and good-bye, but in all the time I never saw them do anything sexual that I would characterize as being passionate. I assume that they must be sexual outside my purview, but it is not in their nature to be publicly demonstrative in the way that you might see a husband and wife nestled on the couch beside one another or a couple walking down the street arm in arm. They just don't behave in that way. It's clear to me that they had sex—they sleep in the same bed together—but I never saw anything erotic between them. At an early age I got into the habit of waking up early in the morning, like most kids do, and I'd climb into bed with my parents. Part of that was fun, and part was an attempt to wake them up. I'd come into the bedroom and they would be asleep, hugging each other or with an arm around the other, but I never saw any erotic excitement.

When I was fourteen or fifteen, the only conversation I ever had about sex with my parents was one which my father prompted on the way home from summer camp. He had come to pick me up at the end of August. And as we were driving home it became clear to me that he had decided, or he and my mother had decided, that it was time to tell me about the birds and the bees, and, as I suppose is generally the case in those kinds of conversations, he didn't tell me very much that I didn't already know. Probably the few things I wanted to know were the things he didn't tell me, and I wasn't about to ask him because it was embarrassing to have that kind of conversation with him. He also elected to conduct the conversation entirely in clinical terms, which made it more difficult because he was not able to use the sort of slang or common parlance that I used with my friends. He explained to me how babies were conceived and proceeded to explain to me what precautions I ought to take if I became sexually involved with a woman, and tried to explain to me about menstrual cycles, and how to put a condom on. I remember staring out the window, wishing that the conversation had not come up in the course of a three-hour car ride because it was going to go on as long as he wanted to and I was stuck in the car.

The import of his message about sex was not the emotional or moral risks of getting a girl pregnant. Either that was too difficult for him to go into or it was assumed from the family values that it didn't even need to be discussed, that I was a good boy and therefore would not do it. The thrust of the conversation was to explain the mechanics of the plumbing so that I understood what could and could not be done, and what was prudent in that regard, and that was it. It was really a conversation about the plumbing. &

The inability to face up to sexual issues at home can result in consequences that Sex Avoidant parents do not expect or welcome: their children become uncomfortable about approaching them for advice when needed and end up directionless. In attempting to avoid repressiveness, Sex Avoidant parents put the burden on the children to set their own limits. When Jennifer was in her teens, her mother, who thought of herself as a modern parent, avoided having any meaningful discussions about sex and refused to acknowledge that her daughter's boyfriends were potential sexual partners. The result of this "cop-out," according to Jennifer, was that she became pregnant at seventeen and married early without really wanting to. Only at that point did she evoke a reaction in her mother:

&§ My mother taught me about the birds and bees when I was eight. She did say a sperm and an egg, but she didn't say penis and vagina. She just told me what reproduction is. As far as sexuality is concerned, my mother was always saying when I was dating, "This is my daughter's little friend." It was never a boyfriend to her. She went out constantly at night and didn't want me alone with one boy. She didn't mind if seven were in the house, but one bothered her. She didn't realize I could go into the bedroom with one. All she ever said about having one guy over was that it could put me in a situation where I might be uncomfortable. She copped out a lot. She never asked me, "Are you doing anything?" Not that she was a terrible mother, but I was pregnant before marriage. Her reaction was, "Oh, how could you." The main thing that she said was, it was not the idea that I was pregnant, but "How long were you fooling around? Was this the first time?" She also really freaked me out when she asked, "Who knows about it?" My best friends knew and she made me lie. She made me promise to tell them I had been secretly married before. She really made me promise to do that, because she thought it was a reflection on her. Not on me, but on her. ﾆﾞ

While the intentions of Sex Avoidant parents are benign, their embarrassed inapproachability tends to stir up angry feelings in their children. Like Jennifer, these children see their parents as hypocritical Sex Repressives masquerading in liberal clothing who have copped out on their parental responsibility. They feel, as we will see, that because of their parents' hang-ups, they have missed out on the warmth and openness in family relationships that would have enabled them to grow up comfortable with their own sexuality.

SEX OBSESSIVE PARENTS

Sex Obsessive parents view sex as a healthy appetite that should be cultivated and satisfied. They make it a point to talk to their children about sex early on and parade, rather than hide, their own sexuality. Some Sex Obsessive parents are people who have difficulty controlling their sexual impulses, and rationalize their inability to do so with the attitude that uninhibited sex is good for everyone. Most Sex Obsessive parents introduce sex into the family setting out of a desire to be "with it" and nonrepressive. They are in active rebellion against the sexual restraints under which they grew up and want to demonstrate that they have no inhibitions about sex. The message they send out is that sex is a "must."

Derrick is a perfect example of a Sex Obsessive father. He

has three children (Susan, nine years old; Steven, seven years old; and a baby girl) and a very stable relationship with his wife, Nina. Sex is a central theme in Derrick's life. He is, as he puts it, very much into sex. Derrick is a jovial and open person who, having grown up in a Sex Repressive environment, makes a point of rebelling against social constraints:

✍ When I was fifteen I got into a very sexually liberated scene. I got a job at a strip joint and got into a sexual area that is very different from the sexual mores of society. I got into scenes with people in the S&M field, and in the sex business. I was into getting laid. It seems as if I've always had some type of contact with the world of sex and the seamier side of life. It was getting out of the house, and being in that area, that seemed to compensate for everything there wasn't at home. I have always been outrageous. Sex for me is very anonymous—the groups and the whole bit. Anonymous in the sense that it was very casual; getting laid was like brushing your teeth. I don't give a damn what society says. I enjoy the freedom, and society be damned about it. If they don't like it, it's too bad. I like the fact that I'm outrageous about it. It's like hiding in plain sight, whereas the freedom you get by just being so open and outward about it is that it outrages society, but so what. Like with Nina, whom I often call a bitch. And it's a very loving way I do it, and I do this in public too. I'd be in a store and I'll say, "Hey, bitch, get over here." And store people would look around, and I sort of get off on that. You know, we've kidded around about that a lot. Nina started getting upset when the kids started calling her bitch so we toned that down a bit. They were led to understand that while we meant it affectionately, most people don't take it that way. We said, "Listen, it bothers your mother because most people don't take it as an affectionate term, but we mean it affectionately." And they accepted that readily because we are very open in front of the kids, and they see that there was never any connotation of anything derogatory in that kind of terminology.

I have a collection of whips and chains, custom-made stuff. The kids love to play with it. I remember one time

Susan put a collar and leash on Steve and she was leading him around. And they play with it in a very innocent game, but the connotations are there and I think they realize it. They know these are toys we play with even though they don't see us do it. They know what they are. When they ask questions about it, we say it's a whip for playing games and for fooling around, and they know that Nina wears lots of lingerie type things—hot corsets and high heels and stockings and garters, and things like that.

I have a huge collection of X-rated tapes. It's right out there where the kids can pick them up and play them. The kids know they're not supposed to, because our position is that they're not old enough to handle that. They've seen bits and segments by accident, so to speak. I guess not letting them see the tapes is a holdover from my upbringing. I guess it's the impersonalness of the tape that I'm not sure they can deal with yet on that level. On the personal level I think they can understand it better, because they tie it all in together with a family and affection between their mother and me. The only thing I try to shield them from is very descriptive violence. People getting shot or murder mysteries is no big deal, but *Texas Chain Saw Massacre* would not be OK. I'd much rather they'd see an X-rated fuck film. I guess primarily my basis with regard to the X-rated film is their mother doesn't think it's appropriate and I go along with that. I'll take them to see anything, the cut-off point being hard-core porn. Not that I consider it bad, but I don't think they're ready for it. Hard core becomes very detached—you have a screen with a dick going into the vagina and that can be the whole screen. There's too much of a detachment there that I don't think the kids are ready to deal with and assimilate.

The kids relate well to our sexuality. We don't close doors around here. The only restriction is it's not done straight in their face. Like they'll walk in on us making love and all we will do is stop any active movements at that specific time, and if they've got something that they want, or they have a question or something, we'll talk to them. We don't try to cover up, but we're not explicit in their face about it. If we're involved in oral sex, we may not necessarily move but we'll stop actively doing what we're doing. And we'll say, "We're in the middle of something. Come back in a little bit." We keep clothes hanging on the door so the door is never completely closed, but sometimes we close it. If they come in while we're at it, I don't make a big deal out of it because it's nothing I consider inappropriate. 8~

The belief of Sex Obsessive parents that "the kids relate well" to their overtly sexual behavior does not always accord with the experiences of their children. Quite the contrary. Instead of allowing their children's sexuality to unfold in natural ways, they tend to propel their children into precocious sexual behavior that is self-conscious and uncomfortable. Libra, who is now in her early twenties, told us about the disastrous consequences her parents' behavior had on her older sister. Both parents agreed to maintain an open marriage, and Libra's mother, though not Sex Obsessive like her father, continued to go along with this arrangement. Neither parent was prepared, however, when their older daughter initiated a Sex Obsessive life of her own. As Libra described it:

~§ Dad had blatant affairs, and the worst part of it was that he tried to make the women a part of our lives and the family. When I was still in grade school, he had one woman for three years whom he brought home to dinner a lot. Dad was obviously sexually involved with her. He'd flirt with her outrageously. One time he took us to visit her at her house. When we were there, she stubbed her toe and Dad made such a production over it. He was bending over her and cooing, and I was disgusted by it. He was so physical, like holding hands, putting a hand on her knee, or whatever. I didn't want to be there but I had to. I think if he was doing it on the side so that nobody knew, it wouldn't have been so disgusting. But the fact that he tried to make us all one big happy family and be friends was what was so disgusting.

It affected my older sister in a very bad way. She became very sexual, and my parents, although they tried to control her at first, absolutely couldn't. There was no way to, and they both gave up. My sister was allowed to stay out all night, and she was very sexual and flaunted it. She hung out with a street gang and had sex with almost all of them. She slept with a whole lot of people whom she didn't particularly care about. Everybody was pretty disgusted or worried about her, but there was nothing to do. Sex was something she could have with the most undesirable people. Having the most open relationships with all these people was her way of outdoing my father. I don't know if my Mom ever gave her a lecture about how sex could be with people you cared about, but my sister wasn't buying it because she didn't have that experience of her parents to go on.

I think she finally burned out. She has a relationship now that's lasted for six months, and that's the longest she's ever been with anybody. She wouldn't ever use the term love. She thought that sex was something you did for physical pleasure. She talks about sex all the time, but much too graphic for my taste. I think she used to talk just to shock me. She talked about how the guy she was dating had a small penis, or what she was using for birth control at the time. She told funny stories about diaphragms shooting across the room and how the jelly gets all over the place. Stuff like that. Dad would just laugh in an embarrassed sort of way and change the subject, and Mom would give her all sorts of feeble advice as to how she was screwing up her life. ❧

Despite their open display of sexuality in the home, Sex Obsessive parents tend to be basically uncomfortable about sex. They broadcast the fact that they are sexual in part to convince themselves as well as others that they do not have any sexual hang-ups, and their children end up paying for that denial. Because many Sex Obsessive parents retain the repressive feelings about sex with which they were brought up, namely that sex is dirty, it is not uncommon for them to become very upset when their children start to imitate their behavior. In our practice we have had many children referred to us by their parents or social agencies because of inappropriate sexual behavior, and a relatively large number come from Sex Obsessive homes. These children talk about having witnessed their parents engaged in sexual acts, which they often describe in graphic detail and then try to copy with younger siblings or friends. When the parents "catch" a son or daughter doing it, they become very angry and sometimes punish the child severely. The message the children take away from the reprimands they get for imitative sexual behavior is that sex is exciting but evil, a game to be played by the powerful.

The problem in Sex Obsessive homes is not that sex is made part of family life but that it is made the focal point of family life. Children in such settings experience their parents' sexuality as intrusive, and it interferes with the children's ability to integrate sexuality into their own lives at their own pace.

SEX EXPRESSIVE PARENTS

Sex Expressive parents view sex as a vital life-enhancing force and are neither particularly embarrassed nor over-whelmed by it. They are able to integrate sexuality into their lives and into the family by dealing openly with the discom-forts that may arise from sexuality and setting reasonable limits on sexual behavior as they do on all behaviors. In this manner they help their children develop a respect for their bodies and sexuality. The message about sex in these homes is that sex is OK and I'm OK.

Mary Travers, who as we saw had a Sex Avoidant mother, is herself a Sex Expressive parent. When Mary became sexually mature, her mother was anything but comfortable with it and tried to turn her head the other way:

◆§ I know she was anxious that I had embarked upon sex a bit early. As a matter of fact, she caught me. I had a boyfriend—I was fifteen—he was a scholarship student at the university and he was home for spring break. We had had sex twice, once in his school when I had gone out to see him, and once at my home. Anyway, he had come over and my mother came home. We had a brownstone, and my room was in the subbasement, in what would have been a garden apartment. My mother came downstairs and we saw her in the door. It was very embarrassing, and there was much shuffling of clothes and I got up and went to the door and asked her was she mad, and she said, "No," but the tone of her voice said, "Yes." She said, "No, but don't make a habit of it," and she went upstairs, leaving us to sort ourselves out. I thought it was so funny—"No, but don't make a habit of it!" ह

In contrast, when Mary's daughters became sexually mature, she opened up discussions with them to help them feel comfortable about themselves and about asking her questions:

ह I can recount a couple of discussions I had with my girls which may shed some light on how I deal with it. When Erica was fourteen, she was very tall for her age and I figured we're going to have something happen. I had my first serious beau at fifteen so I figured there was a reasonable chance it might be the age for Erica. So we had a discussion, and I forget how we started. I'm sure I said something inane about "Soon you'll be having a steady boyfriend. But there are things you have to know." And she said, "What is it really like?" And I said, "Probably very embarrassing and uncomfortable because you're both going to be very self-conscious. If it's his first time, between the desire to do it and the terror that he won't do it well, you will have a young man who will be in terrible conflict about one of the few things one should not enter into with conflicts." And then I explained how it is possible for something that is vertical to cease to be vertical, no matter how much one wants it to stay vertical. And I talked about what you are supposed to do if in the middle of this, with all the excitement and desire to do it, fear interjects and makes a muck of it. I talked about being gracious and supportive; after all, you shouldn't be in bed with this boy if you don't really like him. You have to learn to be kind to him if there's a problem, just as he has to be kind to you if, in the middle of all this, you decide you want to stop. It's something everyone knows they're going to do sooner or later, but when that moment arrives, it's scary and you can be frightened about what's he going to think of you, about getting pregnant, about his invasion into your body. There can be a zillion things that you can be frightened about. To make it a wonderful thing is quite important, and you need familiarity, trust, affection. It's never just right the first time you do it. It's too loaded with the other things, and not to expect the earth to move and the birds to come out and sing, because it doesn't work that way. Those things happen when you love somebody, when you're more experienced. 8≈

With her second daughter, Alicia, Mary was just as open, recognizing Alicia's emerging sexuality and creating an atmosphere that could allow Alicia to express herself sexually in a mature and fulfilling manner:

≈§ When she was about fifteen I said to her, "I know you're not in a relationship at the moment, but I think you really ought to go on the pill, because when the issue comes up I don't want you to have to think about whether it's safe or not. All you should really consider is whether you want to do it or not, and it would be a shame if you get pregnant when you can do something to prevent it. This doesn't mean you should rush out and find a boyfriend. It just means it shouldn't be a problem when you do have a boyfriend. Let me introduce you to the lady doctor in the building, and at some point in the future, if you call her, she can give you an examination and prescribe pills. That way she doesn't have to call me and you can do it at your own discretion. Or I'll go with you if you want. She said, "No, no, I'll do it when I'm thinking about it." So I didn't say anything more, and then when I was on the road I get a phone call from this young man who had volunteered to fill in for my housekeeper and watch over the apartment and the kids. My kids adore him, he's fun. He liked to cook, they liked to cook, he liked to gossip, and they liked to gossip. Anyway I get a phone call from him and he says, "She's gone and done it." I said, "What?" "She went to the doctor and has gotten the pill. I don't know why she can't wait. Why can't she wait until she's thirty-five?" I laughed, and he answered, "Well, it's easy for you to say. You have not spent the last hour sitting at the table reading aloud the directions on the birth control pills to make sure she knows how to take them!" I had this vision of a sitcom—this young man, this surrogate house-keeper, terribly intent that my daughter know how to take these pills! ટ•

Reflecting on her mother's attitudes about sex, Alicia noted how the acceptance of her sexuality helped her feel good about herself and heightened her sense of responsibility:

•ટ When I was fourteen and had my first boyfriend, after the third week of going out with this guy she said to me, "If you're still going out with him in three weeks, I'm putting you on the pill. First of all you have to be protected. And I don't want you sleeping with this guy on a street corner. I want it done respectably, and I want it to be right for you, so we're going to take all the precautions in the world." I didn't ask for the pill, she was telling me. I thought it was extremely liberal. Very cool. She wasn't trying to encourage it, but she was saying it was OK. It made me feel good. ટ•

Alicia feels that the sexual expressiveness and freedom in her home have made her more responsible about sexual behavior than her friends who have been reared in Sex Avoidant atmospheres:

•ટ My girlfriends think I'm a little too open. I have the most freedom of all my friends. I love it. But if you have that freedom you should be a responsible human being. Parents are very uptight people sometimes, but we come from a different age. . . . I've never felt that I had too much freedom. . . . It's never made me feel wrong. It made me feel kind of special because I got that kind of freedom, but it just didn't come out of nowhere; I worked for it. I wouldn't say "I'll be home at twelve" and come home at four in the morning. When I leave this house and my mother asks, "Will you be home?" I'll say, "Most likely, but you never know," and she smiles and says, "OK." If I know I'm going home with someone, I will call her if it's a decent hour, and if it's too late I will always call her in the morning and tell her where I am. I don't want her worrying. I gave my mother every reason in the world to trust me, and children often give their parents every reason in the world not to trust them and then they ask, "Why don't they trust me? Why can't I do this?"

In a lot of families, you mention sex and they say, "I don't want to hear about it," and the kids get into trouble. Some of my friends have had abortions. Their parents aren't the ones who yell at them and tell them what to do; it's always been me. I've been the one who says, "I'll take you down to Planned Parenthood if you're that afraid to tell your parents. You have to be responsible if you want to have sex, because if you do it irresponsibly you're going to get hurt." And it's very important to talk about it with your parents, because whether they like it or not, you're informing your parents about something they should know. A lot of parents don't want to know anything about it, and I think that's horrible. 🙠

Sometimes it is easier for parents to be Sex Expressive with a child of the same sex, but some parents manage to maintain the same openness and affirmative attitudes with children of the opposite sex. Eugene, a friend of ours and Sex Expressive father, described how he dealt with his daughters' sexuality:

🙠 Our girls knew about sex. We had always talked to them, and whenever they had a question they would come to me about, I'd answer it as honestly as I could. They didn't begin dating until fairly late because they would not go out unless they really liked the boy. They were never in this business of you have to go out Saturday night, you can't stay home, and they had their sexual experiences late for the time—I guess my older daughter was eighteen the first time. She called us up at two in the morning, and I picked up the phone and she said, "Now don't get upset. I'm at my friend's house, and I know you always told me if I'm not going to be home to let you know, and I don't want you to go into an empty room. I'm staying over and I think he's going to get me in bed." And I said, "Fine." And the next day, Sunday, we had guests, and she came waltzing into the living room and went like that [made an OK sign].

She had come to me a few weeks before and said, "I'm going with this guy and I know he's going to get me into bed and I think I ought to take the pill." And I said, "I think that's a good idea, but before you do I want you to go to Dr. X and let him do an examination and make sure everything is OK." So she went and had the exam. As a matter of fact, Dr. X was out of town, and I called his associate and said, "Do you know of an obstetrician who is nonjudgmental who will prescribe the pill?" and he got very indignant and said, "I'll prescribe it. Send her to me." So I sent her. After the visit I asked her, "How was it?" and she said, "Oh, he was fine. Of course he asked me if I loved the boy, and I knew what he wanted to hear, so I said 'yes.' " She didn't really love the boy, but I think she had a very sensible attitude towards sex. I believe that you should have sexual experience before you're married, so you know what you're doing. ॐ

In light of the common fear that talking to children about sex and allowing them freedom to have relationships will encourage promiscuity, it is important to emphasize that this is not likely to occur in Sex Expressive homes. On the contrary, children of Sex Expressive parents, like Alicia Travers and Eugene's daughter, tend to be responsible in their sexual behavior. Because Sex Expressive parents are frank in discussing sex with their children, they create a climate of mutual respect in which their offspring can look to them for guidance and for help in defining appropriate limits. And because Sex Expressive parents encourage positive attitudes about sexuality, their children tend to feel more secure about themselves and at one with their bodies. Having a healthy sense of self, they are less apt to succumb to pressure to have sex if they are not ready for it. The openness that exists in Sex Expressive homes creates a generally warmer, more spontaneous climate and avoids the frictions and resentments so prevalent in Sex Repressive, Sex Avoidant, and Sex Obsessive homes. When we look at specific family relationships, between fathers, mothers, daughters, sons, sisters, and brothers, we will illustrate how these four patterns impact on the family members and suggest ways to achieve greater cohesion and happiness in the family.

THREE

THE MYTH OF
THE VIRGIN COUPLE:
DESEXUALIZING MOTHERS
AND FATHERS

When we talked to people about how they saw their parents' life as a sexual couple, it was striking how often we drew an initial blank. Glen, a drama student who grew up in a middle-class suburban family, gave a typical response, saying, "I have no notion about my parents' sexuality at all. My parents were like 'Father Knows Best'—no more than that. Everything you could see on TV they would do; kiss each other, hug each other, but that was it." Betsy, whom we met before, responded more sharply. "We didn't have sex in our house. There was no such thing! My parents never talked about it, and I never thought of them as having sex." Brenda, who grew up in an inner-city area and is the second oldest of twelve siblings, always knew her parents had to have had sex to have so many children, but she still couldn't imagine them as sexual people: "Even though my parents were having babies, I didn't think of it so far as the sex part was concerned. I didn't think of my mother and my father making love; they were just having babies. I never saw them together. When he was in the house, she was always busy doing something—cooking, cleaning, taking care of another kid." Practically all of our interviewees assumed that their parents had a minimal sex life, and quite a few said, half jokingly-half seriously, "Well, I know that my parents must have had sex at least X times" (X being the number of children in the family). No matter what the age of our interviewees or the social mores under which they grew up, most of them saw their parents as passionless people, with little or no sex life. That their parents may have liked sex, and engaged in sex for recreational as well as procreative reasons, was difficult for them to imagine.

When you stop to think about it, this desexualization of parents is quite remarkable because the marital relationship is the one most sanctioned for sex; sex in marriage is not only accepted, but expected. Once married, for the first time in their lives the couple is encouraged to have sex: the bride receives seductive negligees at her shower, the groom is groomed on risqué jokes at his stag party, and the newly-weds are cheered off on a honeymoon designed to heighten sexual passion. The blushes that the couple might have experienced when registering at a vacation resort together before marriage disappear when they sign the register as husband and wife, because they are no longer doing something naughty when they have intercourse; in fact, they are supposed to disappear in the afternoon for a bit of lovemaking and to emerge only for meals. When the couple turns into a family, however, sex somehow becomes filtered out of the home atmosphere. Starting with pregnancy, there is a subtle alteration in mood, and husband and wife may each pull back from the other sexually. The withdrawal is usually attributed to a dampening of desire brought on by increased tiredness, loss of physical attractiveness, or concern about the physical safety of the fetus. With the arrival of the baby, other practical problems are held responsible for the couple's inability to capture their former feelings of sexual freedom and abandon, such as the demands of the infant's schedule or their own exhaustion. While these problems are real, on reflection it becomes apparent that they are not the main reason for the desexualization that occurs in the new family. The presence of an infant, whether as a fetus in the womb or a baby in the room, seems to bring out the couple's self-consciousness about sex and reactivate the old puritanical attitudes that so many parents grew up with. The infant becomes a silent observer of the parents' sexual life, in whose presence they feel called upon to create the myth of the virgin couple.

PASSION ON HOLD

Because people do not like to acknowledge that they are uncomfortable about sex, it is easier for couples to attribute their loss of sexual desire during pregnancy to physical factors rather than to confront underlying feelings. The most common explanation given us by men for the slackening of their sexual desire is the physical unattractiveness of the mother-to-be. The pregnant body is a far cry from what a sexy "number 10" is supposed to be, and because of this, many men find themselves put off by the idea of having sex with their pregnant wives.

For many women, too, pregnancy is a time of reduced sexual passion. The disinterest of their mates adds to their own concerns about their sexual attractiveness, and the excitement of pregnancy can fade quickly as a woman feels her husband finds her unappealing. Madelaine, a very attractive-looking woman and professor of early education whom we will hear from again later, reminisced about her first pregnancy:

◄§ With the excitement of having a baby, I was also looking forward to a time of great sex. We had been having a lot of trouble with birth control. I wouldn't take the pill. Joe wouldn't use a condom, and so we ended up with a diaphragm, which I hated and which always was a mess to use. Finally, sex without care. I don't know whether we were lucky or unlucky, but I got pregnant right off. We must have had intercourse only about three times before I was pregnant, but then after that Joe just didn't want to sleep with me anymore. I mean have sex with me. He was still interested in sex, but he didn't want to have sex with me. It's not that he wanted to have sex with somebody else. He wanted to have sex with me, but not intercourse. He thought of all the different ways I could satisfy him, but he didn't want to touch me. He always denied it, but I think I just turned him off with my big belly. I think he also thought I was disgusting for wanting to have sex, and that I should only be into motherhood. All the time I told myself it was only nine months, but then after Gillian was born and I was nursing her, it was the same thing. It was only after I got her on a bottle that he wanted to have sex with me again. And all the time I felt like it wasn't my body, but belonged to Gillian, and she and Joe were the ones who decided what's what. §►

Sometimes it is not the husband but the pregnant woman who shies away from having sex. Self-consciousness about her body can be intensified by her husband's advances rather than being allayed by them. When a woman fears that he finds her "disgusting," and is "only doing it out of a sense of duty," she often pulls back self-protectively, as if her experienced unattractiveness can be better hidden that way. Edith told us:

❧ Oh, Mark would start fondling me and start kissing me, but I really didn't want him touching me. I never could bring myself to talk to him about it outright, and instead I would just tell him I was tired or not feeling too well so he would leave me alone. In my grammy gown I was safe. I was the mother of our child and he was proud of me, but I was afraid that if my gown came off I would be just a big, unattractive hulk. Maybe he would look at me and get turned off and wish he had another wife. ❧

Not all societies share our view about the unattractiveness of a pregnant woman's body, and in fact not everybody in our society goes along with that notion either. Some men think that a pregnant woman is a definite turn-on and feel aroused by the bulge that attests to their virility. Philip, a cabinet-maker , has three children and wishes he could afford more because he loves the idea of making babies:

❧ I married Ann when I was eighteen, and I got her pregnant the first day of our honeymoon. She didn't believe that she was pregnant until she didn't get her period, but I knew the minute it happened. She had a healthy pregnancy, no trouble, and she never looked better in her life. Her cheeks just glowed. And her bosoms got full, and you could just see that baby growing inside her, getting bigger day by day. What a feeling to see that life there, and to feel the baby kicking. It just filled me with love, with energy, and I just wanted to keep on making love to her, and it was like making love to our baby at the same time. We started on the second kid as soon as the doctor said it was OK and we couldn't wait to have the third. And each time it was wonderful, making a new life and watching it grow and seeing Ann. She looked like the most beautiful woman in the world. ❧

Another reason some hesitate to have sex during pregnancy is that they are afraid intercourse can hurt the baby. While there are some grounds for concern, these apprehensions tend to be exaggerated and many parents sense this. Nancy, a conscientious mother and former nursery school teacher, was quite aware of how irrational she and her husband were about their worries for the baby's safety:

❧ My obstetrician told me that we better not have sex for the first six weeks as it could hurt the baby and maybe cause a miscarriage. I later found out that she was the only obstetrician who recommended that. Anyway, we followed doctor's orders and abstained for six weeks, but after that, when she said it was OK, the funny thing was we were both a little afraid to have intercourse. We decided we were just being overly anxious and should relax and enjoy ourselves, but we couldn't. We did have sex but it was strained. Jim was usually afraid to move or press too hard against me, or else I was afraid he was too wild and then I would tell him to stop so as not to hurt the baby. The best thing was the last month, when the obstetrician told me again we had to abstain. What a relief that was! We didn't have to feel so foolish about not having sex. ❧

After the baby is born, other practical reasons for withdrawing from sex emerge. First there is the prescribed postpartum waiting period, but sexual life rarely reverts to what it was before, even after those six weeks have passed. For the first few months it seems as if the baby completely reorders life according to its own schedule. Sleeping time is broken up into four-hour segments, and wake-up time is ordained to be somewhere around six A.M., no matter what the couple's habitual time of awakening might have been. It seems to parents that whatever sexual life they have is built around the baby's timetable rather than around their cycle of desire. One can't have sex when it is close to feeding time or waking time, and it is better to wait until the baby is asleep again. There is a joke among new parents that every time they start to have sex the baby will wake up. Actually, it's not only a laughing matter. There is evidence* that babies of nursing mothers tend to wake up when the mothers are sexually aroused. The mechanism seems to be as follows: when aroused, the mother starts to lactate, and the baby, through some supersensitivity to the odor of maternal milk, wakes up and cries for its supper. Also, the fact that the mother starts lactating when stimulated is another reminder to both parents that the woman's body now has obligations other than its own gratification. The incessant demands of a baby force many parents to squeeze in their sexual life around the baby's schedule, introducing a new pattern of hurried, anxious sex. Indeed, some parents find that they can only recapture the joys of uninhibited sex if they leave the house and baby and go away for the weekend; many grandmothers have been roped into baby-sitting on such occasions, while the couple absconds to a hotel and an uninterrupted romp in bed.

More basic, though, than the very real intrusions of the baby, whether as bulge in the belly or bawler in the bassinet, are the parents' attitudes about sex. The baby's presence in the home, its innocence, purity, and vulnerability, can bring to the surface all the buried parental feelings that sex is dirty, that it belongs in the motel room or the back of the car, but not at home with the family.

THE SILENT OBSERVER

From the moment that a woman announces she is pregnant, new constraints or, rather, reawakened old constraints color the sexual interaction between the couple. Once a new life is conceived, it is as if there are three people in the bed instead of two. In this particular ménage, however, the third partner does not bring new sexual excitements but instead

---

* As reported by Dr. Richard Krebs, Associate Director, Department of Psychiatry, Sinai Hospital, Baltimore, Maryland, and cited by Bob Gaines, "You and Your Sleep," *Ladies' Home Journal*, May 1972.

brings new sexual restrictions in the form of an additional superego. Where once the couple's parents served as the sexual watchdog, that function is now taken over by the baby. Feelings about sex, which had its own rhythm and tempo before, undergo subtle changes because of the new silent observer. Love between wife and husband may be deeper than before, but a different consciousness develops about sex that causes passion to slacken. Although parents are not clear as to why this happens, many recognize that behind their practical concerns are more amorphous hesitations about having sex once one becomes a parent. Jim, who tends to see things very graphically, perhaps because he is a commercial photographer, expressed his discomfort this way:

◄§ We had a rough time sexually when Martha was pregnant. She wanted to have sex as usual, but I felt very awkward about having sex. It wasn't that she was unattractive to me, which is what she kept accusing me about, but that I felt I didn't belong inside of her. I guess this sounds a little weird to you, but I was picturing Eric inside—I knew it was a boy—and saw him needing his space and felt that it wouldn't be right to crowd him out from the start. I had this awful visual image of him getting drenched by my sperm and shivering and drawing himself up into a tighter fetal ball. I finally decided to use a condom and that made me feel a lot better, although Martha insisted I was nuts. §►

Other men, too, feel as Jim does, that sex during pregnancy is incompatible with fatherhood, but many more women feel that sex during pregnancy is incompatible with motherhood. In her book *My Mother/My Self*, Nancy Friday quotes a child psychologist reflecting on her personal experiences:

◄§ It felt wrong, sex, and me almost a mother. I was into this whole other picture of myself—one of those warm, clean, dedicated mothers you see in women's magazines. Those pretty women don't have sex! They're good mothers and I was going to be one too. . . . Sex became something silly or frivolous, perhaps a bit shameful, that you did before you became a mother.* ミ❦

Having grown up in a world of double standards that make men more comfortable with sex than women, it is not surprising that women are more apt to feel awkward about their sex lives vis-à-vis their children. Among all the couples we spoke to, it was usually the mother who was more reticent about any display of sexuality once there was a silent observer in the home. Susan, who has a daughter now aged four, described how upset she used to become when her husband would relate to her sexually in her infant daughter's presence:

❧ George used to be impossible around the house. I'd be doing the dishes with the baby there playing on the floor with pots and pans and George would come in and "grab a feel," as he calls it. He was a real tease about it because he knew I would not say anything to him while Patty was there, and we would have this silent struggle as I tried to get him to stop without catching Patty's attention. Once on vacation when we went south to visit my folks, we had ordered a crib in the motel room for Patty, and George wanted to have sex. He waited, of course, till she was asleep, but you could never tell what would wake her up. I couldn't even raise my voice to get him to stop for fear she would hear me, and so we had sex, with George grunting away, and I tried not to make a sound or even rustle the covers. I wouldn't speak to him the next day, and when we got to my mother's house we were still not talking. That was the worst trip we ever had. At night in my old bedroom at my mother's house, we had this whispered argument about it and I was furious. As a matter of fact, I still am, every time I think of it. ❦

Other mothers and fathers feel uncomfortable even at more subdued levels of sexuality than that expressed by George.

* Nancy Friday, *My Mother/My Self* (New York: Dell Publishing Co., Inc., 1977), pp.437–38.

Any allusions to sex, talk or gestures that have sexual overtones, become X-rated activities not allowed in front of one's children. A pattern is set that hides parental sexuality from the children and at the same time reinforces the guilt and furtiveness about sexual relations that had only been temporarily submerged. "Careful, not in front of the children" is the parents' way of covering up their embarrassment at being sexual creatures; it also constitutes the unconscious communication to their children that sex is a no-no.

In their need to sustain the myth of the virgin couple, parents find it increasingly difficult to have sex, particularly good sex. Many get locked into the "late-night syndrome," postponing their sexual encounters until the children are safely asleep and they themselves are too tired for sex. When children are old enough to stay up after the parents go to bed, parents feel self-conscious about having sex, as their children might be able to hear tell-tale sounds.

Another complication for parents is the "closed-door syndrome." Ordinarily many parents sleep with their door open, a habit that starts before the arrival of children, when there is no need to close the door, and continues afterwards so they can hear if the baby or child cries out in the night. Once parents and children are accustomed to the open-door policy, it becomes difficult for the parents to close the door again when they want to have sex because they will be faced with the inevitable "Why?" as well as with their embarrassment about the answer. They become concerned lest their children realize that the closed door means sex is in progress. Some parents resolve this problem by keeping their door closed all the time, but others, who close their door only to have sex, disguise their activities with a cover-up such as, "We are both very tired and going to bed now. We'll close our door so you don't have to worry about making noise." Either children intuit that there is something special going on between their parents that they are not supposed to pry into, or else they remain naively unaware of what is going on and end up embarrassing their parents still further by barging in at the most inopportune time. When "caught in the act," parents rarely acknowledge what they are doing and usually try to dissemble with feeble explanations such as "Daddy is giving me a massage because I strained my chest," but their embarrassment alone communicates to the child that he or she has done something wrong. When that embarrassment is too great, parents have been known to become very angry and to yell at their children, thereby upsetting their offspring still more.

On the rare occasions when children are confident enough to ask their parents what was going on behind the closed door, they are apt to be given a runaround. Most of the parents we talked with could not recall a child ever asking them about their sexual lives. The questions about sex that they remembered were asked in general terms like "How do babies get born?" rather than "How did I get born?" Many children are so aware of their parents' discomfort that they consciously withhold questions. Elizabeth, a TV news reporter who grew up in a family where there was a conspicuous absence of any acknowledgment of sex, knew that her mother would be embarrassed, and did not ask what went on behind the closed door because she "didn't want to make a thing of it for her." Maybe Elizabeth's frustrated need to know helped turn her into a reporter!

The few parents we interviewed who remembered being asked questions about their role in the birth of the questioning child tended to evade a straight answer or, worse, to leave their child with incorrect and misleading impressions. Madelaine, the early-childhood expert we met before, understandably held the opinion that a child should be given information when ready for it, and as much of it as the child could handle. Nevertheless, it is apparent from her description of a conversation she had with her six-year-old daughter that the child had to pull information from Madelaine bit by bit, and that she was not given one iota more than what she asked for. While Madelaine felt that she was very forthright in her conversation about sex, she left her daughter with the uncorrected perception that sexual intercourse is disgusting but that one puts up with it once or twice in a lifetime if one wishes to have children:

❧ Mommy, how are babies made? ❧

They are made when the sperm from the father joins the egg from the mother. Daddies' bodies manufacture sperm and Mommies' bodies manufacture eggs.

Where are the sperm and the eggs?

The sperm and the eggs are inside their bodies.

Then how do they join?

The sperm come out from the Daddy's penis.

From his penis?

That's right.

Then how do they get to the egg?

The sperm goes inside the mother's body and meets the egg.

How does it get inside the body?

It goes in through a special hole in the body.

A hole in the body?

Not exactly a hole. It's an opening in the body, right in-between the opening where the peepee comes out and the BM comes out.

You have a hole there?

Yes, every woman has a hole there. You have a hole there too. It's called your vagina.

How does the sperm get into the hole?

The Daddy puts it there.

But how does he put it there?

He puts his penis into the vagina.

You mean he puts his penis into the hole?

Yes, that's right.

Ugh, that's disgusting.

It's not disgusting. That's the way you make a baby.

Then I'm never going to have a baby.&

A little while after this conversation, the daughter came back again to Madelaine and asked:

& Did Daddy put the sperm inside you that way?

Yes. &

There were no more conversations between mother and daughter about reproduction or sex after that for several years.

"NOT MY PARENTS"

As children grow older, it becomes clearer and clearer to them that sex and family do not mix. They get the message that it is better not to talk about sex at home from the fact that their parents do not bring it up as a topic of discussion or turn red when the children bring it up. Children know that sex exists—they see couples on the street, in the park, on TV, kissing and hugging or making love—but they see little or no sexual activity at home. No wonder then that children find it difficult to associate sexuality with their parents. They are programmed to see their parents as a virginal couple who do not relate to each other sexually, and the effect is solidified as the children, for their own reasons, begin to hold on to the notion that their parents are asexual. Having learned that sex is shameful, the thought that one's parents might like having sex becomes upsetting and is suppressed. Bradford, who described the mechanical way in which his father explained the act of sexual intercourse, finds it very difficult to acknowledge the sexual life of his parents. They set him up to think of them as asexual, and he now prefers that fiction to the reality of their rather lusty life together. The thought that his parents have been secretly having sex while he was raised to believe that they were above such shameful passions makes Bradford, even as a thirty-three-year-old sexually active single, feel uncomfortable:

◆§ I don't remember exactly how it came up, but when I was around twenty, my uncle was telling me how much my parents liked having sex and my aunt piped up and said when my parents got married they checked into a hotel and my mother didn't see the light of day until a week. Before that I couldn't imagine my parents having sex, and because they were antagonistic to each other, I certainly couldn't imagine them wanting to have sex. It never dawned on me, the dynamics of it. Not that they had an S&M relationship, but I realize now that is probably what made their sex life interesting for so long—because if you're just friends it's a very boring sex life, but if you have dynamic tension in a relationship you have sexual excitement and interest. Because of their bickering it didn't seem strange to me that they didn't display affection. I never thought of my parents in terms of physical affection, but I would have been startled, even if they had been demonstrative, to know they had a sexual relationship. I know I didn't think about my parents having sex before that conversation with my uncle. Afterwards I assumed that I knew something very private about their life, and that made me feel very uneasy, knowing that they got naked and very intimate with each other. It still makes me uneasy. ଛ➣

The myth of the virgin couple is perpetuated by children not only out of the need to idealize their parents, but also to preserve a childlike attachment to their parents. Acknowledging that parents have a sexual relationship with each other means acknowledging as well that parents have ties to each other that may be more compelling than their ties to the children. Glen, the aspiring actor who had "no notion" about his parents' sexuality, expressed his feelings as follows:

∾ I found it hard to think of my parents' relationship that way. It is like there was a mental barrier to that thought. The thought of it is, like, "Wow!" For one thing my parents weren't very physical, and for another I was close to my mother and maybe had rejected the idea out of some sort of attachment. You know, as if the thought was impossible because she was my mother first and I wanted to see her that way. ∾

Remnants of the old double standard make the concept of a sexual mother harder to tolerate than that of a sexual father. Mothers are supposed to have a primary affiliation with their offspring, and to be caretakers rather than pleasure seekers. It is also more frightening for many children to imagine a mother engaged in sex than a father, as they tend to see sex as a violation of the woman's body. Our experience is that it is harder for boys than girls to acknowledge the sexuality of their parents, particularly their mothers. Maintaining the myth of a desexualized mother seems to be especially important for boys, as they are prone to have erotic fantasies that can threaten their image of their mothers. A mother who can excite sexual interest is too similar to those "loose women" whom boys hold in contempt. We'll look at that more closely when we examine mother-son relationships.

Parents often feel freer to declare their sexuality as their children grow into adults and become sexually active on their own. They may then start to talk about sex more candidly or make allusions to their sexual life together, but to their surprise, the "children," more often than not, become annoyed when their parents do this. Reassertion of parental sexuality is a burden that even grown children do not want to deal with, as it upsets their concept of who their parents are and what they represent. It becomes embarrassing to think of one's parents as sexual if they have previously devoted so much of their energies to maintaining an asexual environment. Many parents we spoke to were taken aback by their grown children's lack of patience for their parents' sexual lives or their children's refusal to acknowledge that aspect of parental existence at all. Bert and Irma are a fairly typical couple in that respect. They are both now in their fifties and have three grown children—a daughter of twenty-five who lives by herself in a different city, and twin sons of twenty-one who are both away at college. Bert is a vigorous man who sells scuba diving equipment and goes diving every chance he gets, and Irma is also quite athletic, although her sport is tennis and her occupation physical education teacher. Bert and Irma think of themselves as "progressive parents," but their attitude about sexual issues has been one of avoidance. While they have not consciously inhibited their children's sexual curiosity, they have been concealing about sex, being careful not to let on that they used their communal bed for anything but sleep. Now that they are ready to swing with the times and let the children know they are keeping up with new mores, Bert and Irma are disappointed that their children are critical of them. Bert told us:

◄§ Our daughter, Beth, often calls us up on Sunday morning just to chat, because the rates are low then and she knows she will catch us at home and not the answering machine. A couple of Sundays ago she called and we didn't have the machine on, because we were home, but we were making love so we just let it ring. We figured it might have been her and made a mental note to call her back, but every five minutes or so it would start ringing all over again. It wasn't the most relaxing sex in the world, but no sooner had we finished when the phone rang again and I picked it up. As I suspected, it was Beth and she was furious. "Where were you?" she asked me accusingly. I told her we were home but just not answering the phone. "Why didn't you answer?" she went on, and I said, in a laughing sort of way, "Beth, what's so strange about two adults on a Sunday morning, alone in bed, not answering the phone?" And then she said, "I still can't see why you didn't answer the phone. You must have known it was me." And I said, still laughingly, "Beth, we were busy, we couldn't answer the phone." And she came back at me, unbelievably, "What were you doing? I thought you said you were still in bed. Why couldn't you answer the phone?" Then I started getting a bit angry and I said to her, "Listen, Beth, your mother and I were in bed doing what people do in bed and I don't see why that's so hard for you to understand." And all she said was, "I can't understand the two of you at all," and then proceeded, very huffily, to tell us what she was calling about. Irma and I were absolutely dumbfounded. Here Beth is—she's twenty-five, I'm sure she's slept with her boyfriend although she never came out and said so—acting dumbfounded that Irma and I are having sex! ❧

PARENTS ARE ALSO LOVERS

We have been describing "mainstream" parents—those who, whether they think of themselves as sexually liberated or not, are at heart unable to integrate sexuality into their family life. Of course there are other parents who do not suppress their sexuality. When parents are open yet unobtrusive about their sexual life, their children seem to accept sex as a normal part of existence, as we saw, for instance, in Mary Travers's family. When parents parade their sexuality, as we saw with Derrick, who lets his children play with his whips and chains, their children tend to react negatively, feeling overburdened by the immediacy of the parents' sexual behavior.

If children are uncomfortable with their parents' sexual attitudes they tend not to talk about it with their parents. This goes not only for children of Sex Repressive and Sex Avoidant parents but for children of Sex Obsessive parents as well. These parents tend to be unaware of the negative impact their open sex behavior has on their children. Charlotte's situation is a case in point. Charlotte grew up in what she described as an upper-middle-class family, very proper to all intents and purposes as far as the neighbors were concerned, but quite disturbing as far as Charlotte and her two siblings were concerned because her parents were engaged in an open and passionate sadomasochistic relationship with each other. Both Charlotte and her sister, now adults in their thirties, feel that their parents' intrusive sexual behavior had a negative impact on their own sexual development, leading to fear of romantic involvement. Because the sisters were unable to understand the loving nature of their parents' aggressive physicality, they were fearful that close attachments would lead only to pain and domination:

⊷ I had a family that did its own thing. I guess on a certain level my parents' relationship was largely sadomasochistic, and they seemed to enjoy it, actually. They had a hot love affair going for about twenty years with each other. When I was with other people's families what I would notice was the peace and quiet, and I used to complain to my mother about it a lot, saying, "Why can't we have more peace and quiet here?" and she would say things like, "Well, what they keep in the closet we have right out here." So they were a volcanic duo—extremely volatile. They were very much in love. They had passion. I suppose in middle-class homes passion is not shown—the less pleasant side of passion, that is. You can call theirs an erotic relationship. It was a volatile love affair. They were not cooled out at all.

I have discussed with my sister the bizarre kind of childhood that we had, its good and bad points. She felt maybe it made us sterile in some kind of way. I don't think she meant biologically sterile but psychologically sterile. I know I never wanted to have a child. I mean, you have to be quite mature to understand what that kind of passion is. Our parents' relationship at a certain level was sadomasochistic, and that would have to scare a kid half to death. It wasn't until I was in my twenties that I started to see men as human beings as opposed to some weird objects that I was supposed to relate to. Then one day I had a revelation that there was a person sitting there, not just an anatomy. It was too much for a child to handle. That's a lot for an adult to handle. I mean they went at it! How do you explain that stuff to a child? I don't know. If this were the island of Samoa or some island where these hang-ups never existed—maybe all these complexes are done away with. I think it affected me more. I think my sister probably got off easier because she was younger, and at the time she was growing up they had already cooled off a little bit. I think it traumatized me, their volatility with each other. I think the big negative for me was fear of closeness. ह❧

Sometimes Sex Obsessive parents start to set boundaries as their children grow older, although this is perhaps done less to protect the children than it is to protect the parents. Nina, a bank teller and mother of three, and the wife of Derrick, the Sex Obsessive father who takes pride in being outrageous, described recent changes she's made in her behavior as a result of feeling intruded on by her children. She is afraid that her children may come to regard her as an outlet for their sexual curiosity, but she still seems unaware of how she is burdening them by being stimulating and frustrating at the same time:

❧ My children have seen me in sexual acts, but now when I want to have sex I tell them, "Leave me alone for ten minutes. I'm going to shut the door and make love to Daddy," and they do. It was kind of accidental when they first saw us having sex. When they were very small it was always natural to be hanging out around the house naked and to be fondling and caressing each other. It set a pattern that it really just doesn't matter. But now that the kids are at the age where there's a sexual awareness on their part, I find myself being more discreet and requesting space when I need it. Susan's body is starting to develop and I feel more conscious of it even if she doesn't, and I think that she does. When they were toddlers they just took it in stride, and they've always just accepted it because that was something that was just given to them. I think they had a sense of what was going on when they were very little because they always left us alone at that time and hung out in their room.

Sex is a thing that people do. It's really nothing to hide. I think they have to see and know at some point because they'll do it, and should not feel it's something shameful. I feel there are certain limits but I'm not sure what the limits are. I've always had just straight sex, and if I feel I want something more, I'll shut the door or go under the covers or ask them to leave us alone. Derrick and I never discussed how to handle sex. We just did it. If they seemed to be content and we were in the mood, we would have sex, and if they would walk in and see, they would walk out and go back to their toys. So it was just a thing that was handled very naturally. I never flaunted it, but I don't think I ever hid it in such a way that the kids would never know that Mommy and Daddy had the same genitals that they did.

I feel ready to change now because of the age of the children and my awareness of their presence. Age comes up at this time because they want to know more about the body, and as a result I just feel that my sexual life should be private. It is no longer something that's just information; it's now more like experimentation and I don't want their parents to be an outlet for their curiosity. I think that it's now time for them to develop their own sexuality and make their own discovery. And I realize now as we speak that I'm getting ready to make my sex more private because it arouses their curiosity more now. If they stood at the door and lingered, that would be totally inappropriate to me now. We're still going around the house naked, but I find myself wanting to be covered and asking Derrick to put something on. They are aware of my body in a different way and mine is not a body for them to share. I don't want them to think I am now an outlet for them. ∂❧

Sex Expressive parents, who unlike Sex Obsessive parents are mindful of limits, are able to acknowledge their sexuality and integrate it into family life without threatening the children. It is even possible for parents in an "open marriage" not to disturb their children if they take care to preserve boundaries. Alice, who describes herself as "one of the original hippies," is such a parent. Although many outside observers might consider Alice's life-style to be shocking, promiscuous, and a bad model for her son, she has been more protective of her child's feelings than have such seemingly straight and monogamous couples as Charlotte's parents or Nina and Derrick. Alice is a youthful person, full of pep and passion and, in her own terms, "very up front." She has an eighteen-year-old son, Reggie, who lives at home with her, and she has been divorced from her husband since Reggie was six years old. Both during her marriage and since, Alice has lived a very free sexual life which was not hidden from Reggie, and he grew up knowing that grownups have fun having sex. Alice, though, has been careful to keep what goes on in her bedroom private out of an intuitive sense that graphic detail would make her son uncomfortable as, indeed, it makes her uncomfortable to be forced to deal with the intimacies of other people's behavior:

ஃ When Reggie was small I was a totally responsible mother until he went to bed. At 7:30 the mother stopped and the hippie came out. If he was still up I was a mother, but when he went to bed it was playtime. I don't mean it was freak-out time. Since I was the only one with a baby and the only one with a house, Reggie always saw people of all ages, because people were always there. We would leave him with my parents for the weekend, go to Washington, get teargassed, and come home, and Pete would go to work.

He saw Pete and me kissing and he saw other people kissing. We had a big house with four bedrooms, and the house rocked. He always saw people sleeping over on the weekends—this couple in one bedroom, that couple in another bedroom. I had to tell Donna at one time, "Please keep the moaning down. We have a kid in the house. Just put a pillow over your mouth—it's not necessary," but Chuck insisted on his girlfriends making a lot of noise. It was the same with Melody when she slept over with Chuck. It couldn't have been because he was so good. One weekend, Pete's brother came with his girlfriend, this was after Pete and I split up, and she was making a lot of noise and that made Reggie uncomfortable because he was old enough by then to know. I think in the back of his head he didn't know what sex looked like, but he knew there was something going on in there that you do when you're older. It's the same thing with me. I don't know what my son does in the bedroom, but I know something's going on in there, and we have a rule: "Just as long as it doesn't make anybody uncomfortable." I don't want to hear bang, bang, bang against the wall. That will make me uncomfortable, and the same rule goes with me. ಶ

Although exposed to parental sexuality from an early age, Reggie did not grow into a sexual monster but into a caring person, very respectful of the young women with whom he forms relationships. As his mother described him:

◄§ He's not of the hippie generation. He started out with a mother who thinks it's very healthy to have sex, but he's a monogamous person. He doesn't bind anyone to monogamy but he doesn't cheat on a girl in a relationship. He is involved in it and respects the other person. Also because I let the girls sleep over, he has had the option to have relationships. He asks, "Can she spend the night?" and I say, "Yes." I didn't have that option. He's had one-night stands but probably in the hope that they would work out and be longer. ಶ

And Reggie confirms his mother's view. He is aware of the way his parents live and accepts their life-style, even though it is not his own. He enjoys having sex and is responsible in his relationships:

◄§ I guess I was around six when my parents split up. I knew they wanted to be alone in their bedroom and do their things at night. That, I guess, you get just from watching a movie. You see a couple, you know every night they go to bed together and they, like at the end of "Hill Street Blues," have a little kiss or something. So you know that leads to stuff. I knew what the idea was. I thought it was fine, OK. Like, they're married and it wouldn't make much difference if they weren't married. Like, sure, go ahead. And all of a sudden they split up, and I wanted a brother to help raise and I wanted them to do it around that time. But when they split up it was like, aw, shit, there goes my chance. No little brother for me.

One thing you got to remember. My Mom was a total hippie when she was young. She used to, when she was married, sleep around a lot and it was just like a nice thing. The attitude I got from my parents is that sex is fun. It's fun and it's nice to be with girls. It's normal. Like everyone I saw was going into the bedroom and shutting the door and having a good time, so I wanted to try it too. I know it always made people happy. And if I ever heard anybody talking about it they wouldn't say anything bad. So I said, "OK, good, this is going to happen to me too."

A lot of the guys I know are into watching porn. I'm not into that stuff. I don't have to. I've always been pretty lucky with girls. My philosophy is everybody should try it. But if you're with a sensitive girl, you got to think about her feelings. I do that. I'm not going to go out and just screw a girl and be like, "Ha, He, Ha. I got her!"

A lot of guys out there sort of rag the girl. There are a lot of girls out there and I look at them and I say, "Wow, how can you be such a slut," because they know they're being used and thrown aside and they don't care. I guess they feel that's the only way they can have sex or be cared for. You see, that's a problem. Another problem is some of my friends they just can't get enough. Or they can't get it at all. There's this one girl in my school and it's really sickening when something like this happens. This girl got really drunk and there were people at this party and they went to the park and to the kiddie's playground and there was a line of people waiting to get her. She just got so drunk and just laid there and let all these guys do it. Her name became "Sandbox Sally" because it was in the sandbox it happened. I don't know how she could let that happen. I know basically what I'm doing. I know if I'm doing something really wrong or if I'm doing something crazy. ৯

Alice and Reggie represent an atypical family, but they illustrate the point that parental sexuality does not have to be traumatic for a child and can, rather, set the stage for healthy sexual attitudes. An example of a more mainstream Sex Expressive parent is Larry. As we saw before, Larry is very open in discussing sexual issues with his children and tries to provide sex education in a natural context whenever the subject is sparked by something on TV, a situation at school, or a conversation they are having. When it comes to his sexual relationship with his wife, Larry is similarly relaxed and open, but within well-defined limits:

⤙ Our children know that their parents are sexual. They say it: "Look, they're going into the bedroom together." I am probably much more comfortable with that than other people. I am perfectly comfortable in saying, "We're closing the door because we want time for ourselves and for our pleasure and fun." And if they say, "I know what you're doing," I say, "You're right. You're probably right. We might surprise you, but you're probably right." It seems to be a trifle intrusive to announce that I'm going to have sex. I don't announce to my kids when I'm going to have a bowel movement. I might say I'm going to the bathroom. I don't think they're requesting that information. That's too intrusive. It's a delicate line. I don't hide it, but I'm protective of them and that accounts for a great deal. My children don't have any trouble knowing that if adults close the door you don't open it. You knock on it. If they say, "What are you doing?" (and I remember them saying, "What are you doing, hee, hee, hee,") I'll tell them what I'm doing—"We're making love." I don't have any problem with that. And then I'll tease them about that. "Did you want that answer?" And they giggle. Other than that, I have never discussed details of my sexual life in front of them nor have I asked them to discuss details of their sexual life with me. I disapprove of intimate sexual conversations between parents and children. I think sexuality needs its boundaries, privacies, specialness. ⤚

Many parents would probably be very happy if their sons and daughters got married, settled down, and stopped running around to singles bars. Nevertheless, they do not set them an example of how gratifying married life can be. Instead they tend to convey a sense of a passionless partnership in which sex has no place and thereby suggest that sex is an extramarital activity or an activity that married people have to forgo. Sex Repressive and Sex Avoidant parents make their children feel guilty about sex and uncomfortable with the idea that their parents might engage in such tainted activity. Sex Obsessive parents tend to overwhelm their children with sexuality, turning them away from romantic attachments in which sexual demands may be made. Sex Expressive parents, by their own example, help children appreciate the role that sex plays in a marital relationship and how it helps glue the family together.

FOUR

DADDY'S GIRL:
THE ROMANCE BETWEEN
FATHERS AND DAUGHTERS

The father and daughter relationship is unlike any other parent-child constellation. Perhaps this is best summed up in the phrase "Daddy's girl," which suggests the exciting connection that exists between the two. While the phrase "Momma's boy" has negative connotations, suggesting an unhealthy relationship, "Daddy's girl," in contrast, conveys an acceptable, close, and even somewhat romantic attachment.

For a long time it has been taken for granted that the major influence on a girl's development is the mothering she receives, but recent findings indicate that a girl's relationship with her father, from infancy onward, has an enormous impact on the way she will experience herself and her sexuality, and on the kinds of attachments she will form later in life. A father, after all, is the first man a daughter knows, and it is through him that she learns how to relate to men. A father's interest in his daughter helps awaken her sexuality, while his disinterest can leave her feeling detached or insecure about her body and her self. Does he find her attractive and encourage her to show affection? Or does he disapprove of her and keep himself distant, making her wonder if she is in some way unappealing to the opposite sex? As she grows up, does he maintain a close relationship with her and participate in her sex education, or does he communicate discomfort with her emerging sexuality?

A father's interaction with his daughter also influences her sexual development in terms of the role behavior that she sees open to her. Does he encourage her to prepare for an independent life and plan career goals with her, or does he persuade her instead to lead a passive existence and look for a man who will take care of her? Does he set up one standard of behavior for her and a different standard for her brothers? Can his son use his tools and help with the carpentry, while she is banished to the kitchen? Can the boys stay out at night, while she must observe a curfew? In myriad ways, a father communicates to his daughter what he and, by inference, other men think and expect of her.

A PROBLEMATIC ATTACHMENT

From the very beginning, fathers are conscious of the sexual difference between themselves and their daughters and relate to daughters differently than they relate to their sons. Studies* show that fathers are more tender and careful when holding girl babies than boy babies and establish more eye contact. This tendency is reinforced by girl babies, who are more responsive than boy babies to the human face. When shown a photograph of a face, for instance, girl infants will smile and make jabbering sounds, while boy infants will not, and this responsiveness intensifies when there is a live face which is interactive and smiles back. Investigators of the early father-child relationship have described girls as exhibiting flirtatious, "vamping" behavior towards their fathers. Girls between the ages of two and a half and three will tilt their heads, cuddle, hug, kiss, lap sit, mold their bodies to their fathers, and make lots of eye contact with them. This flirtatiousness is attributed to the innate sexuality of girls, although it might also be reflecting the sexuality of fathers, who respond differently to the sociability of their daughters than mothers do. Little girls are further encouraged in this type of behavior by the social mores that promote coquettishness—frilled underpants, special lines of "girl's cosmetics," bikini bathing suits, beauty contests, and the like. Regardless of who turns on whom, however, sexual undercurrents are apparent in the father-daughter interaction right from the start.

The father-daughter romance is encouraged by our culture, which puts a premium on female sexual attractiveness

---

* Some of the more recent studies are reported in Stanley H. Cath, R. Gurwitt, and John Munder Ross, eds., *Father and Child: Developmental and Clinical Perspectives* (Boston: Little, Brown & Co., 1982) and Michael E. Lamb, ed., *The Role of the Father in Child Development*, 2nd edition (New York: John Wiley & Sons, 1981).

and highlights the appeal of younger women. Merchandisers look for younger and younger female models to peddle their wares, a trend exemplified by the teenage Brooke Shields proclaiming that there is nothing between her and her jeans. "He's old enough to be her father" is an apt description of many of today's couples, and the older men become, the younger the women they tend to marry. Nobody seems to find it strange that older men, with their greater status, experience, and power, are attractive to younger women, or that younger women, with their svelter figures, smoother complexions, and greater impressionability, are attractive to older men. Male professors often turn to their female students, physicians to their patients, executives to their secretaries, and so on. By the time men become fathers, they have been conditioned to be sensitive to the physical charms of younger females and to be aroused by the awe and dependency of younger females.

For their part, daughters are particularly attracted to their fathers, whose time with them is generally spent in play rather than in caretaking. A daughter tends to regard her father as the more indulgent parent and to look up to him as the more powerful parent because he generally is physically stronger and wields more influence in the outside world. Daughters thus fit right into the image of the female that fathers have been taught to want—except that they have also been taught that their daughters are forbidden objects. No wonder that many fathers find themselves both aroused and repelled by the budding sexuality of their daughters and are often at a loss as to what to do about it. How a father relates to his daughter, and whether he will help or hinder her in feeling comfortable with herself, depends on how comfortable he is with his own feelings about her. The chemistry that makes the father-daughter relationship special from early on also makes it problematical as the daughter grows up.

HOW AM I SUPPOSED TO FEEL?

Despite the dynamic tensions, there is a blanket of silence on the feelings that fathers have towards their daughters.

Sexual acts between fathers and daughters are so destructive that the natural feelings of attraction between the two tend to be condemned as well. The torment many men feel as they become aware of their daughter's sexuality is elegantly described by Joseph Heller in his novel *Something Happened:*

❧ . . . I turn irritable whenever my daughter comes out of her room to chat with us wearing only a nightgown or a robe that she doesn't always keep fully closed on top or bottom. (I don't know where to look.) I either walk right out without explanation (seething with anger but saying nothing) or command her in a brusque, irascible voice to put a robe on or put her legs together, or keep the robe she does have on closed around the neck and down below her knees if she wants to stay. She is always astounded by my outburst; her eyes open wide. (She does not seem to understand why I am behaving that way. I cannot explain to her; I can't even explain it to my wife. I find it hard to believe my daughter is really that naïve. But what other interpretation is there?) Afterwards, I am displeased with myself for reacting so violently. (But there is little I can say to apologize. Where am I supposed to look when my tall and budding buxom daughter comes in to talk to me wearing almost nothing, sprawls down negligently with her legs apart, her robe open? How am I supposed to feel? Nobody ever told me.)* ❧

Many fathers are too anxious about these feelings to acknowledge them, but even though they feel uncomfortable some can, like Joseph Heller's character, describe their distress. The fathers we have spoken to started experiencing discomfort with their daughters at different ages, some as early as age three, some not until adolescence. Kenny, a dashing-looking merchandiser of frames and posters, raised his daughters in the sixties, a period when he himself was experimenting with the freer

* Joseph Heller, *Something Happened* (New York: Alfred A. Knopf, 1974), pp. 175–76.

life-styles then in vogue. He told us he made a conscious effort to create an atmosphere for his daughters in which they could grow up without the sexually repressive feelings to which he had been subjected, so they would feel at ease with themselves, their bodies, and their sexuality. One of the things he did was take baths with his daughters until they were around five or six, when he found himself becoming uncomfortable, just as Jack did in similar circumstances:

∽§ I used to take baths with them all the time. We would get in the tub and splash around together. I was trying to liberate myself. I had never had an adolescence and I was having it then in my thirties and learning how to accept my own body, and I was going through what you're supposed to do when you're sixteen or seventeen. I would say, "There's nothing wrong with it, and how beautiful everybody's body is, and mine too." And I wanted them to grow up with an appreciation of their own bodies and none of the hangups and shame that I grew up with. But after a while it started to bother me. Nothing specific, but it just seemed provocative. §∽

Larry, the psychologist, being more aware of his tendency to become aroused by his daughters, enforced clear lines of demarcation between himself and them by age four:

∽§ When kids are small, fine. I didn't care about nudity. I wouldn't walk into their room nude, but if they walked into my room I wouldn't care. I might not even rush to put on pants. If they opened the door I'd say, "I'm dressing," and if they chose to stay, they'd stay. No child is ever damaged by the opportunity to see her parents have genitals and what they look like. When the kids are very young and they want to jump into the tub, fine. But when they get past age four, I am not going to encourage that. I'll discourage it. I remember telling one of my kids that it was time for her to give up her bath with Daddy, that she was too old for that. I think that as my daughters reached puberty I became more demanding of them and I think that was a reaction against my own feelings. I recall being uncomfortable when my daughter sits with her legs wide open, and her young vagina is sitting out there. I'm uncomfortable and I'll tell her to close her legs. If my kids are sitting in my lap and I'm aware that I have genital contact, I'm concerned about that. I'm a very alert sexual person. I don't walk around with my fly open, and I make sure we don't cross appropriate lines or violate the boundaries. 8⤸

Many fathers enjoy the flirtatious aspects of their relationships with their daughters and do not become uncomfortable until around puberty, when their daughters start developing breasts. Jason, an electrical contractor in his late forties, loves to dance with his daughter, and they would often do so in the living room together in the evening, while waiting for dinner. His daughter Lisa would teach him all the new disco steps and he would teach her the lindy and the tango, but their dancing turned from a time of relaxation for him to a time of tension as she started to mature physically:

⤹ After a while I would find myself watching Lisa instead of just watching the dance steps. She is, you know, tremendously attractive, and I couldn't help noticing her body as she was dancing and it made me feel like a dirty old man. I thought I would teach her more sedate ballroom dancing because it isn't so sexual, but in a way that made it worse. If you're holding somebody you become much more aware of their body than if you are discoing. We'd be doing a waltz or a fox-trot and if I held her too close I would feel her breasts against my chest or sometimes brush against her doing a dip or a twirl. I don't think I was ever so sex conscious when I was dating as I was with Lisa. I had to give up dancing with her for a while until I got used to her new body. 8⤸

What happens when fathers become aroused by their daughter's sexuality? Some, like Larry and Jason, put limits on interactions that make them feel uncomfortable, but still keep themselves available for affectionate and physical warmth and support. Daniel, another aware father, stopped taking baths with his daughter, but he continued to hug and kiss her and be physically close in ways that he found nonarousing:

◄§ I think it's very important for a father to let his daughter know that she's attractive. They can never hear it enough. How pretty she is, how well she looks. I would try to be very careful of affirming her and not undermine her confidence in herself. I am still kind of physical with her. I hug her. When she is upset, she is very anxious to hold hands, to put her arms around me. She comes over and is very affectionate. §►

Other fathers, who are aware of their sexual feelings but feel guilty about having them, tend to pull back in a manner that more radically curtails the way they relate to their daughters. They behave in a Sex Avoidant way, becoming aloof to their daughters in order to defend themselves against their own feelings of sexual attraction. This is most unfortunate because the father's withdrawal can cause his daughter much pain. For the most part, daughters of Sex Avoidant fathers are bemused by their father's pulling back, which they interpret as a flagging interest in them or as a subtle disapproval of their growing womanliness. Either way, it erodes the daughter's feeling of self-confidence and sows the seeds of self-doubt in her about her attractiveness and worth as a female.

THE EMOTIONAL SHUTDOWN

Even worse, from the daughter's point of view, than the father who pushes her away in order to control his sexual feelings is the father who does not recognize his sexual feelings. Consequently, whatever sexual currents there are get blamed on the daughter. These fathers turn against their daughters in self-righteous ways and impose restrictions on them in order to curb their own distress. Sex Repressive fathers are usually patriarchs who rule the roost along clearly distinguished sexist lines. Madelaine, who had the stilted conversation with her daughter about sex we recounted in

Chapter 1, described how her father made life miserable for her and her sister. Not incidentally, her father gave both his daughters names beginning with *M*, after his own name, Marvin:

◄§ I suppose there were happy moments with my father, but I remember him mostly as a killjoy. He was always butting in whenever Mandy and I were having fun, and then there were terrible fights with my mother about how she was raising us. I remember once I went shopping with my mother for a new dress (that's another thing—he didn't want us to wear slacks and we had a big fight about that) and fell in love with this bright red dress that had a big plaid belt. We bought it, and that night when I was modeling it for my father he exploded. "You can't wear that. It's too loud. You look like a little hussy. No daughter of mine is going to go out of the house in a dress like that! Take it off and back it goes." I burst into tears then, not only because I wanted the dress so badly, but because he made me feel like there was something wrong with me. The funny thing is, I almost never wear red. Once I bought a red blouse to go with a tweedy skirt that had red tones in it, and the two really went well together, but every time I wore it I just didn't look right to myself. My friends all tell me that I should wear more red, that it's my color, but I just never feel comfortable in it. To get back to my father, he always complained about my clothes, he wouldn't let me or Mandy wear any lipstick, except when we got to our senior year in high school. And if we ever played in our room with the door closed and he was home, he would just barge in. When we got older and started dating, he made life miserable for us. Mandy had it worse because she was older. He used to wait up in the living room or sit on the front porch till she got home, and call her every name in the book. When it came my turn he was a little better, but not by much. §►

Madelaine feels that her father made her very self-conscious and inhibited about her sexuality. All through high school she turned down invitations to dances because she was afraid of getting physically close to boys, and even now she will only dance with her husband. Her sister Mandy, on the other hand, became the "loose woman" that her father accused her of being. She threw herself into relationships both in defiance of her father and, apparently, in search of the masculine reassurance and warmth that was not forthcoming from him. Both Madelaine and her sister Mandy acted out ungratifying patterns preordained by their father's antisexual attitudes, Madelaine in automatic accordance with his wishes and Mandy in unconscious rebellion against those wishes.

THE BIG DADDY COMPLEX

Some fathers, instead of pulling back from their daughters as they become conscious of the sexual undercurrents, cannot control their feelings, and their delight in the cuteness and femininity of their daughters may take on erotic overtones. In extreme cases this behavior manifests itself in the form of incest, but there are many more instances of what has been called "pseudoincest," behavior which can be characterized as sexually seductive and overly stimulating. Fathers who find it hard to draw a line between noticing a daughter's sexuality and availing themselves of it encroach on their daughters in a variety of ways. Some may become inappropriately physical, insisting that their little girls sit on their laps while they fondle or caress them. Other such fathers may talk to their daughters in a sexually tinged way, telling dirty jokes, relating tales of their affairs with other women, or making passes at their daughter's girlfriends. Charlotte's father, the Sex Obsessive parent who had a sadomasochistic relationship with his wife, talked to Charlotte suggestively and ogled her:

⋖§ When I was in my teens my father would crack jokes about sex. He asked me once if I was curious about what sex would be like. I had a feeling when I was thirteen or fourteen—I developed very young and had very big breasts—I had a feeling that that was the beginning because of the way he looked at me, that perhaps he consciously experienced having sexual feelings towards me. So the question didn't come out of the blue and it came along at that same period of time. For me it was far-out. I mean somewhere deep inside myself it was like I wasn't used to being thought of in those terms. I was thirteen years old. I hadn't experienced anything other than boys jumping on me in the school bus. I mean I wasn't used to my father seeing me in that light. That was the first experience I had with him. At that point he was saying something with his eyes, but I don't know if it was conscious. If anyone had asked him, "Do you want to have sex with your daughter?" he would have died. But that was certainly what was happening at that moment, if only because it made me conscious of myself as a sex object for the first time, in a different kind of way, in a more physical way. &

Charlotte was threatened by her father's intrusiveness, and it created troubling feelings that haunted her for many years:

I especially remember now getting turned on to his smell and the feeling of his tweed jacket. That turned me on. And the smell of his cologne. That was a turn-on. But I repressed all that pretty well. It was only in a dream state that I was aware of having sexual feelings towards him. I don't think I plunged into the middle of my Oedipal trip until I was in my midthirties, when I literally jumped into the middle of it because I had been running away from it for so long. &

Girls react to a father's sexually provocative behavior in a variety of ways. For many girls, a pattern is established whereby they learn to relate to men in a highly sexualized manner, constantly needing to come on to them in order to feel that they are really liked. Other girls cringe at their fathers and other men, perhaps becoming mousey so as not to attract male attention, and some turn away from men completely. When fathers "turn on" to their daughters, it also creates problems in the mother-daughter relationship. Daughters invariably feel guilty towards their mothers, as if they are betraying them, but they may also become angry with their mothers for not protecting them from the intrusive and unwanted attentions of the father.

In our view, one of the most serious consequences for daughters is the tendency to blame the daughter for the father's overly sexualized behavior. From time immemorial, men have found themselves unable to face up to their erotic feelings to their daughters and the finger has always been pointed at their daughters. The Bible, for instance, relates the story of Lot, who is seduced by his daughters after they have induced in him a drunken unconscious stupor in which he nevertheless manages to impregnate them both! The "Lot Syndrome," more recently making a literary appearance as the "Lolita Syndrome," was nurtured by Freud, who gave it an aura of scientific authenticity. What Freud did was to take his female patients' reports of sexual molestation by their fathers and interpret them as hysterical fantasies on the part of the women.* Much of twentieth century "enlightened" thinking has been influenced by his theory of female sexuality, which holds that little girls, because they feel anatomically deprived, turn to their fathers as a way of obtaining a penis. Although fathers' interests in their daughters were not denied (Freud himself had a dream in which he was sexually aroused by one of his daughters), responsibility for arousing sexual feelings was laid on the daughter, with the result that daughters were supposed to become decorous and docile in order to keep the father's sexuality at bay. The old double standard of sexual behavior, which is still quite prevalent, derives in good part from the need of fathers to suppress the normal sexuality of their daughters in order to control their own sexual feelings.

Much of the distress between fathers and daughters re-

---

* Freud first renounced his original belief in the reality of seduction by the father in his letter to Wilhelm Fliess, dated September 21, 1897, which appears in part in *The Standard Edition of the Complete Psychological Works of Sigmund Freud*, vol. 1, ed. James Strachey (London: Hogarth Press, 1953), pp. 259–60. Even his original formulation of actual seduction by the father implied acquiescence of the daughter. Freud never called it sexual abuse or rape, which was probably a more correct description in many, if not all, cases.

flects the father's discomfort with acknowledging that his daughter is a creature of the opposite sex who is growing towards full sexuality and womanliness. This is poignantly illustrated by Anaïs Nin in one of her early diaries when she describes how her father used to photograph her in child-hood while she was sitting in the bath, occasions which she remembers as their most intimate times together. While her father, through this behavior, led her to understand that he admired her displaying her body, he later berated her for using her body seductively. Years after the photographic sessions, Nin was performing at a dance concert and thought she saw her father in the audience, although he was not there. When she told him about the incident he responded, "If I had been there, I would have disapproved absolutely. I do not approve of a lady being a dancer. Dancing is for prostitutes and professionals."*

CREEPING SEXUALISM

Several areas revolving around sex turn out to be difficult for fathers and daughters. The first is "the facts of life." Hardly any fathers we spoke to volunteer information to their daughters about sex. Several fathers did talk to their daughters about relationships and sexual feelings, but they generally assumed that Mom was the preferred source of "technical information." There are many jokes in the folklore about mothers asking Daddy or big brother to tell little brother about the birds and the bees, but nowadays it would seem that fathers are asking mothers to tell their daughters what sex is all about. For example, Kenny, the poster and frame dealer, said:

◄§ I never brought it up with my girls, and unless there's some reason, you wait for them. When they got to be adolescents, there were issues about health and issues about contraception which I was careful to discuss with my wife to make sure she would discuss that with them. Because that

* Anaïs Nin, *The Diary of Anaïs Nin*, vol. 1 (New York: Harcourt Brace Jovanovich, 1966), pp. 87–88.

was her responsibility to do that. I many times asked her if she had discussed it, and what they knew and didn't know about it, so that in my discussions with them I would know where I was with them. ଈ∾

Fathers told us that they feel it is intrusive of them to talk to their daughters about sexual specifics, but what it seemed to boil down to, as we explored that issue with them, was that it made them feel uncomfortable. It was as though they could not help but personalize a discussion and were guarding against imagining their daughters engaged in sex. Jack, who cut off sexual discussions with his daughter as she matured, described how it became too stimulating for him when she had concrete experiences to relate:

ৰ১ Melissa and I had lots of talks over the years, although it sort of diminished by the time she got to late adolescence—eighteen or nineteen—and it got very difficult to talk about. In fact we don't really talk about sex. I don't particularly encourage it. And I don't know why fathers and daughters have to talk about sex after a certain point. I think it's better if they don't. It's her personal business. We talk about relationships a lot, but I wouldn't ask her anything about her sex life. If she brought it up it would depend. A couple of things have come up, and I don't remember anymore what she told me, but it was more than I wanted to know. It wasn't appropriate. Talking about sex is stimulating, and it's not something to talk with everybody about. ଈ∾'

For their part, daughters, too, are reluctant to talk about sex specifics with their fathers, although this is not always the case. As little children, girls are apt to ask questions of either mother or father, but after a while they reserve their questions for Mom. This does not appear to be a natural reticence on the part of growing girls but a learned response to Dad. When fathers talk to daughters about sex or sex-related topics, there is usually a lot of teasing going on which sets up a barrier to comfortable discourse. Girls have the reputation of being teases, but judging from the fathers and daughters we know and interviewed, the big tease in the family is Dad. Some fathers will not talk to their daughters about personal or sexual issues, period, but those who are comfortable enough to carry on a conversation seem to have some residue of nervousness which they cover up with a quip or a crack and a slightly biting edge. This not only deflects their own discomfort but also serves to let the daughters know what Dad's boundaries are. Karen, a twenty-four-year-old graduate student in music education, told us how her father has been joshing her for the last twenty years about her "boyfriend":

≈§ When I was in nursery school, there was this little boy Timmy and we were very good friends. He lived real close by and our mothers liked each other, so we would do a lot of visiting back and forth after school and on holidays. My father, though, always teased me about it. He would come home at night and say, "How is your boyfriend today? How come he isn't taking you out to dinner? Are you sure he isn't involved with somebody else?" And then when I was older and was dating, Dad would kid me or my dates with, "Did you know my daughter had a serious affair before she met you?" Or to me he'd say, "What would Timmy say if he could see you now?" ξ∞

Jessica, now eighteen and an up-and-coming dancer in the ballet corps of an important company, told us a similar story about her father's teasing tendencies:

≈§ I was playing the game of "stinky pinky" with my family at the dinner table one night. I must have been around ten at the time. You know the game? You have to provide a rhyme that matches the definition. Like if I say, "smelly finger," you say, "stinky pinky." We used to play that game a lot. That night, when it was my turn, I used a "stinky pinky" that I heard at school. I asked, "What's a large-sized brassiere?" The answer is, nobody in my family got it, "An over-the-shoulder-boulder-holder." After that, my father was always kidding me about it. He'd say things like, "When you grow bigger we'll have to get you an over-the-shoulder-boulder-holder," and, of course, when I did get my first bra, which I got pretty young because I developed quickly and needed it for dance classes, he made some crack about my finally getting an over-the-shoulder-boulder-holder. Even now, he'll still say things like that if my bra strap shows through my leotard for instance—"Oops, your over-the-shoulder-boulder-holder is showing." He's just like a big boy about it. He reminds me of the naughty boys who used to put girls' pigtails in the inkwells in the old storybooks. ॐ

Daughters are sensitive to their fathers' touchiness about sexually tinged issues and tend, therefore, to go to their mothers for information and advice. Olivia, a college sophomore living at home, described her hesitancy with her father this way:

ॐ I know I can always talk to my father if I want to, but it's much easier to talk to my mother. After all, my mother is a woman like me so it's natural to go to her. Besides, with her we just talk. With him he makes a joke out of everything and he's always teasing me about everything. I don't get offended, really, but sometimes I just don't want to hear his cracks. He's very weight conscious and always is making remarks about how much I'm eating: "Oh, another helping of potatoes? Your bottom will start to look like your Mom's." Or he'll say, "Are you sure two slices of cake are enough for you?" He means well, but it can be such a drag. ॐ

A very touchy issue for fathers and daughters is menstruation. Most daughters prefer not to acknowledge anything about their periods to their fathers, and their fathers learn about their daughters' onset of menstruation through the mother. In some Sex Avoidant homes, menstruation becomes a big secret. Daughters squirrel away their sanitary napkins and tampons, and are careful to purchase them when Dad is not around. If menstruation should interfere with any activities, care is taken by father and daughter to make some nondescript excuse which both know is merely a cover-up. Mary, a homemaker now in her late thirties, recollected her early teens and embarrassments with her father in this way:

◄§ It was always worst for me in the summertime because the family spent a lot of time at the beach. When I had my period I would never go swimming. I used to wear sanitary napkins. It was before I started using a tampon, and you couldn't go in swimming with a napkin. Everyone would run right into the water as soon as we stretched out our beach towels, except for me. My father would say, "What's the matter, Mary? Come on in!" And sometimes he'd start to pull me up to drag me into the water. Either my mother would say, "Oh, leave her alone, Ted," or I would say, "I don't feel so good," or sometimes my father would suddenly say, "Sorry, never mind." I suppose everyone knew what was going on. That always made me feel very peculiar, like he suddenly realized what was going on, and then he would sort of avoid me when he wasn't in the water, like I wasn't supposed to play ball then either or do any of the tumbling-wrestling games we used to do at the beach. §►

Some fathers, in distinction to Mary's father, talk about menstruation, but in the gently teasing way they talk about other aspects of their daughter's sexuality, making such comments as, "Seems my little girl is becoming a big woman now." It is possible for some fathers, however, to take their daughter's menstruation in stride. When Allison married Ben, for example, she was surprised at how relaxed he was in talking to his teenage daughters from his first marriage about their periods, in contrast to how uncomfortable she had felt with her own father:

◄§ Ben and the girls are really very together in that particular respect. Whereas when I was a kid I would be dying of cramps and would never tell my father, and he was a physician, they can do that. It amazes me. He'll say, "I'm going out, do you need anything?" And they'll say, "Yeah, could you pick me up a box of Tampax." §►

For most men the onset of menstruation is experienced as something of a threat in that it announces the sexual maturity of their daughters and forces them to deal with an issue they would rather ignore. Sex Repressive fathers, who cannot face their own feelings, tend to project them onto their daughters, usually in a hostile manner. Many fathers start to become very critical at this point, watching their daughters very carefully and commenting negatively about their behavior: "Watch how you sit, don't cross your legs like that," "You look like a little tramp in that sweater," and so on. When daughters start dating, the verbal assault escalates, as we have already seen with Lynn Caine and Madelaine and her sister.

One of the ways in which a father communicates to his daughter his feelings about her sexuality is by his comments about other women. Many fathers think nothing of making cracks about "women drivers," "the ball-breaker at work," "lady cops," or in other ways denigrating women who are leaving the traditional mold and venturing into new fields. Obviously, such contempt does not encourage girls to aspire to roles which may be competitive with those of their fathers. Similarly, many fathers make hostile remarks about women's sexual behavior and characteristics. Jessica, the ballerina with the teasing father, related the following incident:

◄§ My father was reading in the paper about Marilyn Monroe's affairs with Jack Kennedy and Robert Kennedy and then he said, "She was just a whore." That got me very angry. I told him, "What about the Kennedys? What did they do that was any different?" My father said, "She slept with them because they were powerful, because she wanted something from them," and I told him, "They slept with her because she was glamorous and they wanted something from her too." He thought for a minute and said, "I suppose you're right." §►

Jessica is fortunate that her father is open to what she has to say and can reflect on his own attitudes, but many fathers voice sexist sentiments to their daughters without in any way realizing or acknowledging the damaging effects this has on their daughters' comfort with and acceptance of their sexual selves.

Nudity is another delicate issue between father and daughter in many families. In Sex Repressive homes there is usually strict separation between father and daughter right from birth. Some fathers even prefer not to see their infant daughters naked and leave the bathing and diapering completely to their wives. This attitude, in part, reflects the sexist division of labor to which they adhere, but it can also reflect discomfort about physical intimacy with a baby of the opposite sex. Such fathers continue to be careful to avoid their daughters of any age when not fully clothed, and to step out from their own rooms only in a robe or shirt and pants. The less repressed the father, the less body covering he considers necessary. Some fathers are perfectly comfortable appearing in the house in their undershorts and think nothing of seeing their daughters in a slip, but very few can take nudity in stride. Several of the men we spoke to, who were relaxed about nudity in the home when their daughters were small, started to cover up when their daughters approached the age of four or five. Jack and Kenny, you may recall, used to bathe with their daughters until around that age but then stopped because they thought it was provocative and unduly stimulating of the child. Larry also stopped, but he could acknowledge that the person being unduly stimulated was himself.

ROLE WITH THE TIMES

A father's sexual attraction to his daughter may be denied, ignored, or projected onto his daughter, but none of these strategies makes it go away. They are devices to help the father deal with his guilt and discomfort, but they usually are not very effective and they certainly do not take the daughter's feelings into account. A daughter needs recognition and acceptance of her growing sexuality, and a father needs to separate his appreciation of his daughter as a sexual person from the perception of her as a sexual object. Of course a father's discomfort with his daughter's sexuality is something he has to be prepared to work on directly, but many fathers can use a little help from the family in recognizing and dealing with their feelings. Like Joseph Heller's character who bemoans the fact that nobody ever told him what to feel, fathers often do not know what to make of the sexual stirrings which they experience in front of their developing daughters. Fathers do not want to be aroused by their daughters, they just are; and when a father is too ashamed to acknowledge his feelings, it can be a great relief if someone else can help him do that. William, one of the fathers we interviewed, had a hard time dealing with his daughter Irene's boyfriend, who would smooch with Irene in front of him. When he stalked out of the living room and holed up in his room, his wife followed after him, scolding him for being rude and acting like a jealous lover. This confrontation escalated into an argument between William and his wife that made them uncomfortable for several days. In describing the incident William told us:

◆§ Of course my wife was right. I was overreacting and my male possessiveness was acting up. It wasn't so much that Irene's boyfriend was horning in on my territory, or that I couldn't handle the thought of her being sexual. It was more that I felt isolated, as if no one had any regard for my feelings. Maybe it's wrong to feel that way, but it's very hard to see your little girl suddenly becoming a woman and have her guy carrying on in front of you. If only my wife had said something sympathetic to me like, "Gee, that must be tough for you," instead of rubbing my nose in it. All I needed was a little understanding of my feelings and that it wasn't easy for me. §◆

When things cooled down, William and his wife both talked to Irene about how her father felt. William apologized to his daughter for his surliness with her and her boyfriend, and tried to explain his feelings to her. He told us proudly of his improved relationship with his daughter, and how a couple of years and one boyfriend later, she called him up before bringing her new companion home for the weekend and asked him, "Daddy, do you think you can handle that?" As William described it, he was able to be gracious to her new lover because his daughter had eased the way for him by showing understanding for his feelings.

One of the best ways to create a comfortable relationship between father and daughter is for the father to give up the traditional role of removed provider and take an active role as an involved caretaker. The more a father learns about the day-to-day rearing of his daughter and the more he participates in the act of cleaning the oatmeal off her chin, burping her after a feeding, and changing her dirty diapers, the less likely he is to be disturbed by her sexuality. It used to be that fathers saw their daughters when the latter were washed and fed and all dressed up in their pink pajamas; in short, the daughters were presented to them as objects for admiration or toys for play. When a father has daily responsibility for a daughter and checks out her body for diaper rash, that body will tend to lose its fascination for him. A daughter's growing sexuality then becomes part of her overall well-being and growth, not a thing apart. It is not accidental that Sex Repressive fathers tend to enforce strict divisions of labor and activities in the home along sexual lines and keep themselves aloof from child care, while Sex Expressive fathers tend, for the most part, to be men who see child care not only as their duty but as their privilege.

When a father can relate to his daughter in a relaxed way and treat her as another person in the house rather than as his pet toy, the problematic areas seem to fade away of their own accord. Issues of menstruation and nudity, for example, cease to emerge as issues. A father who is not used to covering himself up, literally, will generally feel no need to do so in his daughter's presence if he is not covering up sexual feelings that he has been unable to acknowledge and work through. In such homes, where the atmosphere is relaxed, nudity is regarded as a natural state and father and daughter are not aroused by seeing each other nude. Olivia, the college student who is uncomfortable with her father when he teases her, thinks nothing of seeing him in the nude, or vice versa:

⊷ In my house we all like to be nude. Not to go parading around nude, but not to have to put something on just to be proper. When I come out of the shower, for example, and go back to my room to get dressed, I don't want to have to take a wet towel from the bathroom to cover myself with and then have to take it back to the bathroom to hang it up. I like to go to my room naked and then get dressed. What's the big deal? If my father sees me, he sees me. And the same goes for him. It is much more practical that way. We only have one bathroom in our house, and there are four of us. If my father has to shave while I'm in the shower that's no problem for me, or for him for that matter. It's different, though, with my sister. She doesn't want him to see her nude. It doesn't bother her if he's naked, but she's very private about herself. I think that's because he used to tease her about gaining too much weight. She used to be a lot heavier and he was always making cracks about that, and I think that she's just embarrassed about her body and how she looks. Even when we get dressed in the morning she doesn't even want me to see her naked. She always turns her back to me when she puts on her clothes. Before she got fat, I don't think she cared one way or the other. ⊷

Another important undertaking for fathers is to open up the lines of communication with their daughters to talk about sexual issues, and without the teasing. When a father is not afraid to talk to his daughter about sex, he is letting her know that he accepts her sexuality as an integral part of her life. Larry told us that although he may have been a bit lax in talking to his sons about sex, he has made a special point of having a discussion with each of his daughters, both to let them know he is accessible and to convey to them his acceptance of their sexuality:

⊷ I'm much more inclined to make sure that I talk to my daughters than I am with my sons. I think that when fathers do not talk about sexuality to their daughters, it leaves them with a sense that fathers are disapproving and not approachable. Fathers are models for their sons, and it is easier for a son to observe his father and see how his father relates. But it's more difficult for daughters, and there is often a sense of decorum that cuts off direct communication. That's why I make it a point to talk to my daughters about sex. ৡ

Larry's discussion with his younger daughter, which he described for us, conveyed a sense of his understanding of her sexual feelings, and reassurances about his support and availability:

৻ Essentially I explained to my daughter that it's very understandable and very desirable that she is interested in and exploratory about her body, her sexual feelings, and the bodies and sexual feelings of her friends, both boys and girls. I told her that I thought it was difficult at her age to have to deal with the different attitudes to sexuality that people have and that she had to understand that the very open attitude we have in this house was not something everybody shared. Therefore she would have to make decisions about how open she would want to be with others about her sexuality, her behavior, and her attitudes. I told her that when she started to engage in sexual activity was entirely up to her, and that I was available for counsel, but that no permission or reporting was necessary.

I wanted to have this conversation before there were any pending issues. I advised her that often young people get very involved in the physical and emotional aspects of sexuality, understandably, without being thoughtful about the consequences. I told her that sixteen- and seventeen-year-old kids were more likely to fuck first and think later—and I used language like that—and that it does not mean you are evil but that you didn't think about consequences soon enough. This is always accompanied by the other side from my kids of "Oh, I know that, Daddy. I wouldn't do that." My daughter has always said, "Daddy, the most important thing is that we trust each other," and I think that's so. I do not supervise my daughter in that sense. I emphasize with her that I know she often feels lonely and wants to be loved and that sex is a way that people get over feeling lonely, but sometimes you fool yourself and she needs to be thoughtful about it. I explained that she had choices in contraception and I would be very happy if she wanted to see a gynecologist, and I emphasized to her that it was her body that would bear a baby, so she couldn't expect somebody else, even someone who cares, to be responsible for that.

I talked to her about promiscuity, and that I felt there were advantages and disadvantages. The advantages are it increases your sense of possibilities of the kinds of experiences that are available, but the disadvantages are very significant in terms of reality factors. Heavy traffic means greater exposure and possibly leads to diseases. These are serious issues that she had to think about. I also told her she should be aware of social attitudes—she might be misunderstood by people if she were sexually more experimental than her friends, and she would have to decide her own personal view and understand that her sexuality is her responsibility. That's the substance of it. ঌ

Although few fathers have the psychological background and training that Larry does, the importance of his message is clear and easily replicated. All a father has to do is address his daughter as another person facing the same qualms and questions about sexuality that he faced growing up, and trust her instincts that he has helped to cultivate through his tender loving care.

FIVE

OEDIPUS HEX:
THE GUILT TRIP OF
MOTHERS AND SONS

The romantic attachment that enhances the father-daughter relationship has a counterpart in the mother-son relationship, but one that is loaded with guilt. Closeness between mother and son is either derided, as in the phrase "Momma's boy," or feared, as in the Oedipus myth. The mother-son dyad is the most talked-about of all family constellations and the only one to be understood in terms of a neurotic "complex" rather than as a naturally occurring attachment. Despite the psychoanalytic smoke about sexual undercurrents between mother and son, there is little fire and mother-son incest is an exceptionally rare phenomenon. Just as significantly, boys who have close relationships with dominant and omnipresent mothers often turn out to be highly successful rather than wimpy men. Franklin D. Roosevelt, Winston Churchill, Douglas MacArthur, and even Sigmund Freud are among the long line of famous men who had exceedingly close maternal ties. In studying mother-son relationships it has become apparent to us that many of the popular theories are out of line with what really goes on.

Most of what we have been told to date about the mother-son relationship comes from men. Freud developed, and his followers keep alive, the theory of the Oedipal complex, which holds that a boy's inevitable desire to sleep with his mother is inflamed by the mother's seductiveness and need to possess his penis to compensate for the lack of her own. Other male writers and commentators have elaborated on this theory, offering the concept of the overbearing mother whose frustrated need for sexual possession of her son expresses itself in "smother love." This version of the Oedipal complex appears under such labels as Momism, The Jewish Mother, or The Devouring Mother, and has gained general credence through the popular writings of novelists and essayists. D. H. Lawrence, for example, in describing the mother in his novel *Sons and Lovers*, said, "She selects them (her sons) as lovers. . . . But when they come to manhood, they can't love, because their mother is the strongest power in their lives, and holds them."* Devouring, sexually motivated mothers also crop up in such best-selling novels as Bruce Jay Friedman's tellingly titled *A Mother's Kisses* (Simon & Schuster, 1964) and Dan Greenburg's *How to Be a Jewish Mother* (Price, Stern, Sloan, 1964). Philip Wylie offered a nonfictional version of the overbearing maternal vampire in *A Generation of Vipers* (Farrar & Rinehart, 1942), later elaborated on by Hans Sebold in *Momism: The Silent Disease of America* (Nelson Hall, 1976). Analysts who posit a psychological basis for homosexuality have long pointed their finger at Mom, and have only recently backed off, recognizing that a father, too, might have some responsibility for his son's sexual development. At base, most of the prevalent theories of mother-son relationships are sexist rationalizations that make Mom the fall guy for unacceptable male sexual impulses.

We see the mother-son relationship as being a good deal less sinister and more human than psychoanalytic theory has made people believe it to be. Mothers, of course, play an important role in the developing sexuality of their sons, and a mother is the first female figure a boy relates to, but she is not inherently the seductress whom sons are warned to guard against. Twice as many mothers, when first pregnant, want to have a boy rather than a girl.** Freud reduced this to the mother's desire to obtain vicariously the penis she was denied at birth, but a son represents much more than that. There is an undeniable added excitement merely in having a child of the opposite sex, and for many women a son provides a connection to the male activities they may be cut off from. As society begins to provide more opportunities for women, we would be surprised if this preference for boys does not drop off.

---

* D.H. Lawrence, *The Letters of D.H. Lawrence*, ed. Aldous Huxley (New York: Viking, 1932), p. 78.
** Study conducted under the auspices of the Population Reference Bureau by Nancy Williamson, demographer, reported in *Ms.* May 1978, p. 20.

Mothers are drawn to all their children in a protective and nurturing way, and many, though not all, are drawn closer to sons by the sexual element that exists in their relationship. But both mothers and sons are programmed to renounce the closeness of their relationship. Thanks to the prevailing sexism that dictates different standards of behavior for boys and girls, the cuddling and coddling that mothers, and fathers, enjoy with daughters is considered suspect when it occurs with sons. As one researcher has noted, a girl is supposed to grow up learning not to be a baby, but a boy is supposed to grow up learning not to be a girl.* After a relatively short time of indulgent nurturing, boys are expected to engage in male pursuits with their fathers rather than snuggle up to their mothers. Indeed, by the age of one, boys show a clear preference for their fathers. Instead of allowing love to flow, mothers feel called upon to push their sons out of the nest and encourage them to follow in the footsteps of their fathers. At the same time, mothers are made to feel guilty for harboring desires for closeness, as if such behavior represents a stoking of the Oedipal flames.

Complicating the picture is the fact that hormones have a life of their own. Sons may be taught that it is wrong to go snuggling up to mother, but it does feel good and, despite themselves, they find it arousing to see her body or brush against the protrusions on her chest. Later, the uncontrollable erections and wet dreams that steal upon boys make them feel vulnerable and exposed. No wonder that they experience their mother's sexuality as a threat and pull back, often angrily, because of what they think she is doing to them. Mothers become, in effect, the prototype of the male concept of "the tease."

In this context it is not easy for mothers and sons to maintain a carefree intimacy and acknowledge each other's sexuality. The mother is left to balance the needs for closeness and sexual affirmation against the potential for overstimulation in the relationship with her son. When mothers and

---

* W. Emmerich, "Young Children's Discrimination of Parent and Child Roles," *Child Development*, 1959, 30, pp. 403–419.

sons feel uncomfortable about their mutual attraction, they tend to withdraw from each other and sons may learn a pattern of emotional disengagement that so many of their lovers and wives will later complain about. And if mothers blame themselves for their sons' natural sexual feelings, as they have been taught to do by Freudian-dominated psychology, they can also unwittingly teach their sons to deny any responsibility for those feelings. When a mother is unaware of a son's discomfort, she may inadvertently continue to excite him, and if she encourages his attentiveness because of her needs for male affirmation, they may well reenact the Oedipal drama. But when a mother and son can appreciate each other's sexuality, the son learns a way of being with the opposite sex that is affirming and close and his mother has the continuing romantic acclamation that can be a vital element in maintaining her positive feelings about herself in a society that denigrates her appeal as she advances in age.

EARLY AWAKENINGS

Mothers have a close physical bond with their children very different from that experienced by fathers. Not only does the mother carry and nurture the child for nine months, but after birth as well she is in close physical contact with the baby, whether nursing it, giving it the bottle, burping, diapering, or bathing it—all daily functions that require handling, touching, snuggling. With boy babies this close physical contact heightens the mother's awareness of the sexual difference between her and her son. Nursing is particularly apt to bring consciousness of sexual differences to the fore, and the pleasurable sensations many mothers experience when nursing an infant may become imbued with erotic overtones when that infant is a boy. As boy babies tend to be more physically active than girls when nursing and to manipulate the breast more, the sensations experienced with boy babies are likely to be more intense, further abetting sexual awareness. Some mothers with a Sex Obsessive orientation find that they are turned on by nursing their sons, and they can be reluctant to give it up because it feels so good. Joan, a single mother who is still nursing her two-year-old son, described that feeling: "I just love it when he sucks at my breast. It is such a good feeling to know he needs my milk so much and that I can provide him with everything. And he grabs hold of my nipple and latches on and sucks so hard, it makes me come." Some mothers prolong nursing out of a need to keep their sons close and dependent, a need which may also have a sexual component. Joan's two-year nursing period is a short time compared to the four years of breast feeding that the novelist Thomas Wolfe enjoyed and the seven years of nursing that industrialist H. K. Hunt was reportedly given by his mother.

Although there is always the possibility of excess, a mother's sexual feelings for a son are not basically injurious. If she can accept those feelings as an expression of her strong involvement and reject the socially induced guilt for having them, they can enhance her experience without jeopardizing his.

A number of mothers (particularly Sex Avoidant women) told us that they felt hesitant about nursing their infant sons. Having been cautioned about the likelihood of Oedipal attachments, they were afraid that they might be guilty of eroticizing the relationship if they became involved in the nursing experience. Their anxieties about possible seductiveness made them pull back and interfered with their ability to make the most of nursing as a time for emotional closeness. Other Sex Avoidant and Sex Repressive mothers, though, were matter-of-fact about nursing. Debra, who is now in her forties and works part time as an editor, nursed both her son and daughter but looked upon nursing as just another aspect of child care, and maintained that there was a total absence of sex awareness as far as her son was concerned:

⩤§ I nursed both my children because I felt it was the better way. I think I felt the same way about both of them. I didn't feel my son was a child I got more satisfaction from or that it was much more elemental or pleasurable. They were both very warm and cuddly children, and I didn't feel I was holding a male child as opposed to a female child. It wasn't at all arousing. That in no way entered into it. He is my child and he isn't my husband and you don't have that kind of relationship. I didn't transfer those kinds of feelings. ֍

It would seem that sex was an irrelevant factor to Debra; however, because of her husband's reaction, which we will explore shortly, we wonder whether it was one that she just preferred not to deal with.

Some fathers become more possessive of their wives after a new child is born, feeling that the infant is competing with them for their wife's physical favors. Such fathers may not only become more demanding sexually of their wives, but resentful of her maternal functions, and they may even seek to interfere with breast feeding. As Dr. Spock, the ultimate authority on child care, has noted, "Quite a few fathers, including some very good ones, object to breast feeding— they can't help feeling jealous. . . . So the mother has to use her best judgment," implying that a mother might have to forgo breast feeding in order to placate her husband.* This jealousy obviously intensifies if the baby happens to be male and, in turn, makes it difficult for a mother to nurse a son with equanimity. Debra, who told us that nursing her son was no different than nursing her daughter, also told us that her husband did not initially take very well to her nursing their son:

֍ I was aware that he didn't really like the idea of my nursing Duncan. I think it may have been different for him because he grew up in a family that was very proper and contained. At least his mother was. But I think the concept was difficult for him to deal with at the time, because even though twenty-three years ago there were women who nursed babies, it wasn't prevalent at the time. It was something I wanted to do. He was supportive of it, but I knew it was something he was uncomfortable about and he didn't like to be present when I was nursing. ֍

* Benjamin Spock and Michael B. Rothenberg, *Baby and Child Care* (New York: Pocket Books, 1985), p. 106.

As Dr. Spock further notes, fathers may also be upset by milk leaking during lovemaking, another potential obstacle to nursing. It sometimes happens that fathers find the sight of a nursing wife or a leaking breast arousing rather than inhibitory of their sex drive. These fathers do not insist that their wives forgo breast feeding but may instead make their own competitive demands.

Many mothers feel more self-conscious handling their sons' bodies than their daughters'. Because women are less familiar with male anatomy, when a male child is born they may be somewhat at a loss as to what to do. Taking care of a girl is like taking care of oneself, but taking care of a boy baby is a different order of experience. Sherry, whose two children are now in their early thirties, described how clumsy she felt when her son, her first child, was born:

✎§ I do think that initially I was more concerned about how to handle a baby boy as opposed to a baby girl. I don't think it was a sexual thing but what do you do with a boy? If I had a choice I probably would have chosen to have a girl, only out of a feeling of more security, but he was such a lovable baby, so I don't remember feeling I wish I had a girl instead. It wasn't a strong thing. I just think it's that a little girl is more like me and I could do things with her and dress her and play dolls and do some of the things that seemed more natural to me. ঈ

Bathing may be an awkward time for some mothers as boy babies are apt to have erections when they are being sponged, making mothers aware of their role in stimulating their offspring. Some mothers may pull back from their sons, others may engage their sons with greater intensity, and still others may take it in stride, but in any event sexuality becomes an issue in their relationship. Sex Expressive mothers notice and appreciate their infant sons' developing responsiveness without interpreting it as a statement about their motherly allure. Alice, the "hippie" Sex Expressive mother, describes how aware yet relaxed she was noticing that her son's sexual equipment was in good working order:

❧ I always thought it was funny that his penis was an exact miniature of his father's—an exact version—the same little thing shrunken down. I didn't look at his erections as a sexual thing. It didn't turn me on in any way. He was just a responsive baby—a very responsive baby, and he still is a very responsive person. ❧

PUSH ME–PULL YOU

Because boys model themselves after their fathers, they imitate the father's behavior vis-à-vis the mother. While parents like their sons to be "little men" around the house when it comes to being brave and developing physical prowess, parents are less tolerant when their sons try to enact the father's husbandly role. When boys become physically attached to their mothers, snuggling, cuddling, and wanting to sleep in the same bed with her, they are often made to feel that their behavior is inappropriate; although this behavior is called babyish, it is the adultlike quality of it that fathers and mothers find disturbing. Veronica, a potter who lives with her husband and teenage son, told us a funny story about her son when he was about five years old, and it was only the humor of the situation which helped her put her own concerns into perspective:

❧ When Jeb was young, he always used to come into our room and hop into bed with us. When he was a toddler, it just used to be a lot of fun and we would play games in bed together, horsing around, having pillow fights, and so on. Then, when he got older, it just didn't seem right to me anymore. I never really stopped to think about it, but one day I just decided, OK, that's it. And I said to him, "Jeb, you're a big boy now and you have your own bed and I don't want you coming into our bed anymore." And he pulled a face and said, "Why not? It's not fair. I don't have anyone to sleep with in my room." And I told him that it's different for married people, that they sleep together but other people have their own bed. And that Daddy and I were married so we slept together. And that he was getting older and someday he'd get married and have a wife and he would have somebody to sleep in his bed. And he looked at me, with his big blue innocent eyes, and he said, "But Mommy, I don't want to marry you, I just want to sleep with you." ॐ

The striving for masculinization of boys interferes very early on with the spontaneity with which mothers relate to their sons, especially on a physically affectionate level. In addition to concerns about being seductive, which have been impressed upon them by the widespread acceptance of Freudian concepts, some mothers are also concerned about their sons becoming too "soft" and "tender," harboring a secret fear that their sons may grow up to be gay. They are on the lookout for any signs of femininity, under which rubric are lumped together such common childhood feelings as dependency, separation anxiety, and the need for attachment. The cuddling, hugging, and kissing which flow naturally from mother to daughter can be inhibited from mother to son when the son becomes old enough to respond in similar ways. Displays of physical affection by a son towards his mother are often labeled "sissyish," and boys then learn to repress this side of themselves. Society accepts physical closeness between fathers and daughters but not between mothers and sons.

The mother-son relationship is taxed further by the overt signs of sexual arousal in boys. The sexual development and arousal sequence in girls takes place on an internal level, except for the development of breasts, but with boys "it all hangs out." The erections that boys experience without concern in infancy start to disturb them when they occur later, seemingly beyond their control, announcing their state of arousal. Similarly, boys are embarrassed about the telltale stains of their wet dreams and discomfited in front of their mothers who are then privy to their personal feelings. When boys grow up in an atmosphere where sex is hush-hushed and their mothers never discuss ejaculation or wet dreams with them, as happens in ninety-nine out of a hundred homes according to a recent survey,* they become secretive

---

* Project on Human Sexual Development, *Family Life and Sexual Learning,* vol. 1, A Summary Report (Population Education, Inc., 1978).

about their sexuality and start to pull back from their mothers for fear of being exposed. The undercurrent of sexuality which enlivens the relationship between father and daughter tends to disturb the relationship between mother and son.

Another problem for mothers and sons is that their timing is out of synch. When boys are small and need closeness with their mothers, many mothers purposefully and literally keep to a hands-off policy in order to avoid being labeled Oedipally seductive and to help their sons become independent. By adolescence boys have learned to keep their distance from their mothers and prefer to keep it that way so as not to become inadvertently aroused by them. But at this point mothers begin to look upon their sons as old enough to relate to them in a closer and more companionable way. A mother may also look to her son, who is becoming a man of the world, to notice and affirm her attractiveness, which she comes more and more to doubt; not only does society disparage her as an older woman, but her son becomes involved with young women, as may his father as well.

The less secure a mother is about herself and her sexuality, the more needy she becomes of her son's attention. This is particularly true of mothers who have unfulfilling relationships with their husbands, and of single women who may have no other male companionship than what their sons can provide. It may, however, also be true of the many happily married mothers who have been brought up to value themselves primarily in terms of their attractiveness to the opposite sex. Society sets up expectations that mothers, as women, should be fussed over: while mothers are supposed to care for their children and see to their needs, when boys come of age they are supposed to take care of mother and see to her needs. The male role still carries with it the requirement that boys relinquish their dependence on mother to cater to her as a member of the weaker sex. The tacit acceptance that the boy should play "little man" to his mother encourages mothers to look to their sons for the attentions they may not be getting elsewhere. Many mothers take it for granted that their adolescent sons should flutter over them and act the role of the gallant. We will get back to this issue in a later section of this chapter.

When a mother has a positive self-image and is not dependent on her son for sexual affirmation, his attentions, rather than frustrating her when missing, help to enrich the relationship for both of them when they are forthcoming. Mothers enjoy, as who would not, the admiration of their sons. Felicia, whose sons are now teenagers, said, "They see me as sexy, because they comment on how well I look. Of course it makes me feel good." Sherry, who was initially wary of her son when he was an infant, told us how she came to appreciate his maleness when he grew older. She has a good relationship with her husband, and one that has been sexually gratifying, yet she gets a special high from being together with her son, Blake. She described how exciting it was for her to go dancing with him, and the romance of receiving a personal gift from him:

☙ I always thought of Blake as handsome, and attractive as a male. I would be very excited at a wedding to have Blake dance with me. I would always feel good about that. I just felt that he was a very handsome, attractive male to me. I didn't want to have sex with him—at least I wasn't aware of feeling that. I guess I was just proud of him as a very good-looking male and as one who was in control of things, as you would with any child. I don't know how much of it was sex and how much it was that he was doing well and looked well and was attractive to people, but I think there was a masculinity aspect to it too. I wouldn't enjoy dancing with my daughter. I enjoyed dancing with Blake. I certainly saw him in a masculine role. I think he sees me as feminine. I think so. Yes, I think the way he hugs me and the way he'll enjoy buying me a blouse for a birthday and seeing me wear it shows that. "Oh Mom, you look terrific." I have the feeling that he sees me as a woman and it's just a very warm feeling at that moment. My husband doesn't go out and buy blouses or clothes for me. His attitude is more if you want something let's go out and get it together, and we'll just go and buy it. But one of the charming things about Blake is that he likes to surprise people. I have three blouses that he's given me over a period of time, and whenever I wear them someone will always say, "What a beautiful blouse." He has exquisite taste. There is something very romantic about him. ᑐ

No wonder women who do not have a solid sexual relationship with a husband or lover are tempted to seek this kind of ego gratification through their sons.

GETTING THE MESSAGE

Because of sexual tensions in the relationship, mothers often leave the job of "formal" sex education of their sons to fathers, just as fathers leave the sex education of daughters to mothers. As with all other questions, boys tend initially to refer their sexual queries to their mothers until they pick up vibrations that this is a subject to be handled "man to man." When a question about sex is asked, mothers usually deflect it in some way such as "Why don't you ask Daddy about that when he comes home?"

We illustrated before a tendency among parents not to offer sexual information spontaneously and, when confronted with questions, to provide no more than what is specifically asked. In responding to sons' questions, mothers usually limit conversations about sex to the physiology of reproduction and the importance of acting responsibly with girlfriends. Debra is fairy typical in the way she has handled sexual issues with her son, Duncan, providing minimal essentials when confronted directly and passing the buck to his father, Philip:

ᑐ When he was small, I took him and his sister to see a lot of animals so they would know about where kids came from and how people were born. I think they really started to have questions when they were about six or seven about how it happened. Our discussions were more about how babies were born than how they were made, and it was only as they got older that we talked about that. I didn't bring it up. If they asked a question I would answer it. They started to have questions of how it happened and how the sperm got into the mother's body. We discussed it, that the father injects his penis into the mother. I told them what they asked in a way they could understand, and if they had any more questions they could take it from there. At eleven or twelve, Duncan brought up questions again, but Philip talked to him then. The only thing I said to him was that he was to treat girls that he's with with the same kind of respect he had for his sister. Philip wanted to talk to him about it. I didn't feel I had to be the person. If Duncan had wanted to talk to me about it, he would ask me the questions and say, "I want to talk to you." ᚼᴗ

Usually the message that sex is a taboo topic with Mom is conveyed subtly, but sometimes a son is made to feel guilty for asking a question. The memories of such encounters linger on for a long time; even adult men whom we interviewed remembered the shame they were made to experience because they asked their mothers questions about sex. Vincent, an advertising executive who is married and has children of his own, reported such a conversation with his mother:

ᴗᚼ I recall when I was a little boy I raised those questions. When I raised it, it was with my Mom and I recall that vividly. I can remember saying, "How are girl babies different from boy babies. What's the difference?" And my mother, I remember she whispered it. There was nobody else in the room. She whispered, "By their penises," and that was it. I think she must have changed the subject. It was a topic that was not decent even though my Mom was raised on a farm with many sisters and brothers. This incident I was talking about, I couldn't have been more than three or four. It was one of my earlier memories. I felt I must have said something terrible. ᚼᴗ

While married mothers can get away with minimal responses, single mothers have a harder time with their sons in this regard. Women who have never been married, or who were divorced or widowed when their sons were young, usually find themselves called upon to field more questions than they feel comfortable with. This comes about because their sons do not have another parent to turn to and also because the mothers' dating behavior arouses more questions in their sons' minds about what goes on between men and women. Stephanie, the divorced mother of a nine-year-old boy, described her acute chagrin at the questions her son brought home to her:

& 3 I've been asked a lot of questions. They come up after peer input. For instance, when he was about seven he said to me one day, "Mommy is it true that ladies have to suck men's penises and lick their balls and men have to suck ladies' vaginas?" And I sort of said, "Who told you that?" I wanted to crawl beneath the cement and die, and I said to him, "You don't have to do any of those things. When you get older and find a lady that you like and she likes you, whatever the two of you decide to do together, that's OK." And that was the end of the discussion, but I was totally horrified at what these kids were passing on to each other. When he was younger he once asked me, and he put it so crudely, "Do you and my father hump?" So I asked him what he meant. And he said, "Do you have sex?" And I said, "Yes, we did. That's how I got you." And he said, "Oh," and then he asked me, "Do you and my father still hump?" And I said "No." And he said, "Why?" And I said, "Because we don't feel the same way about each other that we used to." And he asked, "Why?" again, and I said to myself, "Oh God, why is the sky blue?" and I told him "Because people change and they want different things out of life, and sometimes the people they are with change and sometimes they don't, and sometimes it wasn't always so clear-cut," and that was where we left the discussion. &

Because Sex Expressive mothers feel freer about answering questions, they are comfortable providing more than the minimum necessary technical information. Reggie told us that his mother spontaneously talked to him about a wide variety of sexual issues, and sometimes with a great deal of humor:

◆§ By the time she started talking to me about sex, I already knew mostly everything because, like I said, there were always people around, so I guess I had, like, interest in things before most people do. She used to tell me things like, "There are different ways to go about it, without getting a girl pregnant," and she'd just talk a lot about sex. She'd talk about jerking off, going down, and using a rubber. . . . My father, he had weird ways of going about things. Once we were out driving and there were a bunch of guys walking with their hands pointing down, just like this, and he pointed at them and said, "They're all faggots." He didn't explain why he called them faggots. He just said, "That's a faggot," and I saw the wrist like this, right? So I said to myself, "Oh, that must be what it is." After that, for a couple of years, anytime I caught myself like this with my hand down I said, "Oh, no, my Dad's going to think I'm a faggot." It got me paranoid, because I didn't understand exactly what he meant. He didn't explain faggots very well. But my Mom, the way she explained it to me was with this guy who lived in our building. He was married to this girl and then he got divorced and started living with guys. And she explained to me that he was gay, that some people called him bisexual but he's really trisexual—"He'll try anything. He'll even try a donut." I said OK, that means he's trying guys, you know. And that's how I figured out about him. §◆

Shaping the information that mothers provide their sons about sex is, of course, their attitude about sex and its role in life. It is generally assumed that boys are into sex for sex's sake but that for girls sex is a more central experience. When it comes to daughters both mothers and fathers are concerned that their daughters are not used sexually or hurt emotionally, and when it comes to sons mothers are primarily concerned that their sons behave in a responsible manner. They are afraid that their sons might let their sexual impulses get the better of them and lead them to use a girl sexually or contract a disease. Before, we saw how Debra preferred to keep a low profile on sexual issues with her son and let her husband Philip do most of the talking. In one area, though, she initiated the conversation, and that was on the issue of responsibility vis-à-vis the girl:

❧ When Duncan started to go out seriously with a girl, I asked him about his attitudes towards the girl, and just that I wanted him to have a sense of perspective about that, and what his feelings were and whether he could keep them in check in terms of being respectful of the girl. I raised it with him before he asked something of me, because I wanted him to know he had to think about the other person in the relationship. I think what I was trying to communicate was the sense that there was a certain amount of responsibility in the sexual act and being able to assume that when you were together. That it wasn't a one-way street, and that both of them needed to feel comfortable about what they were doing with each other, and have a sense of responsibility that if you're going to have intercourse with someone it wasn't just to satisfy an immediate sexual urge. It was a mutual agreement and that it wasn't something that was done just out of a supposed great passion that afterwards they'd both regret it. And I told him to be sure that he knew that the girl was either taking the pill or that he used a condom, and we talked about venereal disease and the responsibility. ❧

BOYS WILL BE BOYS

Mothers' worries about responsibility in sex seem to come from a feeling based on common earlier experiences with boyfriends or husbands that males cannot be completely trusted. Many mothers tend to be leery of their son's sexuality to the point where some identify more with the needs of his girlfriend than with his needs. These mothers fear that their sons' sexual urges can get out of hand and be hurtful to their girlfriends. Much of mothers' behavior towards sons is motivated by a tacit acceptance of the notion of lurking sexual impulses that need to be restrained. Some of the reticence in talking to sons spontaneously about sexual issues comes out of a concern that it might be titillating and encourage sons to let go the reins of their impulses. Sons pick up the idea that their mothers don't want them to look upon sex as an inviting possibility. Eddie told us how his mother tried to diminish the importance of sex by talking about it, when she was pressed, as an infantile, undignified activity:

◆§ My mother didn't like to talk about that stuff. She called my penis my doo-doo. She would call sex—she has a problem even today—she calls it kid stuff. My mother was very asexual. I never really saw sex being presented as—and this could really be me doing dime store psychology now— but I never saw sex being presented in any kind of attractive light. It just wasn't a thing that cultivated and mature people would stoop to. §◆

Because mothers take it for granted that their sons have urgent sexual needs that are difficult to control, they try to be accepting of masturbation as a necessary outlet. Stephanie, for example, described her laissez-faire attitude to her son masturbating:

◆§ He doesn't exactly hide it from me per se. He masturbates now. We have cable TV. Sometimes he'll be watching something at 11:00 or 12:00 and it becomes more adult, and occasionally I'll be in the other room and I will come in and find he's awake watching some overt sex on the TV, and between that and I guess he's at a point where he's also changing so he's masturbating more. Sometimes I see him actually fondling his penis, other times he just lies on his stomach rocking. If he's aware that I'm in the room he'll stop, but most nights he will go to bed playing with himself. I don't take that from him. I don't comment. §◆

Mothers are far less accepting, however, of sexual play between their sons and age-mates, whether male or female. It is very hard for them not to interfere with a son's exploratory sex play with other children because it arouses their anxieties that it may get out of hand. Mothers are particularly upset when sex play involves a girl as they fear that the girl might be pressured into compliance. Julius Fast told us how his aunt, who acted as a part-time surrogate mother after his own mother died, "caught" him playing with girls, an event which had unexpected repercussions:

❧ When I was about four or five years old, after my mother had died, I spent some time with my aunt, and one day I went into the weeds in back of the house with a couple of little girls and we played a game called "Doctor"—which meant you examined each other and looked at each other—and one of the little girls went and told my aunt, and she was furious. This was the middle of the week and my father was coming on Sunday, and all week long she would say, "Wait till your father comes. He's going to kill you. I can't imagine anything worse than what you've done." My father came on the weekend, and oh, great satisfaction! She proceeded to tell him, "You know what your son did? He was playing doctor with little girls in the weeds." And my father said, "Doctor? When he grows up he'll be a doctor. That's wonderful." ☙

Usually the aftermath of being caught at sex play with a girl is not so pleasant. Stephanie, in contrast to her relaxed acceptance of masturbation, was very upset when her son Richard was caught playing with a female cousin:

❧ He had an incident with a cousin. He spent the night with this cousin and they were playing, and the following day at one point they got very quiet and his aunt went to see why it was so quiet and she found the kids lying naked on the bed next to each other and she was quite concerned. Her girl is four years younger. And I was surprised that he would do this kind of thing because he never struck me as being sexually precocious. But she explained what she saw happening, and I said, "OK, I will deal with him." She said she told them this was inappropriate behavior and that they should not take off their clothes and lie down together. Sometime after, I approached him on the subject. I said, "Your aunt told me about the incident that happened, and

I'd like to hear what you have to say about it. Whose idea was it to take off your clothing?" And he said, "It was her." And I said, "Are you sure it was her idea, not yours? I mean, you're older than she is. Where did she get such an idea?" He said, "But you asked me and I told you. It was her idea." And I said, "So you followed her." And he said, "Yeah." And I said, "Well, don't you think you should have said 'No'? After all, you are older and supposed to know better." He said, "I never thought about it." So we had a long talk, and I said, "No matter what anybody tells you, you better think about it because you have to be responsible." And we talked about not allowing anyone to touch him in his private places, not to touch his penis, not to touch his rectum, not male or female, and for him not to do it to male or female, and especially not cousins, 'cause it was against the law. &

In her concern about Richard's sexual impulses getting out of hand, Stephanie made a mountain out of a molehill. Although Richard's interaction with his younger cousin would have been inappropriate if Richard had pushed her into doing things that were uncomfortable for her, in and of itself their sex play was not unusual for children. Stephanie assumed the worst and blamed Richard for the scenarios she imagined, whereas what he needed was help in working out guidelines for evaluating the appropriateness of sexual behavior in different situations. By denouncing all sexual exploration and touching as not permissible, Stephanie instilled guilt in Richard for his sexual curiosity, and by stretching the truth and invoking "the law" as the authority rather than her own standards of right and wrong, she eroded the sense of trust between mother and son. Stephanie may have set up additional barriers to future communications with Richard by first blaming him for what happened and then suggesting he was not being honest.

Within Stephanie's message to Richard is the same stress on the importance of responsibility that we saw before with Debra and her son. This issue is particularly relevant to Stephanie as she is continually reminded of how her ex-husband behaves in an irresponsible manner with her:

✑ I don't want him to think he can get away without being responsible. Yes, you can go out and do all the things you imagine, but don't lose your protection. You're going to have to pay for the things you do. You will have to pay the consequences, so the message I want to give Richard is responsible sex. You must be responsible for the protection, just as she is. If she's not, then you must be responsible. Be prepared to pay the consequences. Part of the problem in my household is that I receive no financial aid whatever from Richard's father, and when Richie wants things and makes demands on me I'll tell him, "Look, there's only one salary, your father sends no money." And the message is clear: "Look, this man is not responsible." And on the other hand I'm saying, "You're a boy and you have to take responsibility for everything that you do or don't do." So there's a contradiction. If he's a boy and must be responsible, then why isn't his father sending money? Why isn't his father responsible? That's a tricky thing to try to teach a child. ✑

Paradoxically, mothers who stress responsibility to their sons often also convey the belief that their sons are not fully responsible for their sexual behavior. When a mother emphasizes to a son that he should "keep his feelings in check," she is also implying that his sexual urges are so strong that he might not be able to master them. As we will see, mothers try to control the environment so their sons will not find it sexually provocative rather than teach their sons to control themselves. In this fashion, mothers unwittingly relieve sons of responsibility for their sexual behavior.

Although most Sex Repressive and Sex Avoidant mothers want to curb their sons' sexuality because they fear that it can get out of control, some take pride in their sons' masculine prowess and encourage them in macho behavior. Despite their verbal disapproval, these mothers appreciate sexual questions as signs of masculine precocity, and sexual play as evidence of masculine irresistibility. As these boys become older, their mothers propel them into sexual encounters. While other mothers tend to identify with the girls with whom their sons get involved, these mothers are more

identified with their sons. Even those who have had unhappy sexual relationships themselves when younger seem
to get vicarious pleasure in the exploitative role in which
they cast their offspring. Dolores, for instance, has had a
very trying relationship with her husband, Mike, who is a
"ladies' man." He travels a great deal and tries to make
sexual conquests wherever he goes, taking more pains to let
Dolores know about his affairs than to cover them up. She
reacts by trying to make herself more appealing to him and
acting in a seductive way when he is around, including
doing the black-lace-nighties routine. Although his behavior
hurts her and makes her feel insecure, she encourages her
three sons to follow in Mike's footsteps:

❧ My two younger boys, Curtis and Ian, date a lot and
never get serious with a girl, like Mike Jr. Mikey is the least
like his father, and he is always wanting to go steady and
have a real girlfriend. I tell him the girls are just after him and
he better watch his step and make hay while the sun shines.
His brothers are out getting theirs but Mikey is too good for
his own good. He's a regular prude. I tell him his brothers
are more like M&Ms and he's more like a marshmallow. He
has to be hard as nuts inside and not all mushy. Curtis and
Ian are so popular they can have any girl they want, and
believe me, they do. ❧

When mothers identify with masculine sexual exploitation, it
obviously interferes with their sons' development of responsible attitudes about sex.

NOT MY MOTHER!

We described earlier how most children grow up denying
the sexuality of their parents, but boys in particular have a
strong need to see their mothers as asexual beings. There are
at least two reasons for this. One is that the traditional
double standard which tells boys that sex is all right for men
but that "good" girls like Mom don't "do it" is still hanging
in there. Boys' locker room talk about making out and their
contempt for the girls they make out with apparently hasn't

changed for generations. Here is Darryl, a fifteen-year-old high school student, commenting on that scene, *anno* 1987:

◄§ They say that if the girl enjoys it more than the boy does, then it's like she's doing it a lot. They don't like girls like that. Guys say, "Hey, the more he gets the better he is." It's like girls they know are loose and seem to have sex a lot, they don't want to talk to her. They want to talk to the girls who don't seem to have sex a lot. The quiet ones. If a guy does it they say, "Wow," like it's great. If a girl did it, "She did it. That's a shame." ξ~

Boys still resist recognizing sexuality in their mother so that she does not fall into the category of "a girl who did it."

Another reason pubertal boys want a desexualized mother is more directly self-protective. When a boy experiences his mother as a warm, sexually attractive creature, he may find himself aroused by her, a very threatening feeling if he feels guilty about it and if those feelings cause him to depreciate his mother. As we will see with Darryl, a boy can become angry with his mother when this happens and try to get her to downplay her attractiveness to him. Mothers pick up on these messages and may become overly cautious and hide their natural appeal.

The sensitivity boys develop about seeing their mothers as sexual beings is reflected in attitudes towards nudity in the home. At first, mothers and sons tend to be relaxed about nudity. Many mothers are at ease about it in the early years, keeping the bathroom and bedroom door open when bathing or dressing and unconcerned about being seen in various stages of undress. During these years a mother's bath time is often a favorite time for talks as she is then relaxed, accessible, and not busy with chores. Most mothers, however, including those who feel that nudity is a natural mode of being, find that their sons, on reaching puberty, start avoiding them when either is in any stage of undress. Even Alice and her son, Reggie, who are Sex Expressive people, experienced this onset of modesty. Alice told us:

⊷ It seems like one day he wanted me to stop bathing him. It was the same thing with my brother who is nine years younger and who I used to take care of. I think it is when they start getting hair. I figured it out. They start wanting you to stop when they have hair. I wasn't allowed to come in while he was taking a shower anymore. He used to come in when I was taking a bath to ask me a question or to talk, but he stopped doing that. We only have one bathroom so now I use the shower curtain around the tub. That makes it two separate rooms. He won't come in and pee when I'm in there, but he will come in and brush his teeth. ⊷

Most of the young men we spoke to could not tell us why they did not like to see their mothers in any stage of undress, other than that "it just was not right," but some were quite angry about it. Very likely much of the anger these young men experience is anger that they find themselves aroused by their mothers and are brought face-to-face with these feelings in themselves. Darryl expressed it this way:

⊷ My mother will walk around with her bra on, and I say, "Hey, why don't you put some clothes on." I don't like it! She's supposed to wear clothes, set an example. When I walk around I wear an undershirt and pants. Or she'll take off her clothes and put on a gown. I don't want to see it. It turns me off when I see her in her underwear. I don't want to see her like that. So I tell her to put on some clothes. ⊷

By and large, mothers pick up these cues from their sons and make it a point to keep themselves carefully clothed if and when their sons express discomfort. Occasionally mothers are made to feel guilty by other people about letting themselves be seen nude, including professionals in the mental health and child development fields who feel that maternal nudity is seductive and inappropriate. That happened with Debra when she sent her son to therapy because of a learning disability:

⊷ Duncan was in therapy, when he was about six, because he was receiving medication for his learning and his social behavior. The psychiatrist was very Freudian and he said, "If there's anybody walking around nude, just don't. It's a very critical time in his experience and it's a critical time for boys. And he may feel inadequate in relation to his father, and he may be threatened by you and the invitations you are sending out." It was a turning point in family habits because before that there was the feeling from the whole movement in the sixties that if people go around with no clothes on it's a good idea not to have those inhibitions. It used to be very natural for us. There wasn't any exhibitionistic quality. &

Some boys have difficulty with their mother's sexuality not just because of guilt about their tendency to arousal but because the mother is, indeed, invasive. This tends to occur more often with married mothers who are disturbed by flagging interest on the part of their husbands, and single mothers who lack male companionship. The mother's emotional neediness makes her look to her son for the acknowledgment of her womanliness that she doesn't receive elsewhere. In effect, these mothers turn their sons into surrogate boyfriends, dressing up for them, going out with them to dinner or the movies, and proving to onlookers that they are admired by an eligible young man. John, an aspiring rock star who makes his living playing cocktail piano, is one young man who was burdened by his mother's neediness. His father, who is twenty years older than his mother and lacks her vitality, has become very sedentary, leaving John's mother feeling bereft of a suitable companion. John felt so encroached upon by his mother that he moved out of the house as soon as he could afford to support himself. His initial anger at her demands and guilt over refusing them became modulated only after several years of therapy:

&§ All through high school it seems and in my first year of college when I was still living at home, my mother was always there, always wanting something. It was "Drive me here" and "Drive me there," and "Your father is no help, he doesn't care." Or it would be "Let's go to the movies. I want to see this picture. Your father never wants to go out." And she would always be getting tickets to a concert, or a play, or to a visiting opera company and expecting me to go with her. And if I didn't want to go, she would complain about me being selfish and uncaring and how she couldn't go alone, or couldn't get there if I didn't drive her, or something like that. After I moved out I thought that would be the end of it, but she still expected me to come for dinner, or she would invite me out for dinner or call me up for lunch. Sometimes it would be fun. I'd have a good meal at her expense and we would gossip or talk about a movie or a play. She was always interesting to listen to and was very charming. But often she would go off on a tangent about my father and what a clod he was and that used to get me very annoyed. She was right about him, but when she complained it was always as if she wanted me to fill in for him and set it all to rights. It also bothered me how she always got dressed for dinner and wanted me to get dressed too. I figured we were just meeting to eat, but for her it was like we were out on a date. She wanted me to show up in a suit and tie and take her home afterwards. When I was feeling angry and didn't really want to meet her, I would show up with my five o'clock shadow and T-shirt and she would get really riled up. I guess I was never aware of what I was doing until we talked about it in therapy and I saw I was using that as my protest. ஃ

Roy, a divorced systems analyst, had a mother who was more sexually intrusive and more blatant in her needs than John's mother. According to Roy, she used him "to fill the emotional gap" left by the unsatisfying relationship she had with her husband, and she became even more demanding of Roy during her temporary marital separation:

ஃ When I was very young, I'll say six for want of a better number, my mother used to run around the house without too much clothes—certainly in her underclothes. She would continually adjust herself in my view, putting on her bra, her stockings, taking them off, stuff like that. Also she would just grab me and hold me close—closer than I wanted to be with her, and all that did was arouse me and there was no gratification. It was uncomfortable just because of the sexual business. I'd pull away, but she was always watching me— I felt spying on me. It was a weird situation. She had no compunction about barging in when I was in the tub. She did that when I was in my preteens. When I was a teenager it stopped. There was a time when I was young when my father wasn't in the house. He was living elsewhere. At the time they explained it in terms of work, but they had split up and they had really violent arguments. My mother and I were very close then, and I think she used me to compensate for the fact that my father wasn't there, and I think that's when my sexual feelings were aroused. Later on when my father returned to the house, I don't believe she was as close but she was still provocative. I remember the extreme closeness when he was away. &

Roy's mother put him in a state of almost constant arousal, seemingly oblivious to the effect she was having on him. For a long time, even after he left home, Roy found that it was difficult for him to establish relationships with other women:

&§ I had managed to get out of the house and was living in the dormitory, and then my father died and she said come and live with me. There was a definite attempt to latch on to me. When I got older I was able to have sex with other women. It was just when I was younger I was really not able to relate to any women. I wasn't able to relate to anybody and I had no way of socializing. She had made me very uncomfortable. I wished she would have let me alone. Considering how much she did to arouse me, I felt the least she could do was have sex with me (laughs). I was angry at her for running around in a state of undress. She would have pooh-poohed the whole thing. But also, that would have been an interest which I wouldn't have wanted to admit to. &

THE ONLY GIRL IN THE WORLD

Sexually seductive mothers, like John's or Roy's, are more apt to be found in families that consist only of boys. When a mother is the only female in the household, father and sons often feel called upon to take on the role of the strong and gallant male protector. Such mothers are treated like the weaker sex and fussed over, almost like a family pet. The male ethos of the family makes it easy for the mother to give up her caretaking functions and hasten the independence of her sons. Without daughters to coddle or to share the male adulation, mothers are freer to cater to themselves, and if a mother has a narcissistic streak, she may end up the center of attention in the family. For some women, having attentive sons to fuss over them also provides an acceptable way to play out Oedipal desires.

The relationship between Erik Lee Preminger and his mother Gypsy Rose Lee illustrates the kind of role reversal that can occur between mother and son when a mother is the only female in the household. Until he was six, Erik lived with his mother, his stepfather, Julio, and his mother's "homosexual factotum," Boyd. After his mother broke up with Julio, she and Erik lived alone together until he went off to school as a young man. Erik was his mother's constant companion and assistant, traveling on the road with her, helping her in the dressing room, running her errands, and acting like her caretaker. Their life together was centered on Gypsy's needs, rather than vice versa. As Erik describes their interaction, his mother looked to him for affection rather than being able to provide it:

◄§ This is going to sound more hostile than it is, but I think my mother did not have a lot of experience in her life of healthy, nurturing, loving relationships. The closest I think she ever came to that was with her animals, and I had a feeling that in a way she related to me almost as a glorified lapdog when I was younger. Just like you see these women who will carry their dogs into restaurants and hotels and parties. I think I sort of went along as part of that syndrome. I don't mean that in a negative way. I think that just was what this woman knew. You have to remember that my mother started working when she was four years old . . . and she just had to have been raised under the most peculiar circumstances, backstage in vaudeville theaters for most of her life and burlesque at the age of fifteen. . . . God knows when this woman had the chance to develop and learn about a relationship between two people. . . . She was very, very aloof. There was little hugging and touching, and once we had a big fight about it as a matter of fact. . . . We were having a fight about something, and I remember saying, I think I mentioned it in the book (*Gypsy and Me*), "How can you call this family? We never touch, we never hug." She said, "Well, you've never been a very demonstrative little boy." And you know, that is just a very telling comment because the dogs were slavishly devoted to her and jumped on her all the time. I suppose if I had done that I would have broken through that reserve. ❧

Although Erik does not feel there was any conscious sexual need on his mother's part, he recognizes that this must have played a role in their relationship:

❧ When my mother broke up with Julio, when that relationship ended, we left for Europe, where she was playing in the London Paladium, and for the next year and a half my mother and I were together constantly, but I mean we hardly separated for a moment. We shared the same hotel room, we shared the front seat of the car. . . . At that age, at six or seven years old, what more could a boy-child want than to be his mother's constant companion. . . . I remember now as I'm talking to you . . . that I used to play little tricks on her. I put little slithery things—little rubber spider things—in her bed, and I'm sure that anybody who is into Freud could do really big things about that. So I'm sure that was there, but neither of us was aware of it. But I'm sure it led to a foundation that probably had its effects in the storminess of the breakup during my adolescence. ❧

This breakup was occasioned by Gypsy's fury at finding out that Erik was sexually involved with his girlfriend, an affair which she tried to stop by threatening Erik. As Erik said, he had become "the man in her life," and his mother was not able to share him with anyone else:

⋖ It threw her for a loop. She didn't approve. She thought that for a fifteen- or sixteen-year-old boy to be having sex was absolutely appalling, and she was going to try and stop it, even if it meant sending me away to a military school. . . . It's certainly a control issue, but that's not an uncommon way for a parent to sort of slip sexual jealousy into a role that's more comfortable. For instance, it wouldn't have been acceptable for her to say, "I'm jealous of Erik having sex with this person," but in fact she felt that she should be in charge of me until I was twenty-one years old, I suppose. Or even later . . . She really wanted to keep her hands around me. But of course I was the only man in her life. ⋗

YES! MY MOTHER TOO

Some mothers, who are Sex Expressive, are able to integrate their sexuality into the day-to-day life of the family without creating waves at home. This goes both for married mothers and for single mothers who have sexual partners. The mother's attitude to the expression of her own sexuality is acceptable because it is part of a total attitude towards sex that includes an openness and respect for her son's sexuality as well. These mothers, unlike Sex Avoidant mothers, make it a point to talk to their sons about sex just as they do about other important topics, and to keep open lines of communication so that their sons can come to them whenever they have questions. These mothers also convey to their sons a sense that sex is a life-enhancing activity to be shared by women as well as men, and mothers as well as fathers. They do not set up sex as a raging force which sons must struggle to control and against which they may be powerless. Instead they help their sons achieve a balance between responding to the sexuality within themselves and others and recognizing everyone's legitimate boundaries.

When mothers hide their sexuality from their sons because of concern that it makes their sons uncomfortable, they not only limit their relationship but also help perpetuate the attitude of male irresponsibility that they fear. A mother who feels she must deny her own sexuality because of her son is giving him the message that she, not he, is the source of his sexual feelings and behavior: she is telling him that he is not expected to control himself and that other people must modify their behavior for his convenience and comfort. This type of interaction between mother and son, in fact, sets the pattern for later sexist male behavior. Boys who think their mother must at all times appear fully clothed so as not to excite them also feel that women whom they meet in the street must not dress in a "provocative" fashion unless they want male reactions. When a mother shields her son from having to deal with his own sexuality and takes on responsibility for his behavior, she sets the stage for a mentality that allows such offensive acts as making obscene gestures to women on the street, smacking one's lips as they walk by, and coming on to unknown women in public places. Ultimately, such a mentality excuses rape as an act invited by women. A son who learns from his mother that his state of arousal is her responsibility can easily assume that women who do not soft-pedal their sexuality are "asking for it." A basic lesson a mother can teach her son is how to be appreciative of a woman's sexuality without feeling it is there for him to partake of. In our society we are so used to deferring to male needs that it sounds at first a bit shocking to suggest that a mother be open in her sexuality and let her son adapt to the fact, yet that is what maturation is all about. Mothers do not deny their sons a visit to Santa Claus in a holiday-decorated department store because there are many enticing toys that their sons cannot have. Nor do mothers not allow their sons to look at the candy display or the cookie counter because there are goodies they may not be allowed to buy, or keep them from a museum because there are exhibits that they may not touch. Rather, mothers want their sons to see what life has to offer and to learn how to make judgments as to what is appropriate and inappropriate for them.

Jeanette, a divorced mother of two teenage boys, has tried to raise them with accepting attitudes about sexuality in men and women. She has been relaxed about letting the boys see her nude, and they have learned to regard her body as a body rather than as a sexual object for their use. Jeanette's appreciation of her sons' sexual attractiveness is matched by their appreciation of her attractiveness, and they can enjoy this quality in each other without it threatening them. She feels it is helpful for the boys in their relationships with their girlfriends to know that their mother finds them appealing:

◦§ We are very free. Since they were born the boys have seen nude people of every age on the beaches. They have seen that from the beginning because we travel a lot, and it was never a big problem because I am free with them. They realize how a woman's body is built. They don't have to ask questions. They accept it normally. There was little discussion because they saw it. Nothing was hidden. We were every year on the beach and the men and women were more or less nude—not only topless but nude—so they knew right away that a man is not the same as a woman. A very natural thing.

My boys are terrific. I am constantly in love with them. They are great—very handsome, and they look very much like their father. Especially the younger one looks just like him. The older one is stronger and taller and he took the place of his father after a while. He has an incredible body. It is so beautiful. I just can't help admire him. He is so strong, so like a man. . . . I used to go places with them a lot, but lately they are busy with their own friends. I took one of the boys to the ballet recently, and he spoke to the people sitting next to us and he said, very proudly, "You know my mother is a dancer." He was real proud. I feel proud of them too. It's a nice, very simple relationship. I am not perfect, but they have a picture of me that I really love them. The boys hug me and kiss me and say they love me, and I try to give them loving affection and I hope they do the same with their girls. ◦❧

As we will see later, Jeanette, despite her overall Sex Expressive manner, has been very reticent about letting her sons see her with any of her male companions. Although she wants them to see her as a sexual person, she is not yet prepared to let them see her as a sexual person with a partner other than their father.

Cecilia has been even more successful in helping her sons come to terms with her sexuality as well as their own and allowing it to enrich their relationship. Her two sons, Andrew and Paul, are twenty-two and twenty, respectively. Andrew is engaged to be married and lives in an apartment he shares with two other young men, and Paul, though he is very involved with a girlfriend of long standing, still lives at home while he is finishing school. Cecilia was always very open about the fact that she was a sexual person and enjoyed a sexual relationship with her husband, Victor. She also has been very accessible to her sons, talking to them about sexual issues, and she has tried, through her own casual style of life, to make them comfortable about their bodies and hers. Cecilia feels that her older son, Andrew, is temperamentally less sensual than Paul and that he never had any difficulty reconciling himself to the fact of his mother's sexuality. Paul, on the other hand, has a heightened sexuality and had to struggle to come to terms with his feelings towards his mother. Cecilia was very aware of his situation and helped him with that, not by denying her sexual nature but by helping Paul develop ways of dealing with his sexual urges. As Cecilia describes it, Paul's sexual nature manifested itself already in infancy, creating strong mutual awareness:

≈§ When I had my second child he had been in an incubator, and when he came home eight days after birth, he started to suck and I definitely felt a tickling down underneath. It was very funny, and I said, "Strange, I'm supposed to be the Mama and giving him the breast, and it is provoking another feeling." But that is the only time I felt that. I think the fact that I am very sensitive there, more than any place else, and love to be sucked on my breast helped to arouse that feeling. I guess it was a mechanical thing. And then I saw that my son Paul was very sensual, definitely. When he was three or four months he would rub his little penis with his diaper and provoke an erection, and he would do that very often. And very early on his approach to me was very sensual. It was not like Andrew, who would come and give me a kiss and hug me like my son. Paul definitely had another way of expressing his feelings. I did not feel a sexual attraction, but I felt that I had to help him change his attitude. I wanted his relationship to me to be very much like Andrew's, and I wanted that to be very clear. When he used to hug me and embrace me very sensually, I told him, "Paul, if you want to kiss Mommy, hug me real hard and give me a nice kiss, but don't feel all over my body." I thought it was very interesting how soon the sexual life is awakened.

Victor and I were always very open and relaxed in the house, and we both would walk around nude, as would the boys. When they came into my bedroom, and still now with Paul, and I am naked, that is comfortable. When Andrew was home, if I would go into the bathroom because someone was phoning him and he was drying himself, he didn't feel ashamed or cover himself, nor the other way around. With Paul it used to be different. He was very much more sexual. But I was aware and didn't let it go out of limits. Friends used to say, "That's awful! How can you let him see you in the raw. That's so seductive. You should stop!" But Mama didn't change; Paul did. With Paul it was a stage he went through, but now that he is older he has learned to be comfortable with me sexually. Before, when I was naked he used to look at me very intently, and it was not because I had big hands or big feet or a belly button, but because he liked to see my breasts. He still sees me, but he doesn't need to stare at me. He will notice if I put on a little weight and rib me about it, or when I am in good shape he will say, "Mommy, you look terrific!" ❧

Cecilia has kept a running dialogue with both boys about sex that has enabled them to integrate their sexuality into the life of the family. They all acknowledge one another's sexual nature and sexual needs, being supportive and respectful in this regard. The boys appreciate that sex is an important part of Cecilia's life with Victor, and she appreciates that sex is an important part of her sons' lives:

∾ When Paul first started dating, he came to me and said, "Mommy, you have to teach me how to dance and hold a girl." And I said, "Be soft," because he sometimes used to grab me very forcefully. He was interested in knowing how to hold a girl and all those things, but by that time there was no hint of anything sexual there with me. I told him, "If you have a relationship, don't be pushy. Don't push yourself. Let things happen a little bit. Be attentive to what the girl really wants, but don't be persuaded if you don't want." They saw that sex is important in my life and that a woman needs to be loved and caressed. Victor and I are very open about sex all the time. It was always very natural, and they knew about sex and they knew how it is done. They even saw us once or twice. Andrew saw us making love. I remember once he came into the bedroom and I said, "We're busy right now. Come back later and tell us what you want." I haven't felt they have been shocked because they see it is a natural and beautiful thing. ∾

A respectful attitude, and how it helps a son put his own sexuality into perspective, is illustrated also by Faith, a single mother who works for a public relations firm. Faith's son, Joey, is now eleven; he is the product of Faith's second marriage. Since divorcing Joey's father, Faith has had a series of affairs, and two long-lasting live-in relationships with men, one of whom is currently in the home and wants to marry Faith. Joey visits his father on alternate weekends, and his father also has had a series of live-in lovers. This is the way Faith described how she handles sexual issues at home:

∾ I knew that if I'd be comfortable with myself he'd be fine. If I started making concessions that I wasn't comfortable with I might start taking it out on him. I have the greatest pleasure from him now. It's very good. When he saw "The Brady Bunch," that was the first time he realized parents were supposed to live together. Half his class is divorced and there's quite a lot of talk that goes on there, and there's quite a bit of questions from that. When he was six or seven years old, he asked me questions like, "Do you and Fred sleep together?" "Yes." "Does his penis go into your vagina?" "Yes." Those questions started to emerge. There's nothing in our relationship that he can't come to me and ask about. He'll come to me and say, "So-and-so called up and he wants to know what the word 'sodomy' means. His mother won't tell him," and I'll explain it to him. To me they're natural questions, they're learning for him.

In the same way, I don't have any problem with my sexuality. Two men lived here for a year at a time. He remembers them both. There were questions like "Does that mean you're going to marry him?" He wanted to understand if you have sex or somebody lives here or you have a relationship, does one follow the other, and we talked about it. He wants to know the feeling, smell, texture of ejaculation. He's going to be twelve soon. "What does it smell like, what does it taste like, tell me." He probably might have had an ejaculation, and in fact he might want to know if he really did. "Is it OK to masturbate?" he said. "I tried it, but I don't know if it was the real thing." It first came up after his friend said that his older brother masturbated and that he learned from his brother and he could do it too. So he asked me, "When do you start, when is puberty?" I told him sex is a natural feeling, that it's healthy, that emotionally and physically you have feelings for people and you have ways of expressing them, and touching is one way, giving pleasure, receiving pleasure. He said to me, and right now it's kind of scary for him so what he said was, "I don't have to worry about that now." And I said, "No, you don't." And he said, "When am I supposed to?" And I said, "Joey, it's like an infant walking. Some walk at ten months, some at fifteen months. It's not something that you'll wake up one day and say, 'OK, I want to touch a woman.' I can't say to you that there's a certain date that all of this is going to happen." I told him it's a physical and mental evolution that will happen, but it's not something that you have to concern yourself about or dwell on. It comes with living.

In terms of my relationship he has asked, "Do you do this or do that?" or "Does it feel good or hurt?" That was a few years ago. I remember thinking, "God, isn't this early to be asking those questions?" He was interested a little more in the physical than the emotional part of it, the sensations. When he was younger, one of the first questions he asked me was, "Does the penis go into the vagina? Is that where the baby is?" I said, "No, technically it's in the womb." Wherever possible I try to use the correct terms. It's hard to remember specific conversations. I do know, "Does it hurt? What makes it hard? Why does a woman suck on a man's penis?" And I said, "It feels good, they're sharing something together. They're giving up part of themselves."

He's told me about some boys who have talked to him about sex and asked him about it and tried to rub against him, and I said, "How did it feel?" And he said "It was uncomfortable," and I said, "Take your cue from that." I said, "This is a very natural things for boys and girls to want to discover and understand, so don't freak out, but listen to your own feelings. You have your own feelings and choices to make, so discover for yourself." ਨ

What emerges so clearly in Faith's interaction with her son is the place made for the expression of sexuality in both her life and his. Because of the openness between them, he can express his feelings and concerns to her and she can help him to put them in perspective. Joey is not threatened by his mother's sexuality both because he sees it as an enriching aspect of her life and because he understands that she is cognizant of his sexual needs. Faith does not flaunt her sexuality, but she does not hide it either and Joey is growing up aware of the fact that his mother is a complete human being.

SIX

THE SPITTING IMAGE: SEXUAL ISSUES BETWEEN FATHERS AND SONS, MOTHERS AND DAUGHTERS

Parents have special feelings towards their children of the same sex. A father's son and a mother's daughter are extensions of the self in a much more intense way than are cross-sex offspring. Through one's "spitting image," a parent can hope to live out unfulfilled fantasies and gain vicarious sexual pleasures. By the same token of close identification, a parent may also become acutely aware of personal inadequacies when seeing a same-sex child succeed where he or she has failed. In such a case, identification can lead to competitiveness and envy. And sometimes parents run the risk of "overinvesting" emotionally in their same-sex offspring. Fathers may seek to provide their sons, and mothers their daughters, with all the love, affection, and indulgence they felt deprived of in their own youth. As a result, the parent-child relationship may become too intense and eroticized; or if these strong feelings are hidden, they may surface in masked form as aloofness or hostility toward a child. The happiest route for all is when the loving feelings of fathers for sons and of mothers for daughters help the children develop as separate beings whose lives can be enhanced by their emerging sexuality and ability to form relationships with others. As we will see, gender differences influence the way parents relate to the sexuality of their same-sex offspring. Certain aspects of mother-daughter interactions are not shared by fathers and sons, and likewise, the father-son relationship has its own unique features.

Two common expressions are used to characterize the similarities between parents and their progeny: "A chip off the old block" and "The apple doesn't fall far from the tree." We like to use "chips off the old block" to describe the son-father relationship, and the "apple-tree" analogy to describe what goes on between daughter and mother. The visual image of chips flying off from the block of wood as it is being split aptly characterizes the way in which sons are expected to go flying off in new directions, as their fathers give them the freedom to "let the chips fall where they may." The attitude that mothers have towards their daughters, however, is much more protective and restrictive. The daughter, as apple, may fall from the tree, but until recently, she was supposed to stay under the protective shade of her mother.

FATHERS AND SONS: CHIPS OFF THE OLD BLOCK

Practically all expectant fathers, seventy-five to eighty percent, hope to have a child of the same sex,* as fathering a son is the closest a man can come to perpetuating himself.

Not only do fathers want sons, but they want masculine sons, sons who are embodiments of the male ideal—strong, independent, adventuresome, and virile. Fathers treat their sons differently than they treat their daughters—their involvement is more intense. For instance, fathers are more active with sons than they are with daughters, touching them more and talking to them more. Fathers also engage sons in more rough-and-tumble activities and more unpredictable types of games than mothers do, with the result that boys soon turn their attention from their mothers and come to prefer their fathers. By age two, most boys would rather spend time roughhousing with Dad than playing quieter games or having diaper changes with Mom. Fathers often discourage closeness between their sons and their wives, fearing that sons may become too soft and not assertive enough if they stick too close to Mom. Sons are also taught to turn away from home activities and to place their interests outside. The breakdown of traditional gender-related behaviors has, in this sense, primarily affected girls; they are now freer to pursue activities outside of home and to enter realms formerly reserved for males, but boys are still dissuaded from entering traditionally female domains and are not expected to model themselves after their mothers.

But although fathers maintain a more active relationship with sons than with daughters and spend a greater propor-

* Nancy Williamson, Population Reference Bureau study.

tion of time with their male children, their relationships often lack closeness and warmth. Fathers, for example, typically hold their infant sons at waist level and on folded arms rather than against the chest. And as actively engaging as they may be, a father's pastimes tend to create physical distance: when fathers throw their sons into the air (a favorite game for both), they are tossing their sons away from them and creating a physical space between them. Relegating caretaking to the mother also reinforces the lack of closeness between father and son; while the characteristic play pattern between fathers and sons generates a preference for fathers over mothers, the absence of consistent fatherly input and daily care can interfere with a son's sense that his father is always there for him as a source of support. A lack of paternal nurturance has also been demonstrated to hinder the ability of sons to form a strong masculine identity.* Ironically, a "toughen 'em up" psychology can boomerang, interfering with gender role modeling instead of reinforcing it. Research indicates that overemphasis on stereotyped masculine behavior produces feelings of inadequacy in boys who are not able to fulfill role expectations. Further, their lack of strong masculine interests tends to alienate their fathers and these boys grow up starved for male attention.** Thus the latent fears of many fathers that their sons might manifest feminine traits can inadvertently come to pass. Fathers who are preoccupied with machismo may not only help propel their sons towards other males but also impede a son's ability to relate on an emotionally engaging level to women. The distance fathers create between themselves and their sons often becomes a model for a son's other close relationships; the male aloofness in heterosexual relationships that is a common complaint among women replicates the dynamics between fathers and sons.

Because the traditional double standard allows greater

---

* Some of these studies are summarized in Lamb, *The Role of the Father in Child Development*.
** Evelyn Hooker, "Male Homosexuals and Their Worlds," in *Sexual Inversion*, ed. Judd Marmor (New York: Basic Books, 1965), and Richard Green, *The "Sissy Boy Syndrome" and the Development of Homosexuality* (New Haven, CT: Yale University Press, 1987).

sexual freedom to males, a father's attitude to sexuality in sons is usually permissive, regardless of his general attitude to sex. All fathers tend to instill in a son a healthy respect for his own sexuality, but their sexual orientation, whether Sex Repressive, Sex Avoidant, Sex Obsessive, or Sex Expressive, will impact on the respect their sons develop for sexuality in others and, therefore, the quality of the interpersonal relationships they form.

LOVE AT ARM'S LENGTH

For a father, part of the excitement of having a boy is the joy of having a male heir, but there is also a more immediate erotic excitement generated by the overwhelming love many men feel for their sons. Just the sheer intensity of his love for this cuddly and vulnerable little boy can awaken a father's sexual feelings for his son. As we saw before, Julius Fast, a Sex Expressive father, experienced this with the birth of his son. To quote Julius again, "When my son was born I felt the same kind of sexuality toward him [as toward my daughters], a tremendous love, and you almost felt you could embrace the kid sexually. But I think that's a normal feeling that fathers get and just push down." Sex Repressive, Sex Avoidant, and even Sex Obsessive fathers tend to squelch these feelings so quickly that they never even enter consciousness. As Larry, the psychologist said, "I've always thought little boys are adorable, especially my little boys. I think they're cute. I think that's a sublimation of sexual responsiveness. I don't recall any erogenous feelings towards my sons and I think it's probably because of my own background. I'm probably too well-defended against it."

The difficulty that fathers have in acknowledging the passionate feelings that a son can arouse is exacerbated by men's reluctance to express themselves in a physically demonstrative way with another male. Fathers, as men, are not used to hugging and kissing other males. They find such behavior unnatural and are loath to let their sons feel that physical closeness between males is appropriate. Sons' early relationships with their fathers are typically characterized by Indian wrestling, ball playing, waxing the car, or mowing the lawn, but not by lap sitting, back scratching, or intimate discussions.

Although physical touching is out, fathers usually feel free to undress in front of their sons and they think nothing of their sons being naked in their presence. Locker room mentality dictates that male nudity in Dad's bathroom is perfectly acceptable even when modesty about the body prevails elsewhere in the home. One consequence of this familiarity is that the son tends to become intimidated by the father's sexuality. Many of the teenage boys and men we have talked to said that seeing their fathers in the nude was an awesome experience. As boys, they tended to be impressed with the size of their fathers' penises and concerned about the smaller proportions of their own. James Jones, the novelist, carried those memories into adulthood and related stories to his children about how inadequate it made him feel. According to his wife, Gloria:

≈§ Jim used to tell stories about looking up at his father's penis and saying, "I'll never be a man like that," and feeling terribly inferior when he was little—five or six. He used to tell all sorts of stories to the kids. I think every kid goes through that once in a while. They seem to. ε≈

Blake, the architect with the Sex Avoidant parents, had a similar experience:

≈§ When I was little I would go in and out of the bathroom when he was urinating. He didn't walk about naked, but I would see him changing clothes, and I would see my mother too, although there was some point at which she put the lid on that. I do remember as a kid thinking my father had a huge dick. I don't know if I envied it, because I had a sense that I would grow up, but there was something exceptional about his and I wasn't sure it would happen to mine. I was just amazed at how big it was, and fascinated with the notion that that was what a man's size was like, but I think I had a fairly clear sense that I was going to get there. ε≈

Eddie, the grade-school teacher whose mother called his penis a doo-doo, also found himself impressed but intimidated when he saw his stepfather's penis:

◄§ I remember I was in the bathroom and he came in and urinated and I was really frightened by the size of his penis. It was so big, and a lot of it came out. It was so furious, it made such a loud sound. It was really ugly, dark. He was a very docile man. He was tall and big. We were having a rather pleasant conversation and he was being very sweet actually at the moment, but it was just like a big ugly fist. The size, the darkness, the speed that the urine came out. I didn't want to have one. I didn't want to do that. §►

It seems very likely that these concerns about their sexual organs and eventual development stem from the early stress on masculinization and resultant fears of "falling short" of the father's expectations. Boys who have Sex Expressive fathers are less apt to worry about their penis size as their fathers are less involved in sexual differentiation. These fathers, by not emphasizing masculinity, do not add to their sons' anxieties about measuring up. Also, unless boys have a Sex Expressive father, they do not feel free to talk with their fathers about their sexual apprehensions. For a lot of boys, male nudity is part of a superficial camaraderie that exposes the body as it covers up the feelings involved. The experience that boys have with their fathers in the bathroom, with its secret comparisons and unasked questions, foreshadows the locker room exhibitionism that inevitably follows later on. Eddie's description of his physical education class at school is reminiscent of his experience with his stepfather:

◄§ I was always sensitive to swimming class because we had to swim nude, and if I were a phys ed teacher I would insist that the boys wear bathing suits. It's really traumatizing for kids. All of a sudden they have to take off their clothes in front of each other in seventh grade. If that always goes along developmentally, that's OK, but in seventh grade some kids have huge organs and some don't and it becomes a source of jealousy. 😂

The lack of real intimacy between fathers and sons is revealed by their inability to talk with one another in a meaningful way about sex. In a recent survey* a majority of the boys interviewed said it was hard for them to talk to their fathers about sex, and we found that to be true for the sons we know. One of the reasons boys don't feel comfortable talking to their fathers is that fathers do not feel comfortable talking to their sons, and therefore when they do talk, they tend to lecture on in a clinical, mechanical way. What most of these talks boil down to is a few precautionary words about preventing pregnancy, disease, or homosexual entrapments, with nothing about the excitement or passionate aspects of sex, or about the nervousness that attends the first experience. As we saw in two conversations described earlier, Bradford experienced his father as a professor who left out all the emotional aspects of sex and Blake said the conversation with his father was conducted in technical terms rather than in boys' slang.

Even when fathers are Sex Expressive, conversations about sex tend to be stilted. Thus Larry, for example, who has moved far away from his own father's repressive attitude, will answer sexual questions in a straightforward manner, but when it comes to his son's sexuality he talks about it in a teasing way, and with a slightly condescending tone:

😂 My son will ask me very direct questions like "What do homosexuals do?" and "Can a man really fuck two women at once?" Things like that. I give him straight answers about what a blow job is, what ass fucking is. I will tease my son because he's a little tight. I will say, "You've got hair on your lip. Any other place?" I feel that teasing and joking helps. Whenever he masturbated I have never interfered, except jokingly. "Don't do it at the dinner table because Grandma wouldn't understand. And other people might get jealous."

* Coles and Stokes, *Sex and the American Teenager*.

Masturbation is a private matter. If children are not embarrassed at that, I'm concerned. They're supposed to be embarrassed—not devastated. Their resources in this area are not completely developed. I had a funny experience with my son. He had a girl in the house. And I know he feels more comfortable with me in the house than with his mother. We're both good-humored about it, but I'm more relaxed about it than she. And I happened to walk in on him, and they jumped up and down the way kids do, and I just apologized and turned around and walked out and said, "I hope I didn't come in at the worst time." ठ∼

These comments are not that different in tone from the comments made by Julius Fast's father when he learned of his son's sexual liaison. First Julius's older brother, who played the role of father surrogate, joshed him, and then his father teased him too:

∼§ My older brother found out I was fooling around. I don't think he gave me any advice at all. . . . I knew that he thought it was great, as far as I was concerned. I know how he found out. I had an exhibit at the junior science fair, and I took my girlfriend to see it and my brother was there. I invited him to come too with his girlfriend, and it was obvious what was going on. I wouldn't have told him, but he would have found out. I might have boasted about it. . . . I know that the attitude was joking, sort of kidding around. . . . Even when my father found out he made a few cracks— "You're a big shot," and that kind of thing. . . . I suppose there was an approval, but at the same time putting me down—"Don't think this makes you a man!" ठ∼

When it comes to his own son, Julius is very open, but he recognizes that his talks with his son on sexual issues do not have the same relaxed tone that prevails in his talks with his daughters:

∼§ When my daughter went off to college, I suggested that she go on the pill, and she did. She had questions. I can't

159

think of any specific questions, but we talked about menstruation and the whole process of ovulation. I think she was a little bored with it all. My son never asked me. He did what I did. He got the book. I had a shelf that wide full of sex books that I used for my writing, and he simply went to the books and read everything. I made it available and I suggested stuff he could read, but I think he liked to find out by himself. I think it might have been more embarrassing, oddly enough, for him to talk about sex to me than it was for the girls, who seemed to have no problems at all discussing things. I suppose it's part of the father-son relationship; there is a kind of challenge between the father and son. The kid is trying to find his way to manhood, and he sees the father as an obstacle. 〰

In fact, when Julius's son had his first sexual affair, he did not, like his sisters, tell his father but let it be known through the family grapevine, via his sister:

〰 The first thing he did was to call up his older sister, and tell her, and the first thing she did was to call her younger sister, who was in a college dormitory full of girls. She let out a scream: "My little brother got laid!" And one of the girls said, "What kind of a family is that?" He was very proud of it and he knew that his sister would pass the word to us immediately, and sure enough she did and I thought that was nice. 〰

As suggested by Julius, there is often a competitiveness between father and son that interferes with their ability to talk in a spontaneous way about sex. Perhaps part of this competitiveness is fear of self-exposure in an area of particular vulnerability to men. The teasing, joshing tone about sex is also present when fathers talk to daughters about sex, as we saw before, but it is very uncharacteristic of the way mothers talk about sex to their sons or their daughters. In fact, when we come to mother-daughter interactions it will become clear that when these two do talk to each other it tends to be in a detailed and personal way.

Another reason fathers and sons are more reticent to share sexual information than mothers and daughters are that men, in accordance with the old double standard, have been taught not to endanger a woman's reputation by implicating her in talk about sex. Although some fathers talk about casual sexual encounters, few are open about their sexual attachments to women they care deeply for. Erik Preminger, who is sensitive to this issue, said:

◄§ I have always been very careful to discuss with my son things like birth control. Now, for example, I think the problem with transmittable disease is a very serious one for anyone coming into a sexually active age, and so I discuss this with him. But the part that involves the interrelationship between two people, I wouldn't. If he has a date, I wouldn't think of asking him anything about what happened on the date, because I think that's his business. But if he asks me a question, I certainly would tell him. I remember when he was ten years old he started to ask me about sex, and I realized in retrospect that I was perhaps too detailed about it with him for that age, but again, he wanted to know what it was like, and I told him. I went into details about oral sex and all the rest of that stuff, and he got this glazed look in his eyes and went to bed and didn't bring it up again for another few years. I tried to never lie to him about anything, and that was just another area of it. It is interesting. I think part of it is that old lesson that you don't talk about your women. Certainly when I was younger, the one thing you wouldn't want to do is tell your friends about your girlfriends. If you were sort of listening to Dear Abby and treating women properly, you didn't want to ruin their reputations and so you tended to be very quiet about it. §►

Erik is also very careful to avoid giving his son signals that could spur him to imitate, or rebel against, Erik's own behavior:

◄§ I have no idea if my son is sexually active or not. I don't know. I just don't think it's any of my business. Part of that

161

is I am a very sexually active person and I think one of the problems that children have with parents is that parents give their children messages that you have to be like me, you have to do it my way, and I don't want to do that. I think it's up to my son to develop his own sexuality in his own way, and I want to leave him all the room in the world to be however he wants to be sexually, so I think it would be a bad idea if I got too involved with messages in that area. ठ✖

THE COMPETITIVE ROOTS

Fathers and sons seem to take it for granted that they represent a challenge to each other, but of course that striving does not materialize out of thin air. There is some biological evidence that males are more aggressive than females and that the level of the male hormone androgen is related to the level of aggression. Evidence also abounds, as we earlier discussed, that boys are reared to be aggressive and competitive. Both father and son have been trained from infancy to compete with other males, and so it is only natural that they feel competitive with one another. With some fathers the competitiveness starts very early in the game, and they may even take exception to their infant sons' nursing in the arms of their wives. These fathers feel threatened when the woman's maternal role seems to take precedence over her marital role, and they may become more demanding in bed as their jealousy of their sons increases. While sons are too young when this pattern sets in and fathers too defensive to be aware of it, mothers are sensitive to what is going on and sometimes hard put to balance the needs of their husbands and sons. Laurel, a homemaker who has four sons ranging in age from preteen to early twenties, found her husband both gloating at his masculine prowess in getting her pregnant so often and demanding of her sexually when she was attentive to the children:

✒§ Bill liked me to nurse the children and he loved how big my breasts were then, but at some point he was envious. He liked me to nurse them when they were very little, but at some point he didn't emotionally like it. He used to say,

"Isn't two or three months enough?" He always wanted me to leave a bottle so the baby-sitter could feed the children, and he wanted us to stay out longer. I think it was a reminder to him of someone else making demands on me. It was a mixed thing. He was pleased that he made me pregnant, pleased that he had caused those changes in my body, pleased that I was lactating because he had set the machinery in motion, but as proud as he was of having sons he also resented their intrusions on my time. When we were away and sharing a room with the kids, he would want to have sex, and we argued about that a lot. He said it didn't matter if the kids woke up. He said they should learn it's a perfectly natural activity and there's no reason not to do it before them. But as soon as they were old enough not to need me so much, he wouldn't have dreamed of them seeing us in a sexually compromising way. ॐ

The initial jealousy that some fathers experience over the close physical bonding of sons with mothers is relatively short-lived as sons tend to be pushed out of the maternal nest fairly early. Sexual jealousies crop up again in adolescence when sons start dating and making conquests, thereby reminding fathers of their own waning potency. At an age when sons come into their greatest strength and sexual vigor, most fathers enter their middle years and begin to witness a physical decline along with the appearance of a bulging rubber tire around the waist. At this point some fathers start their own extracurricular sexual life with younger women, to keep up with their sons and convince themselves of their manliness. It is an interesting commentary on the male ethic that still dominates our society that men who have achieved a high place on the status ladder are likely to have had very competitive relationships with their fathers. The intrafamilial sexual jealousy of father and son seems to be the stuff out of which political and corporate titans are made.

If a father always tops his son, he runs the risk of stifling competitive ambition. Fortunately for their sons, fathers also take pride in their sons' accomplishments and derive vicarious pleasures from their sons' masculine prowess. They may not discuss sexual details or romantic feelings with their sons, but they are pleased when they know that their sons have another notch in the belt. Reggie's father, for example, never talked to him about sex except to prod him on and to warn him about getting a girl pregnant: "The only thing my Dad ever said was 'Go out there, get the girls, have a great time, get yourself laid. I just don't want to be a grandfather, not yet!' "

THE FEAR OF HOMOSEXUALITY

On the other side of the coin of fathers' pride in the machismo of their sons is their fear of homosexuality. They want sons to be manly, and dread any signs of traits associated with femininity—weakness, softness, sensitivity, emotionality. This concern is particularly marked in Sex Repressive fathers, who because of their moralistic and sexist attitudes tend to be very homophobic. Sex Avoidant fathers are disturbed by the possibility of homosexual tendencies in their sons but are more apt to deny it. Sex Obsessive fathers, while sometimes approving of bisexuality as an avenue for more complete sexual experience, are not generally accepting of homosexuality because to them it means their son is not a complete man. Sex Expressive fathers, in contrast to the other types, tend to be more accepting of nontraditional behavior and homosexuality. They do not demand that their children, either male or female, adhere to predefined sex roles and believe that the child has to be comfortable with his own sexuality rather than follow society's definition of what sexuality should be.

Alice described in a very humorous way how Reggie's father fearfully looked for signs of incipient homosexuality, and expressed her relief that their divorce freed Reggie from this paternal anxiety:

⋘ If my husband and I had stayed together, Reggie would have been a totally different person. The best thing that happened to my son was that we split. My husband, even though he was a hippie, had a lot of old ways. Once Reggie was walking in my clogs and my husband freaked out because Reggie was walking in my shoes, wearing women's shoes. I said, "This has nothing to do with women's shoes. To him they are big shoes, lying in the middle of the floor." My husband didn't like that Reggie's friend when he was younger was a little girl. It should have been little boys. However, when Reggie was twelve or thirteen, if his best friend was a boy my husband would have gotten mad at that because it should have been a girl then. Like, what would he want him to do? Have a best friend that's a boy until he's thirteen and all of a sudden forget about the guy and get a friend who is a girl? ঌ

Fear of homosexuality in boys makes fathers leery of sex play that their sons have with other boys. While sex play with girls is looked upon with pride, when it occurs with boys it is very often suspect. Roy, who as we saw before was troubled by his sexually intrusive mother, was also beset by his homophobic father:

ঌ There was a time, I may have been around ten and my brother was seven, when we had come back from the country and my mother and father were lying on the bed cuddling. Incidentally, that's the only time I can remember them doing that, and my brother and I were playing farm. My brother was going to play the cow, and I was going to milk him. Just as I was about to grab his penis and milk him, my father jumped up and said, "NO, NO!" and interrupted us. No explanation or anything, but he just frightened me and made me feel very guilty about the whole thing. That was the only sex play I can remember between my brother and myself. ঌ

A more serious incident was reported by Eddie, whose stepfather sent Eddie's stepbrother to live elsewhere out of fear of what Eddie and his stepbrother were doing:

ঌ Very early on I had sexual feelings towards girls and boys. I fooled around at home with my stepbrother when I was in third grade, and I also played with girls a lot. I wasn't aware of what sex was, actually. To me it was just that I wanted to touch people, so I touched them. I remember once we were going to the beach and my brother and I were in the back of the station wagon and I remember my father stopping the car to stop us. I wasn't aware of any wrongness in what I was doing. And it took me many years—I don't think it was till I got to college that I figured it out—why my stepbrother was taken away and sent to live with his married sister. The question came up in my mind, and of course I would never ask my father, but one of my theories of the reason they took him away is because of what we were doing to each other. They were probably afraid of what was happening. At the time they told us not to do it, it was wrong, but I wasn't sure what it was that we weren't supposed to do. ও

Paternal homophobia probably has a lot to do with fathers' difficulties in showing physical affection for their sons, as if such interactions somehow might make it seem acceptable that men can hug or kiss each other. Sons thus are doubly deprived of the warm cuddling that their sisters enjoy, being pushed away by mothers and given a handshake by fathers. It is not surprising that many boys, as they enter manhood, have to be educated into the nuances of foreplay as that is not a type of sensitivity that stems naturally from their childhood experiences.

The physical and emotional distancing that fathers create out of fear of homosexuality does not deter sons from becoming gay. It merely creates a void and leaves unsatisfied the desire for male warmth and companionship. Gary, who is in his late twenties and recently announced his homosexuality to his family, feels his father did not provide an emotional context that made it easy for Gary to come to him. Gary experienced his father as a man who could not relate on a genuine level either to Gary's sexuality or to his own. Although Gary feels he was always basically homosexual, he also thinks his father's emotional unavailability helped steer him to the greater freedom of sexual expression gay life represents to him:

One of the things I found myself sorting over occasionally now, as I look at how deeply revolted my father is, is how I turned out to be gay and if that is genetic. I never saw my father as a sexual model. The things about my sexuality now that I am proud of and which are facets of my physicality or sexual expression are not like the way he is. So from that point of view I guess I didn't want to be like him. I never saw him as sexually attractive. I think the fact that I never wanted to emulate his sexuality had a lot to do with the fact that he never demonstrated much enthusiasm or sexual warmth in my presence. He never acted in a sexually demonstrative way in front of me; it wasn't in his nature to. He did not like to do things that were physical. I never learned to play sports or anything like that. He kept trying to encourage me to do it, but I just didn't have any natural aptitude. My father never did any of those things for his own pleasure. I don't mean to put sports and sexuality in the same bucket, but there is a certain continuum on which they all relate, which has to do with a certain celebration of the use of your physicality, whether for sexual purposes, or athletic purposes, or aesthetic purposes. The only time I ever saw him pick up a baseball bat was to try to show me how to do it, but never for his own pleasure. I don't think he ever set out not to do those things; it was just not in his vocabulary. I think that on my father's side, the lack of his physicality, warmth, and sexuality contributed less to my being gay than it did to my being uptight about sexual expression. I'm not sure [my gayness] was an issue of gender choice as much as it was freedom to do whatever I wanted to do.

MOTHERS AND DAUGHTERS: THE APPLE AND THE TREE

Given the traditional roles that women have played, it is not surprising that most wives, when first pregnant, share their husband's hope of having a son, who they expect will be more likely than a daughter to conquer new worlds. Recently some mothers have started to think that their daughters, as well as their sons, may be reared as chips rather than apples—that is, as independent persons who can carve out a new life-style not defined by limiting sexual stereotypes. However, most daughters today have been raised by mothers who are still waging their own struggle against sexism, if indeed they are fighting it at all, and as a result, many daughters continue to learn role behavior even from their mothers that is self-negating, particularly in the area of sex.

A daughter's first relationship is with her mother, and that relationship generally continues to be her closest family tie while she is growing up. Boys are urged to relinquish their ties to mother in order to follow in Daddy's footsteps, but girls maintain their ties as they learn to model themselves after their mothers. Because of this, daughters usually have a closeness with their mothers that sons do not, and the daughter-mother relationship continues to deepen while the son-mother relationship becomes more distant. One of the first lessons a girl thus learns from her mother is the importance of union with another person, an intensity of relatedness that many daughters, as women, will find lacking as they form ties with men later in life. A daughter also learns that part of closeness is caretaking and attentiveness to another's needs, for a major portion of her mother's time is usually devoted to others rather than to herself. Still another lesson that is part of the daughter-mother relationship is seriousness. A mother's time with her daughter, as with her son, is usually taken up with chores and with caretaking, and play is what children do with their daddy. Although women have the reputation of being flighty, especially when they are together, it is clear that the prototype of women's relationships, the mother-daughter bond, is heavy stuff.

In addition to lessons about her role in relation to others, a daughter is also provided lessons about her body and her sex. Mothers begin toilet training earlier with girls then they do with boys, fuss and fret more about the appearance of little girls, and take greater pains to keep them neat and tidy. It is not long before daughters are taught they must dress to please others. Worse, daughters also learn from their mothers that their bodies are shameful. Girls are expected to stay properly attired and not let too much of their bodies show.

Their little brothers may urinate in the street, but girls must be decorous and wait until they get home, lest someone see them. As a girl starts to mature, she learns that menstruation is a "curse," that sex for girls is dirty, that intercourse hurts, that pregnancy is ungainly, that childbirth is painful, and that she better watch out that no one tries to take advantage of her. Fortunately, many of these attitudes are in a state of flux and counterbalanced somewhat by the notions that the body is beautiful, that sex is to be enjoyed by all, and that women can have an important role in the world outside the home. Old messages die hard, however, and those daughters whose mothers have taught them to be self-expressive have to contend with a society that contests their rights to abortion, equal opportunity and protection under the law, and freedom from sexual harassment. Mothers bear a unique responsibility to their daughters as role models. A mother who fulfills the traditional role for which she herself was probably trained, as do Sex Repressive and many Sex Avoidant mothers, provides her daughter with a model of a woman uncomfortable with her sexuality and deferential to men. A mother who is striving to create a new role for herself and a new role model for her daughter offers her daughter a pathway that is, as yet, not totally explored and is therefore replete with many pitfalls as well as possibilities.

MATERNAL HOVERING

The joy of having a daughter is, for many mothers, mitigated by concern for that daughter's well-being. A mother's general—and usual—anxieties about her child's health and development are accompanied by additional worries about a daughter's special vulnerabilities. Although these worries may not be well articulated, they often hover in the background, making many mothers feel especially burdened by their daughters. A daughter's physical appearance, neatness, and cleanliness loom as more important than a son's, and mothers may worry as well that their daughters need to be protected from the dangers that lurk in the outside world. Daughters are often at a loss to understand why their mothers see them as so much trouble as compared to their brothers, especially as they feel their brothers have been more difficult. Nina's situation, while extreme, highlights this feeling. She has two brothers, one older, now in his thirties, and one younger, now in his late twenties. The older brother has psychological problems and has been in therapy for a long time, and the younger brother is a junkie. Yet her mother insists that it was Nina who gave her the most trouble:

◄§ It still comes up, even now. My mother refers to how much trouble I always was. When I asked my mother, "Which kid gave you the most trouble?" she said to me, "You." "Why me?" I asked her, "Rob is a junkie and Buddy is afraid to leave the house." And she said, "You, because you were a girl." She never elaborated and I never asked more. I assumed that because I was a girl, I could have gotten pregnant, so I was more trouble and I was of more concern to her than the boys. I don't know. If my mother only knew what I did to please her! §►

Mothers deal with fears about their daughters in various ways. Sex Repressive mothers avoid all discussion of sexual issues with their daughters, in the hope that their sexuality will simply disappear, but they closely supervise their daughters anyway, just in case. As a result, such mothers do not prepare their daughters for puberty, including the onset of menstruation. Brenda, for instance, has explained menstruation to her fifteen-year-old son, as he is on the verge of sexual activity, but she has kept her nine-year-old daughter in the dark, afraid of the latter's reputation and malleability:

◄§ I talk about a lot of things with my daughter, but we haven't gotten into menstruation yet because she is only nine years old. She doesn't need to know all those things, because she is always supervised and I know where she is. And I don't want her spreading a lot of that talk around either. She spends a lot of time with other girls. My mother told me when my daughter was a baby that she was a very strong girl and would have her own attitudes, but I think she could be influenced by others. ৪৯

Sex Repressive mothers look upon the start of menstruation as a time in which their daughters will require new restrictions to contain their sexuality. Faith's mother made her wear a bra at the start of menstruation, with the caution that "Once you wear it you always have to wear it," and Lynn Caine's mother, as described before, greeted the commencement of her daughter's menstruation with the injunction not to take gym.

Fortunately, many mothers are more relaxed about menstruation and able to take this sign of their daughters' sexual maturation in stride. They explain the function of menstruation, and keep the lines of communication open so that their daughters can come to them for advice when menstruation starts. Sex Expressive mothers try to go beyond merely technical information and provide their daughters with a positive attitude about menstruation. Mary Travers tried to create an "eager, excited, and anticipatory" mood when she thought her daughter Alicia's period was "around the corner." When we asked Mary how she did this, she said:

৪৯ You take out the box of Tampax, and you talk about babies and the fact that they ultimately need that nest there, and that's what all that is—a spongy little nest that gives nice protection against the outside bumps, and when you're not using it, it sloughs off. [Getting pregnant] isn't something you have to do, but it just means your body is revved up for a time when it will be ready, and the only reason you have your body ready long before you're ready to do it is because the natural versus the civilized animal has a different timetable. Culture plays a role in when you're going to do it, but the body doesn't pay much attention to culture. ৪৯

Whether a young girl looks forward with positive anticipation to menstruation as a sign of maturity or dreads it as a bloody "curse," the onset of menstruation represents a significant milestone in a daughter's relationship with her mother. Menstruation is the undeniable sign that one's little girl is also a sexual being—and that the time has come when others may find her a desirable sexual object.

NO, MY DARLING DAUGHTER

When a girl crosses the threshold into puberty, a mother's concerns escalate and with them usually comes a flood of warnings to her daughter. Whereas Sex Repressive and Sex Avoidant mothers may not have talked about sex before, at this time they generally do broach the subject, even if in a veiled manner. After Debra's first period, her mother gave Debra her first, and only, lecture on sex, in the form of a warning that did not spell out just what it was Debra had to fear:

◄§ My mother gave me one lecture and I was absolutely hysterical, and it came after the fact. I must have been around thirteen or fourteen. She said, "Just don't go and sit on a boy's lap." I couldn't figure it out. I had gone to a party and this guy was there who went to school with me, and anyway I sat on his lap and we were horsing around and talking with no romantic intention whatever. I sat on his knee and my friend Marilyn got jealous because she regarded this boy as her property. Because she got angry, she had her mother call my mother, who said to me, "You get into trouble when you sit on a boy's lap." And I could never figure out why. At the time I had no idea what she meant, and it was only in retrospect that I knew what she meant about the lap—that it could be very arousing to a guy and he could get a hard-on. She always said to me, "Just try to be in control of your emotions, don't let them get away with you, and don't let anybody lead you down the garden path, and always feel you can look at yourself in the mirror the next day." She never said, "Don't have sexual intercourse." ξ►

While Debra is fully aware that her mother was overanxious about the potential dangers of sex, she is nonetheless almost as anxious about her own daughter's sexuality. Debra, too, cautioned her daughter about falling prey to sexual feelings,

172

though she did not think that necessary to do with her son. Interestingly, Debra told her daughter, as she had heard from her mother before, to make sure she could look at herself in the mirror the next day:

◆§ When Ruth was twelve, she came home from a Halloween party where the girl host had gone off into a room with a boy guest and they had been feeling each other up. The girl's mother called the girl a slut, and Ruth asked me what that meant. I told her that you get strong feelings being with the opposite sex and that one has to know how to handle it, that sometimes when you're twelve or thirteen you don't have enough handle on your emotions and it can lead you to do things that you should wait to do until you are more mature. When Ruth was a little older I had a talk with her. She said, "Don't worry, I know how to handle myself," before I could get a word out. But I said, "I have to give you a little talk anyway, and you need to listen to it." And we talked about how to conduct yourself so that she wouldn't be taken advantage of by the other person so that she could look at herself in the mirror the next morning. And I told her to be sure about her feelings towards the other person and that person's feelings towards her. The only thing I told her brother was that he was to treat girls that he's with with the same kind of respect he had for his sister. §◆

Mothers view their sons' sowing a few wild oats here and there as a natural phase of masculine development, but when it comes to daughters they are fearful lest their daughters end up on the receiving end. To a degree, a mother's concern about sexual entanglements is a byproduct of her tendency to push her daughter into relationships. A mother's eagerness for her daughter to be popular with boys conditions the daughter to value herself in terms of male acceptance and makes her easy prey for men. In these circumstances, mothers understandably feel that their daughters are vulnerable to being used sexually by some uncaring male. Allison described how her mother, who is in all other respects a highly sophisticated and wordly woman, placed much greater restrictions on her, even at the age of nineteen, than on her younger brother:

❧ I had to be home by eleven. My mother would say, "Where are you going?" And I would say, "To a party at someone's house," and she would call the house to see if the parents would be home to supervise the party. When I met an older man who had a car, my mother wouldn't allow me to go in the car with him, and told me an older man wouldn't want to be home by eleven. My mother said things like, "What do you have to talk about to spend so much time together?" and "You will just get into trouble and into things that shouldn't happen." I would say, "Ma, it takes fifteen minutes to do it—I can do it between eight and eight-thirty," but she did not think that was very funny. She told me sometimes men get very excited and can't control themselves. She didn't say what would happen but just that I should understand that it wasn't appropriate and that I wasn't emotionally ready for it. It was never said exactly what "it" was. With my brother it was different, because he was a male. There were different standards about leaving the house. With my brother there was no "Where are you going? When will you be back?" or calling up to see if there would be an adult on the premises. ❧

Even Sex Expressive mothers, who respect a daughter's sexuality and want her to be able to integrate sexuality into her life, feel that a daughter needs more protection than a son. Lynn Caine expressed the different feelings she had with regard to her son Jon's and daughter Elizabeth's sexual awakenings:

❧ I don't think you worry so much about a male child as a female child. I thought it was my job to make Jon aware of how you can get somebody pregnant and get into trouble picking up diseases, but I didn't feel uncomfortable because for one thing it is different for a boy and for another it is different because of the way I was brought up. I was more fearful for Elizabeth in that girls are more vulnerable emotionally in this area, that girls can get pregnant. I just worried that she would not have a satisfying emotional experience. I wanted her to have somebody who cared about her and was tender to her. I did not feel that way with Jon. . . . I think it's good to have sex, not when you're twelve, but you learn from experience, and what I know of life is that you learn the art of falling down and picking yourself up. So while I would not encourage a kid to have sex just for the sake of having it, I did talk to her about it in the event that she did, that she must be protected, and that she must be prepared. Sex, like other experiences, I wanted to be rich and fulfilling, and I raised the children to understand that. The double standard was that I wanted Elizabeth to be with somebody who loved her and would be tender to her. 🙠

Because the signals Sex Repressive and Sex Avoidant mothers send out to daughters about sex are primarily warnings rather than reassurances, they reinforce the usual anxieties all young people initially feel about sex. Even when mothers say that sex is a natural function, or go so far as to indicate that it is pleasurable, the emotional tone and cautionary nature of what they say is much more powerful than all the nice talk. Consequently, many daughters find it hard to imagine that their mothers or other women, including themselves, could find sex enjoyable, and think women have sex only to please men or to have babies. As Allison described the feeling:

🙠 Even though from the time I was ten I knew my mother was pregnant a lot, I didn't think she had a sexual relationship. In my mind it was only for procreation, and I was appalled and embarrassed about it. I remember once my brother finding a box of prophylactics in my father's night table and I was grossed out. The act, as it was described to me, did not seem in any way, shape, or form pleasurable. I think my mother did once tell me it was pleasurable, but I couldn't believe that, I couldn't fathom it. I think the reaction of most children is that it is gross, disgusting. I remember when my friend and I realized how babies were made we sat in the backyard and decided it was really vulgar. We knew we were going to get pregnant someday—you can't do it by remote control—but it was just something disgusting. &

The expectation that sex must be unpleasant if their mothers are so worried about it often mutes adolescent girls' natural curiosity about sex. Girls are much less apt than boys to explore their own bodies, to masturbate, and to want to experiment sexually with another person. When they do become sexually active, it is more often at the urging of their boyfriend rather than at the urging of their own libido. Nina's situation was fairly typical in this regard. Although she was curious about sex, she never really wanted to get sexually involved with anyone and it wasn't until she was in her thirties and in her second marriage that she was able to integrate sexuality into her life:

<§ I never had penetration before my husband. I never even had petting before I was married, but I had sexual awareness. I had some contact with older boys, but we never did anything uncomfortable. Sex was never handled openly in my house, and rather than deal with it, I just stayed away. There was an older cousin I once became sexually aware of. He wanted to see my private parts and touch me. I think I was a teenager, maybe even younger—eleven or twelve. He put his hands up my dress and played with me. I never saw his private parts and he didn't see mine. I didn't feel very comfortable with what I was doing, but I've come across girls that have had sex play at an early age and did feel OK about it. But I couldn't do it. I couldn't follow through.

When I started dating, my parents would wait up for me, but I didn't stay out late so that was not an issue—it was protection for me. I guess if I thought it was something that was natural I would have gone farther. But I didn't think it was right, but I wasn't really clear about it because my mother never said it was wrong. She never said it was right. I remember a guy wanted to go steady with me but he didn't press hard enough. Boys just never got anywhere with me, and the most sex play I ever had was with my cousin, until

I was married. That first taste of sexual freedom when I got married was just OK. It wasn't something special and I didn't know about orgasms and I thought that everything was OK. I learned to feel comfortable with him, given as much as I knew about my body, and I thought that's what it was, and there wasn't anything else. It was pleasurable enough, but there was no thrill about it. He was always in the mood for sex, far more often than I. I think at the end of my relationship with him I became aware that life should be more than this, and that sex should be more than this. I didn't come out sexually till I remarried, and only now, and I'm thirty-five, am I really sexually aware and having orgasms. I didn't even know that a woman had orgasms until well after I was remarried. ✌

Of course, many teenage girls have not been scared off from sex by their mothers and do become sexually active. Nevertheless they approach sex far differently than do boys of their age. According to the Coles and Stokes survey of teenagers mentioned earlier, girls are much less likely than boys to have casual sex and a majority of girls expect to marry their current sexual partner. Girls are also likely to express sadness or ambivalence after their first intercourse, while most boys are pleased about it. Girls tend to be disappointed that the experience was not pleasurable or upset that it hurt, and many continue to find that sex is a painful experience. Significantly, most of those girls who have learned nothing from their mothers about sex never achieve orgasms, while most of those girls who have been taught that sex is healthy do achieve orgasm. Thus, a mother's fearfulness about her daughter's sexual involvements seems to increase the probability that a daughter will have unsatisfying sexual encounters. With the changing social mores, mothers are coming to accept as inevitable that their daughters will sooner or later have sex. While historically mothers used to fear the stigma of lost virginity and the possibility of pregnancy, now they fear the emotional consequences of sex as much as the act of sex. Once a mother becomes convinced that her daughter can hack it, her attitude towards her daughter's sexuality is apt to change. For many mothers and daughters, a daughter's entry into a sexually active life-style is a turning point in their relationship and, surprisingly, one for the better. If a daughter can survive her first encounters, a mother's fears are largely put to rest, and the two enter into a kind of sisterhood, including new dependencies and rivalries.

TURNING THE TABLES

While many mothers are prone to guard their daughters' innocence, once it is gone the barriers to their communication are apt to go with it. The reticence to talk about sex fades away, and mothers not only start to share confidences about their own sex lives with their daughters but are often eager to hear about their daughters' sex lives as well. A new closeness often emerges, but unfortunately for many mothers, all they have to tell their daughters about is the lack of sex in their own lives. Carrie, a recent college graduate, and her mother started to share experiences with one another once Carrie became sexually involved. While her mother's attitude was initially repressive and full of fretful hovering, it is now one of respect and mutuality, which enables her mother to confide the frustrations of her own sex life to Carrie.

◄§ When I went away to college and started having this affair, Mom couldn't do anything about it. I told her about it, and now we have a very close relationship. I talk to her about sex, and about love and relationship problems. And it's wonderful. Now that the barrier is down, there is much said. She's now as much a friend as a mother, and I really value it. After the initial "I refuse to deal with your sexuality" business which lasted through high school, she realized when I started to live with Bob in college that she had to let go and let me live my own life. She told me she only interfered because she didn't want me to get hurt, and I told her people always get hurt and that's the only way they learn. I don't think parents can shelter their children from any kind of harm, and they shouldn't. I mean they should try to, yes, but sexually if a parent doesn't approve, it is just going to make the child rebel more. But I think I did prove something to her. I was relatively together and I think she knew she couldn't do anything about it even if she wanted to, and she started to trust my judgments. That was important, plus the fact that I was older and we could talk about things more closely. She knows I'm sleeping with someone and that I'm happy with my boyfriend and the relationship. I haven't talked to her about sex in too much concrete detail. We talk more about the emotional side of it. I told her when I had a yeast infection. I told her about when I was wondering about going on the pill and if that was a wise move, and all sorts of things like that, but I don't think we ever talked about enjoying sex. I asked her once whether sex was good with my father, and she was reluctant to answer. But she did tell me that they hadn't had sex for a long time. She says sex is not a priority in her life right now. &

Sometimes a mother has happier news to tell her daughter about her own sex life. Gloria Jones's mother, whose strict Catholic background prevented her from discussing sex while Gloria was growing up, did share information with Gloria after her husband died, as a way of helping her daughter appreciate the depth of the marital relationship. As Gloria described it:

&s My parents slept in the same room, but I didn't know if they ever had sex or not. Obviously they did. I hoped so. My father died when I was about seventeen. . . . I wondered about whether they had sex or not. After my father died, my mother told me they had sex, that she loved him, and that they had a very nice relationship. She did tell me that. &

Despite the willingness, or almost eagerness, of many mothers to talk to their daughters about sex after the daughters become sexually involved, daughters do not always welcome this newfound camaraderie. If a mother has been Sex Repressive or Sex Avoidant in the past, her daughter is likely to harbor anger about this and to be unaccepting of her mother's belated overtures to open up communications. These daughters may find themselves unsympathetic to their mothers and somewhat contemptuous of their mothers' unintegrated sexuality. For instance, Colleen, a divorced mother of three grown children, found her daughter Kathy to be very annoyed when she started to share sexual information about her male friends, as if this was inappropriate in light of the earlier attitudes Colleen had espoused when she was still married to Kathy's father:

✎ I was talking to Kathy one day while we were fixing supper. I've forgotten exactly what I said but it was something like, "I'm seeing this guy and I'm not sure I really want to sleep with him," or something like that. And she said, "MA!" And I said, "What?" And she said, "MA! You're not supposed to talk like that to me!" And I said, "Oh gosh, Kathy, I'm sorry. I didn't know you'd get upset." I guess she does not want to hear me talk about it because I have probably given her the impression over the years that I was repressed sexually. I think that's how she got to know me as she grew up. And I think as I've changed, she doesn't seem to be comfortable taking in that I have become sexual, like herself. ✎

Mothers, on the other hand, may find themselves looking up to their daughters for the latter's savoir-faire about sexual matters and eager to hear details of their daughters' sexual lives as a way of making up for their own lack of experience. Thus the tables turn: the mother's former reluctance to educate her daughter about sexual matters gives way to the daughter's reluctance to educate her mother about sexual matters. But while daughters may not tell all, they do talk, and mothers and daughters establish a level of shared confidences that fathers and sons rarely seem able to achieve.

What do mothers and daughters talk about? As we saw, they talk about their sexual frustrations, they talk about yeast infections and birth control, and they talk about how sex can add to a relationship. They also talk about whether or not a guy is nice and how it hurts to be rejected; they talk about orgasms and whether a boyfriend goes down on you. They talk about everything and anything, and sometimes they laugh and feel conspiratorial. Depending on where they started from, mothers and daughters have different areas about which they feel free to converse but, whatever the starting point, the exchange of information seems to grow exponentially.

Mothers and daughters who have had a Sex Expressive relationship all along have a head start in their communication when the daughter becomes sexually active. Mary Travers talks to her daughters with candor about their mutual experiences. According to Mary, "We have discussed relationships, especially when the girls got to be a certain age: 'He was great in bed,' 'He was chintzy,' or 'a male chauvinist . . .' We've gotten more graphic—coming, knowing your body and how it works, you may have to show somebody how it works. We had those kinds of discussions." From Alicia Travers's point of view, these discussions with her mother express her mother's interest and concern for her well-being:

➔ She is very open about sex. We have always had conversations. Once my mother started to discuss, "Do you know what I mean by did he go down on you?" She started to explain oral sex and playing around, which I didn't really understand then, and she said, "You'll understand that later." What she was telling me was exactly like what it was. She was just making sure that I knew what it meant. And I said, "I know what you're talking about, Mom, but no, I haven't done that." She just wanted to inform me, and if I hadn't done it, she just wanted to prepare me. We have discussions like who you slept with, was he good, was he good for you, did you like him. We have discussions like that and I don't feel uncomfortable with my mother. ➔

In a similar vein, Lynn Caine is able to have open interchanges with her daughter, Elizabeth, about their sexual experiences, which serve to clarify the meaning of these experiences:

181

◄§ She asked me a lot about sex with Martin [her father]. "Did you and Daddy do it a lot? How did it feel?" I was pleased because we grew up being very much aware of what was wrong in our childhood, and I just think it's wonderful to be living in a time when you don't have to be crazy over sex. Sex is normal, sex is healthy, sex is ecstasy, or whatever it is. But it's not a big deal. I don't believe in recreational sex . . . in general, I really don't like hopping in and out of bed. It offends me. I know women who do and women who don't, but just to go and have orgasms isn't what a sexual relationship means to me, and I want my daughter to understand that. Some young women I know are satisfied with fucking and promiscuity, but I think there are a lot of things involved besides fucking. §►

Those mothers who are most open in talking about sex with their daughters also manage to preserve their mutual privacy. Questions are answered when the responses inform rather than titillate. Mothers and daughters can swap a story and have a good laugh together, but still preserve their own space. As Lynn goes on to express it:

◄§ I don't want to bring in all the details. I think that's personal. I wouldn't deny having a relationship, but when Elizabeth asks me graphic details, I don't think that's any of her business. If she asks me about oral sex, I'd tell her, "Sure, it makes you gag," and we can laugh about that. We laugh a lot. We can make jokes about that. I don't mind her having questions, but I'm uncomfortable when Elizabeth would like to hear about every relationship I have or how somebody is built or something. I don't think that's any of her business. If it's a funny story, or if the story or circumstances have information that in any way can be helpful, of course I would tell her. §►

RIVALRIES AND ATTRACTIONS

When daughters are more reticent than their mothers to share sexual information, a variety of feelings may be at work. Sometimes daughters are still too angry over former

Sex Avoidant or Sex Repressive behaviors on their mothers' part, sometimes they sense lingering criticism from their mothers, and sometimes they come face-to-face with their mothers' sexual jealousy. When a mother has been sexually frustrated herself, it can be difficult for her to see her daughter living in a freer way. She may not want to deprive her daughter of this important aspect of life, but if it reminds a mother of her own deprivation it could make her envious and hostile. It is not uncommon for daughters to relate incidents of their mothers' jealousy. Before, we saw how Alice's mother found it upsetting when Alice took showers with her husband. Similarly, Cecilia told us her mother becomes upset when she sees Cecilia cuddling on the couch with her husband, Victor. Describing it from her perspective as a mother Debra said:

◄§ When my daughter Ruth brought her first boyfriend home I had no idea they were having a sexual relationship, but I realized, when I saw them together, how different things were for them than they were for me. Here my mother was afraid I would sit on some boy's lap, and Ruth and her boyfriend felt perfectly free about walking around the house with their arms around their waists, embracing in my presence. A few times when I walked in on them, they didn't stop or seem at all uncomfortable, but nodded "hi" and stayed locked together. It was a little shocking to me and I don't think it was appropriate, but I also know that I found myself wishing that Philip and I still had that sense of sexual urgency in our life. I didn't talk to Ruth about it because I wasn't sure in my own mind why it bothered me, although I do know that later with Ruth and with her brother I made it clear when they were involved in relationships that there was to be no sex in the house. §►

When mothers are not aware of the extent to which their jealousy is aroused, they are apt to interfere more actively in a daughter's relationships, as we will see later.

Some mothers find that their own sexual feelings are aroused by the budding sexuality of their daughters. A mother does not always feel in competition with her daughter but may instead resonate with her daughter's emerging sexual vibrancy. As part of this reawakening of sexual interest, some mothers find themselves having erotic feelings towards their daughters, feelings that tend to be suppressed because they are usually very upsetting to a mother. Melissa, a mother of two teenage daughters who works at home designing greeting cards, was surprised by the recurring sexual dreams she had about her older daughter, Ashley, when Ashley entered into puberty:

◦§ After Ashley started dating, there was a period of several months when I would have these dreams about her. The two of us would be lying around on my bed, which we often do in real life, just chatting or talking about her boyfriends, and in the dream she would ask me what is it like to French kiss. I would then kiss her and it would feel very warm and cuddly. She would say, "That feels nice," and then without talking anymore I would start to make love to her, very gently—caressing her breasts, running my hands over her body, feeling her legs, and finally very gently caressing her clitoris and then inserting my fingers into her vagina and very tenderly stimulating her until she had an orgasm. At that point I would usually wake up, very aroused, and always absolutely stupefied about what I was dreaming. . . . I mean, I have never had any conscious sexual thoughts about Ashley and I still don't know what to make of those dreams. The funny thing is that even though the dreams were sexual as hell, the mood in the dream was not that sexual. It was always just a very warm feeling, very protective and motherly feeling, like cuddling and feeling good rather than feeling sexy and passionate. I thought at the time that maybe the dreams were about my fears that her boyfriends wouldn't treat her right or that they would try to have sex with her in a clumsy, unpleasant way, and that I was trying to or wanted to let her know what sex could and should be like. On the other hand, the dreams were very arousing to me and I still don't know what was going on with me at the time. I have never had any dreams like that since and I certainly am not turned on by women. §◦

Although Melissa's dreams clearly express the strong sexual component that is part of her deep love for her daughter, Melissa cannot allow herself to make contact with these feelings in her conscious waking state. It is difficult enough for family members to acknowledge sexual attractions to each other when these feelings are aroused between opposite-sex relatives, but much harder when they occur between same-sex relatives. Because Melissa's love for her daughter is an all-encompassing love, it is to be expected that she would experience it on a physical level, just as it is to be expected that this love keeps Melissa from expressing her passionate feelings directly to her daughter.

OUTWARD BOUND

For mothers and daughters, sex education is a two-way street, and in some respects mothers are learning more from their daughters than vice versa. Perhaps the biggest learning experience for mothers of teenage daughters today is that sex is not such a big deal as it has been made out to be. In their concern about keeping a daughter from harm, many mothers have distorted the role of sex in a girl's life. Although sex is not to be taken lightly and requires a responsible attitude and informed approach to avoid unwanted consequences such as disease, pregnancy, or heartbreak, it is nonetheless an experience which many adolescent girls can not only survive but enjoy. They neither fearfully avoid sex nor compulsively indulge in it, but accept it as a wholesome part of their lives that can enhance their relationships and their good feelings about themselves. While their mothers hover over them, waiting for them to fall, daughters are demonstrating that they can take sex in stride and that their mothers can relax. Julia, a caring and concerned mother, hesitatingly went along with her fifteen-year-old daughter's decision to start a sexual relationship because she could not offer any intellectually sound arguments against it, and even helped her daughter obtain birth control, but she had a hard time controlling her anxieties. It wasn't long, though, before Julia came to realize that her worries were more reflective of her own vulnerabilities than her daughter's:

◆§ I was very aware that Christina was sexually active when she was fifteen and I wanted to make sure she had birth control. There was a boy she was going out with, and she made some vague remark, and I asked her if she wanted birth control and she said, yeah, it would be a good idea. I don't remember what she said exactly, but she really wanted to let me know. I immediately said to myself, "She's sixteen," not fifteen, and added a year to her age. Even though I knew she was very responsible, I think I was very afraid of her getting pregnant. I also thought her being in a sexual relationship was much more emotionally involving than she thought it was, and I remember her saying, "You're making such a big deal of it. I'm not such a vulnerable kid and I won't get hurt." It made me feel old that I had a daughter who was sexually active. I didn't want to think about her getting pregnant. I remember it being very upsetting for a week or so, but once I decided that she was being responsible and that she didn't seem as emotionally involved with it as I thought she was, I got used to it. But I do remember it being very amazing and upsetting to me. I thought that it made her tremendously vulnerable, but it didn't seem to, and at some point I decided, OK, that's my bag, it's not hers. ౭✍

While most mothers are still learning from their daughters that sex is not a hurricane they may not survive, Sex Expressive mothers have been able to instill this attitude in their daughters and help them overcome the cultural barriers that stand in the way of girls' accepting sex as a normal part of their lives. These mothers try to demystify sex and give their daughters support in coping with lingering social stigmas and roadblocks. Gloria Jones described how she helped her daughter, Kaylie, obtain birth control despite the objections of the gynecologist and how she gave her approval to her daughter to live with her boyfriend despite objections from friends:

◆§ There was no overt sex until my kids were sixteen and we were in Miami. In Miami, Kaylie went to a terrible high school and started to smoke grass but Jim stopped that very quickly. She had her first affair there. Kaylie wrote a funny short story about it; I hope it gets published. She told me she was going to have an affair with this fellow, and then I took her to a doctor. I picked a lady doctor, and we went upstairs and I said, "I think you ought to teach my daughter about birth control because I think she's going to have an affair." Then Kaylie looked at me and said, "I think we're in the wrong place," and I said, "Why?" And she said, "Look at the Virgin Mary" (hanging on the wall). It was too late to run and the doctor gave me such hell. She said, "This child is too young and what are you doing!" and so forth and she refused. That was her right. So we went to another doctor who agreed with me, and he said, "If you think she's going to have an affair, it's better that she doesn't get pregnant, so we should show her how to use the diaphragm," and that was that. The kid she had the affair with came up and stayed with us when we moved to New York. He was cute, a very nice fellow. All my friends were horrified that I let her sleep with this fellow, that we let her have this affair. Jim said if she was going to do that, she was going to do that, and it was better at home than out in the fields and better with a diaphragm than without. 8≈

Similarly, Mary Travers, in talking to her daughters, tried to reduce the anxieties about sex that filtered through at various stages of their development. She consistently focused on helping her daughters maintain a positive attitude towards sex as an important and enhancing part of life:

≈8 After my daughter's first experience, she said what probably every girl says, "It wasn't quite what I thought it was going to be," and then we talked about the work involved in sex and that you have to work on it to get it right. . . .

When I would tell stories about childbirth, I never made it a scary subject but talked about the exciting aspects of watching a baby being born. I didn't weigh it heavily with pain, because they were so far away from having one and why should you load them down with that kind of anxiety? When they get closer to the date of having a child, then they know there is pain accompanying it, but they also know it doesn't last very long. . . .

I had a very interesting conversation with my daughter when her six postpartum weeks were over. "Well," I said, "it should be pretty soon," and she said, "Don't talk about it. I don't even want to know about it at this point. I'm still feeling the episiotomy." I said, "You shouldn't wait too long." "Oh," she said, "I heard from my girlfriends it's not going to be good," and I said, "Right. The first time is not going to be good, but it's one of those things you just have to get through and hope it will be better the second time. But you know you have a husband who has been without sex for a considerable length of time, so you really ought to think about it. You may not feel like you're into it before the fact, but there's always that wonderful quality of sometimes you get into bed and you don't really feel like making love and all of a sudden in the middle of it . . ." And I used the sewing machine analogy: the needle threaded on top and the bobbin thread on the bottom inside. "If the needle doesn't catch the thread on the bobbin it goes in and out and it never catches—and sex is like that." And I said, "Sometimes you make love and you're not really in the mood and you think the bobbin is not threaded, and you get around midway and all of a sudden the bobbin catches and you're sewing. And it's like that," I told her. "You just have to get back into it and it will be fine." ❧

Mary Travers and Gloria Jones come from the world of show business and publishing, a world that has always been freer in setting its own standards and being a standard-bearer for others. But the enlightened attitude they express towards a daughter's sexuality is one that more and more young mothers are coming to accept. Tracy, who was raised in a Sex Repressive home, has made a conscious effort to bring up her children to be more comfortable about their sexuality than she was with hers. This was easier for her to do with her sons, but she is also attuned to her daughter's sexual needs. Tracy wants her daughter Meridith to be able to accept herself sexually and enjoy a full sexual relationship with a partner:

❦ Meridith is a little tight as a person, and I don't always experience her sexuality. Maybe I was stricter with her than the boys. I would like to encourage her to enjoy herself and her relationships more. I worry that she isn't enjoying sex, and I care if she has orgasms and enjoys it. I have told her things out of my own experience, like being concerned about sleeping with a man and not getting enough pleasure for myself from it. I have told her to explore her body, masturbate, get to know yourself really well. All that has evolved through the years for me so that now it is really comfortable and orgasmic and I'm comfortable about my own sexuality, and I talk to her about the same things—about getting pleasure for herself and reaching orgasms. ❧

SEVEN

SIBLING RIVALRY,
AND LOVE

Until recently, most of the research and theories about family sexual attitudes in relation to child development focused on the role of parents vis-à-vis their children, and sibling relationships were largely ignored. Now it is recognized that the family exists as a system in which each person has an important effect on the others, and siblings are starting to get the attention they deserve. Most people, after all, are siblings: over eighty percent of the population grows up with a sister or brother.

Sibling relationships, like all family relationships, are usually characterized by intense feelings. The very nature of the nuclear family contains the expectation of strong commitment and attachment. Parents foster close sibling ties by encouraging their children to love, protect, and share with each other. Just the circumstances of living in the same house bring sisters and brothers close to one another: they play together, watch TV together, talk about Mommy and Daddy together, explore together, and often sleep together, providing each other with companionship and emotional support. In this context it is only natural that early sexual feelings are directed towards the person with whom siblings are closest, namely their sister or brother.

How parents respond to sibling relationships has a powerful effect on the growth of healthy sexuality and the possibilities of developing future fulfilling relationships beyond the family confines. Many parents find it hard to accept the sexual pulls and tugs which emerge in the family setting. They are upset when they see their children expressing natural curiosities and longings, and try to nip these feelings in the bud, often in a way which communicates disgust and horror. These siblings learn to approach each other furtively, and they grow up feeling guilty and ashamed of their sexual impulses. If parents interfere with spontaneous sibling interactions, and especially if they withdraw approval, siblings can become overly dependent on each other for love and lose interest in outside emotional involvements. Contrary to what many parents believe, suppression of early sexual play between their children is more rather than less likely to lead to incestuous behavior later on.

In Sex Expressive families, where parents take the emerging sexuality of their children in stride, siblings are unlikely to feel shame because of their loving feelings towards each other. For them, the sibling relationship can be a safe place for learning about one's body, for swapping information, for modeling behavior, and for developing confidence in relation to others. Under these circumstances, sibling relationships provide a springboard for establishing satisfying relationships outside the home.

SISTERS AND BROTHERS

When we think of sibling love, the relationship between sisters and brothers comes to mind, and when we think of sibling rivalry, we generally think of same-sex siblings—sisters and sisters, or brothers and brothers—but both feelings play an important role in opposite-sex sibling interactions. Parents, however, seem to be more anxious about sibling love than rivalry as far as their daughters and sons are concerned, although this is largely an unspoken fear. As a result, brothers and sisters are usually kept apart from each other once they pass the age of three or four, and sometimes even before that. Sisters and brothers are taught not to appear unclothed before each other, not to engage in exploratory play together, not to bathe or go to the bathroom together. Gloria Jones let her children bathe together until the age of four or five, and she got flak, even from strangers, when *Life* magazine showed a photo of her son and daughter together in the bathtub:

◄§ We got so much critical mail about their bathing together I said maybe it is not such a good idea. At six o'clock they used to come home from school, and the maid and I would put them both in this big tub and get them quickly ready for supper and then they had homework to do. I was just kidding about that [stopping the baths because of the letters], but I did realize that people had a deep puritanical streak and maybe we didn't have such a puritanical streak. &

Children pick up early from their parents not only that physical intimacy is wrong but that sex play between sister and brother is especially wrong. Nobody, parents and children alike, can articulate why close brother-sister relationships are wrong, only that they just are. Of course the underlying fear is of incest, an act that by definition is to most parents, and therefore their children, morally repugnant. Nevertheless, sisters and brothers do engage in various levels of sexual activity with each other, ranging from the exploratory play of childhood to actual sexual intercourse in adolescence. Casual sexual contact between brothers and sisters is estimated to occur in nine out of ten homes; serious sexual contact between brothers and sisters is much less common, but it is still the most frequent type of incest.*

With most cross-sex siblings, sexual play is an outgrowth of curiosity. Sisters and brothers wonder how and why they are different, and they learn about each other by way of comparison and play. Through better knowledge about their uniqueness, children also develop greater security about their gender identification. Some parents do not mind sisters and brothers looking at each other when they are young, but find it hard to stay cool when they see sisters and brothers touching. The "don'ts" and disapproving scowls teach children quickly that it is bad for them to engage in any play that involves the body. Reactions vary, however, depending on the relative ages of the children. When the sister is the older child, and already mature enough to help in child care, parents generally feel it is proper for her to clothe and bathe her younger brother until he enters into prepuberty. Sisters,

---

* Although exact figures are hard to come by because of people's reticence to acknowledge incest, most investigators in this field agree that brother-sister incest is the most common form. See, for example, Blair and Rita Justice, *The Broken Taboo* (New York: Human Sciences Press, 1979); and Stephen P. Bank and Michael D. Kahn, *The Sibling Bond* (New York: Basic Books, Inc., 1982).

too, feel comfortable about relating to their young brothers in a maternal rather than sororal way. Alice, for example, compared the experiences of helping out with her younger brother to those of raising her son, and Colleen said that she loved taking care of her baby brother because it made her feel "real grown up."

Sexual interest between brother and sister becomes most troubling for parents when the brother is older than the sister, and indeed this is a potentially touchy situation as most incidents of sibling incest occur between older brothers and younger sisters. It is rare that parents will leave an older brother to care for a baby sister when the care involves intimate physical handling like bathing, for example. Instead, parents of older brothers and younger sisters tend to make it clear that the two are to keep a distance, and separate rooms are considered mandatory even when space is limited in the home.

Several factors make sexual exploratory play between an older brother and younger sister problematic. First, as with any relationship involving an older person and a much younger one, there is always a question of coercion. Younger siblings are primed to "go along" with older siblings, having been taught to look up to them and in general wanting to model themselves after their older brothers and sisters. Older brothers are not only used to giving orders, as are older sisters, but they often do so with the added authority vested in them by parents as the male sibling. Brothers are expected to be more demanding, while sisters are expected to be more accommodating. In this way, the stage is set in many homes for power-oriented sexual involvements of older brothers with younger sisters. Actual intercourse may not result, but even sexual play between older brother and younger sister can have a coercive tone. Cecilia, for example, described how her older brother Martin introduced her to sexual play and tried to force himself upon her beyond the point at which she felt comfortable:

◆§ I got my education from my older brother. Very much indeed. He would play with me sexually sometimes, but I

194

wasn't so aware really of what I was doing. Maybe I liked it too. Yes, I think I did. He would say he liked me very much, and I was very excited about the idea of that type of acceptance in my life. It was new to me. I didn't have a sexual relationship with him, although he tried several times and I had to push him away. It wasn't acceptable at that time. I felt uncomfortable about it. I think first of all because he was my brother, I felt it was a taboo, and then it felt aggressive. It was strange—he being an adolescent, going into adolescence, and me not even being a grown girl. I was slow in my development into adolescence. That took me a while. ಒ

Older brothers rarely recognize the exploitative element involved in their sexual activity with a younger sister and dismiss such incidents as casual experimentation. Of course it often is, from the older brother's point of view, but the younger sister is used as a guinea pig. Bob, an acknowledged homosexual who grew up with an only sister six years his junior, recognized how important it was for him to have his sister as a sexual playmate, but he did not ponder on the effect of his behavior on his sister:

ಒ We had one or two kinds of sexual experiences together— sort of undressing and playing around a little bit. It was at my instigation, but I was six years older. I must have been about twelve or thirteen and she was six. We don't talk about it now. We didn't talk about it then. I don't know what the feeling was on her part. On my part it was a degree of exhibitionism. You have to understand that if you grow up as a gay young man in this society, your avenues for sex exploration and testing out the normal feedback that one would want to get about one's sexuality are nil. So a thirteen-year-old boy who is reaching puberty, and is feeling his oats, he isn't going to the dance to feel up some girl in the back seat of a car. The boy in that circumstance doesn't really have the social rituals of that age to allow a homosexual boy to practice those things and see what kind of response he is going to elicit from others, and I think there were probably more actual contacts with my little sister largely related to just needing to do that with somebody, and she was handy. I think in the case of when that happened, the simple direct part about it was she was interested in seeing my penis and I was interested in showing it off, because I knew I had one and she didn't, and she knew likewise. I don't think she had ever seen one in her life and I don't think my father ever let her see him. There was a reciprocal need. She was curious, and I was exhibitionistic. It had to happen so it seemed accidental. We couldn't sit down and say, "Let's do this." It had to occur accidentally. 8≈

When sisters and brothers are close in age and still young, parents see their play together as cute and appropriate unless it involves bodily exploration and fondling. Colleen, who rejected the Sex Repressive style of her parents, acknowledged that she had her own difficulties accepting the mutual sexual interests of her children. Although she never saw her sons and daughter engaged in sex play together, she knew she would have interrupted it if she had come upon them:

≈§ We had lots of books around and animals for them to learn about sex from, but in terms of their own sexuality I guess I was more repressive. They probably did fool around with each other, and because of our lifestyle they had plenty of time when I wasn't at home. They had private places, and private times, and their own rooms. If they were young now and I came across them, I probably would say, "Let's not do that and let's look at pictures and books instead and I'll show you what it's about," but I'm not sure how I would feel. I think today I would probably be sympathetic, but if I had come across them at sex play when they were young I probably would have been more curt than I would have hoped. I think I had grown more intellectually than I had emotionally. I probably would have reacted strongly even though I knew better. I probably would have said, "Stop it! Get your clothes on and get out of here. I don't want you to do that." I wouldn't have said it was something wrong or disgusting or anything like that, but I think they probably would have gotten that impression from my voice. ෴

At the other end of the spectrum is Nina, who rebelled against her Sex Repressive inheritance by adopting a Sex Obsessive orientation. She and her husband, Derrick, are perfectly comfortable about their daughter and son's exploratory play, even when it includes the whip and chain collection. Nina feels their interaction on this level is perfectly natural and that it is safer for them than experimenting with children they do not know well. Although purely speculative on her part, she thinks she could even be accepting of her children having intercourse with each other:

෴ I think it's perfectly natural for them to explore sexually with each other. I think that would be a safe place for them to start. Their awareness is at about the same level. She's two years older, but as far as exposure and awareness goes, I think they are at the same level. If they tried to have sex, I would say that is their business. That would be perfectly natural, and it would be a lot safer with each other than it would be with anybody else. I don't think it would bother me. She's nine and more mature than I was at twelve or thirteen, and I know that I had sexual awareness of my body at that time but I didn't know how to direct it. It's a thing that happens. I think that human beings are ready a lot sooner than society is ready. Of course a certain amount of intellect has to come into play. ෴

Gloria Jones, another mother from a Sex Repressive background, established a Sex Expressive environment for her two children. With good humor, she recognized that mutual sexual exploration was a perfectly natural activity for her son and daughter when growing up and she always felt confident that they could set appropriate limits by themselves. When we asked Gloria if her children engaged in early sexual play, she responded:

෴ They never told me. They probably did, but I don't think they ever did anything you could call deep penetration! They might have done some fiddling around, but I never saw them doing anything. I think it's implicit that you don't screw your sister, and that your sister doesn't screw you. I'm sure they did play with each other. ❧

Sex play between brothers and sisters close in age may continue past the time when parents feel it is right, especially when the two children are emotionally tied to each other. Usually the incest taboo is strong enough for sexual explorations to stop short of intercourse, but quite a number of adolescent siblings engage in mutual masturbation. The biggest inhibitor of incest between brother and sister is, interestingly enough, not the injunctions of the parents but the emotional availability of the parents. Studies of sibling incest indicate that siblings turn towards each other when their emotional needs are not met by the parents. The more distant or rejecting the parents, the greater the likelihood that sibling sexual experimentation will lead to sibling incest. As one researcher put it, when parents are unavailable to them children turn to their sibling as the "second-best" love object, and find that she or he is "even better."* Unfortunately, most instances of sibling incest, even between age-mates, have disastrous consequences, leaving both brother and sister feeling guilty and with damaged self-respect. When children are given sufficient nurturance by their parents and feel secure within the family, they are able to put the brakes on their erotic feelings towards one another. Cecilia is a good case in point. While, as we just saw, she was pushed by her older brother into sexual experimentation that she did not really enjoy, she and her younger brother, who had a very strong emotional and physical attraction for each other, were able to set boundaries that limited their sexual interaction:

❧ When I was thirteen, my younger brother was seven and he would sleep in the same room with me. He was attracted

* Luciano P. R. Santiago, *The Children of Oedipus: Brother-Sister Incest in Psychiatry, Literature, History and Mythology* (Roslyn Heights, N.Y: Libra, 1973), p. 7.

to me starting at a very young age. We played a little bit, some sexual games, but he was too young. I think that was when I awakened sexually. It was nice to be with him, but we stopped. He was eager, but we both knew it was not right for us to play those games anymore together. ठ~

Naomi, who is now twenty-five and works as a cashier in a restaurant, has a brother who is five years younger. They have been sexually drawn to each other, and Naomi has been careful to avoid situations that would be too arousing for either of them:

~§ I remember once playing with him. I once passed by naked and he touched my breasts. He was very young. He was eight years old, and I remember I felt that it was forbidden, but I enjoyed it. I felt, though, it was something that shouldn't be done. It started out he was just tickling me, but then it became more like a caress. After that I always wore my underwear; I didn't go around nude anymore. When we grew up a bit, when I was sixteen and he was eleven, I don't think I ever felt comfortable in my underwear again. Since then I have always covered myself in front of him. ठ~

Sometimes the incest taboo is experienced with such strength that sisters and brothers cannot acknowledge their sexual interest in each other until they grow up and move out on their own. Maria found that her attraction to her brother Peter only entered her awareness after she was married and safely away from him:

~§ A couple of years ago I started to have moments of attraction to Peter. For the first time I thought of him as a man, not a brother. I don't know why, but he is very sweet with me, very patient, and he helps me. Sometimes I look at him and say, "Gee, if he were not my brother, it would be great!" I think he feels the same way towards me, but being a brother, that is the end. One should not think of it; after all, it is taboo. We were brought up like that. You don't make

199

love to your brothers, your father, your sons, because it is incest. I saw a wonderful film where a mother makes love to her son, and you go out of the film feeling it shouldn't be, it is better not to be. And I am clear on that and I haven't let anything happen. &

Because love between siblings becomes difficult to handle when it begins to take on erotic components, opposite-sex siblings sometimes try to mask erotic feelings under a veneer of hostility. The nasty interactions between sisters and brothers that often occur in adolescence—teasing, deriding the other's physical appearance, and other such gambits— that parents interpret as a loss of familial feeling quite often cover a growing attraction that the siblings involved can only handle by artificially distancing themselves. To emphasize this distance, siblings may even go after each other's friends, as if this proves disinterest in the sibling. Charlotte reported that her brother literally jumped on her girlfriends when she would bring them home to visit:

&§ My brother is two years younger than I am. When I was around twelve, thirteen, somewhere in those years, I had a bedroom and there was a ledge outside the windows and my brother came crawling around on the ledge. He was always trying to get a look. When my brother's sexuality really came on, it came on hot and heavy. He stopped badgering me after a while and became a really nasty pest. When my girlfriends came over, he would jump on them, and grab them, and stuff like that. It really embarrassed me. &

Another way of dealing with erotic feelings towards one's sister is for the brother to take on the role of father-protector and keep other boys from acting on feelings for his sister that he cannot express himself. Many sisters complain about how bossy an older brother became when they started to date, checking up on them like a surrogate father and passing comment on the worth of the boy or how late they came home at night, and in other ways standing guard.

Although parents are concerned about the sexual aspects of brother-sister love, they tend to be unaware of the sexual aspects of cross-sibling rivalry. Yet the biggest source of rivalry between sisters and brothers is probably differential sex-typing by the parents, and the more stereotyped and sexist the parental attitudes, the greater the clash between sister and brother. As we discussed earlier, parents tend to prefer boys and to accord them greater freedom and opportunities, while girls are raised in more restrictive ways. Marked differences in parental expectations of their sons and daughters create not only rivalries but sexist patterns of interrelationship between brothers and sisters that pave the way for sexual exploitation.

The effects of sexist child-rearing patterns are quite subtle in the early years. Girls enjoy their dolls and boys enjoy their trucks, and neither may feel deprived in terms of the accoutrements of childhood. In some homes girls are even given construction sets, just like their brothers, even though one does not hear that boys are given dolls, just like their sisters. What does start to bother sisters, though, are the patterns of deference to their brothers that girls experience on the part of their parents. Not only do fathers and mothers usually hope for a boy when expecting a child, but when this wish comes true, they tend to give the boy more attention. Complementing the studies on young children which demonstrate that boys are given more encouragement than girls are studies of adults which demonstrate that women who are successful tend to come from families where there are no brothers to deflect attention. The twenty-five top business women studied by Margaret Hennig and Anne Jardim for *The Managerial Woman*, for example, all come from families of all girls.*

Favoritism towards boys manifests itself in many ways, sometimes glaring, sometimes more subdued, but usually discernible at some level. In Colleen's family, the favoritism shown to her brother was extreme. As the firstborn child,

* Margaret Hennig and Anne Jardim, *The Managerial Woman* (Garden City, NY: Anchor Press, Doubleday, 1977).

Colleen retained a special status through the birth of her younger sister but lost that status when her brother, the third child, came along:

◄§ My mother became very attached to my brother as soon as he was born. My sister and I were just jealous of it. If there were a favorite piece of meat and we all wanted it, she would say, "No, no, it's for Patrick." And I can remember she'd say, "He should have it. He's a growing boy." ϑ►

Feelings of rivalry between sisters and brothers usually escalate in adolescence when girls become resentful of the greater freedom allowed their brothers to make dates with friends, come home late from school, and go on excursions or to parties unchaperoned. Sisters are bothered by the inequity of their treatment as well as by the interference with their social life. They find the double standard demeaning and feel it puts them at a disadvantage vis-à-vis their brothers. Allison's mother, as we saw earlier, was very strict with her when she started dating, but allowed her younger brother much more leeway:

◄§ It was different with my brother because he was a male. There were different standards. It eased up a little with my sister, because she is five years younger and by the time she started dating they were a bit more used to it than they were with me. I'm not certain, but I think they gave her less of a rough time than they did with me. But with my brother there were big differences. He had much less supervision and "where are you going, when will you be back" and calling up to see if there would be an adult there on the premises. My sister went through much the same routines they went through with me. They were really very strict with all of us. My brother couldn't come to the dinner table in a T-shirt, for instance, and once when my sister came to the table in a bathrobe and with rollers in her hair, my father said, "It's a sin for a young lady to be a slob." The way they expected us to behave was very clear, but with my brother they were more relaxed. ϑ►

202

The situation was much the same in Harriet's family. Harriet, now in her late twenties, works as an assistant in the physical therapy department of a large hospital. She has a sister who is two years older than she, and a brother who is eight years younger. Harriet feels her brother was always the favored child, and that her mother, who thinks of herself as a progressive woman, allowed much greater freedom to Harriet's brother than to Harriet. The twofold message that comes across to girls in such situations is that they should learn to defer to males, and that they should respect male sexual needs but not their own:

◄§ My brother was what I would call spoiled. He got everything he wanted. He insisted, and was not resisted. It is a sensitive area for me to speak about. I don't know why my parents had such a long span before my brother was born, and it took me some time to realize my mother was pregnant. She announced it very happily, and both my mother and my father were very happy to have a son. They used to treat him very differently. I don't remember exactly how, but he was treated like a boy. I remember a conversation I once overheard my mother having with a neighbor. Our neighbor was telling my mother that her daughter was masturbating. My mother said, "Oh, it is natural. It is this age," and she told her my brother was masturbating. Years earlier, when she saw me masturbating, though, she had gotten very angry and she made me feel bad. When I told my mother I slept with a man—I told her around the age of twenty although I actually had done it at seventeen—she was shocked. She was angry with me and said she had only one man and that was my father. When my brother was about fifteen he dated a girl called Beverly, and my mother said to me one day, "I think he is sleeping with Beverly." And she said it with concern because she wanted him to sleep with her. I knew he did because he had told me about it. She wanted him to be social and make out. §►

SISTERS AND SISTERS

In families where there are only sisters, parental child-rearing practices are influenced by birth order rather than by sex, as is also the case in families of all boys. Usually it is the oldest sister who is given parental attention and encouragement that in brother-sister homes is reserved for boys. In terms of freedom, however, especially in sexual behavior, it is the youngest sister rather than the oldest who is usually favored. Parents tend to be more restrictive of the oldest sister when it comes to sex and only little by little learn to relax the reins as the younger sisters come along.

Generally, the firstborn sister models herself after her mother but later-born sisters model themselves after the firstborn sister. The older sister tends to set the pace and determine the joint activities of herself and her sisters. If a girl has an older brother she is more likely to play and work alone, but if she has an older sister she is more likely to play with and learn from that sister. Same-sex siblings have been found to have much closer relationships than opposite sex siblings, and sisters tend to have closer relationships than brothers. These ties can be so strong that in later years husbands are frequently jealous of their wives' involvements with their sisters.

Because of the close modeling of younger sisters on their older sister, the degree of self-confidence of the firstborn sister is a very influential factor in the life of her younger sisters. Consequently, when the firstborn sister relates to others in a comfortable way and is "popular" with boys and girls, the younger sister has a much better chance of establishing rewarding relationships herself. When it comes to sexual behavior, the firstborn sister is usually the sexual pioneer. She is the one who will initiate exploratory sex play with her sisters, and she is also usually the one who will begin experimenting with boys as well. When younger, sisters' sex play with each other tends to consist of exploring each other's body, and playing with and identifying the various parts. Perhaps because girls are more verbal than boys, such exploratory play is often accompanied by a lot of talk and sometimes also with a "secret" language. Sisters love to have their own private communication system and special names for things, which extend to their body parts and sexual functions. In her book on sisters, Elizabeth Fishel reports how Carly Simon and her two older sisters, Joanna and Lucy, made up their own special vocabulary for sex. According to Joanna, "We liked to talk about sex so much that we made up substitute words. One particular thing, for example, was that we loved to talk about having our period. We just thought that was terribly interesting when we were quite young. And we made up a word called 'sponking,' which meant having your period. And to this day, we will say, 'I'm sponking,' and supposedly, nobody knows what that means. And we made up the word 'kettles' for breasts and 'logs' for penises."*

Sisters can be particularly helpful to one another in talking about sexual matters when their mothers are Sex Repressive and Sex Avoidant. In such families sisters provide the only outlet for sexual curiosity and the only intimate channel for obtaining information. Cindy, now in her late twenties and recently divorced, grew up in a Sex Avoidant home with an older sister to whom she is very attached. When they were younger, Cindy often tagged along with her big sister, who introduced her to matters sexual:

◄§ I suppose I started becoming aware of sexual activity when I was nine or ten. My sister had a girlfriend who had a wonderful collection of books on sexual practices. Her parents had them, and the parents were away a lot of the time and their housekeeper didn't pay much attention to it, so we had the run of their library, and as soon as we discovered it we spent a great deal of time looking at books and discussing it with one another. And we would talk about whether our parents really knew all that stuff. We were pretty sure her parents did, but we weren't sure about our parents. Sometime around then my sister and I started experimenting. I just liked the experience of touching and of being touched. I didn't so much like touching her, but I liked being touched, and that is when I started

* Elizabeth Fishel, *Sisters: Love and Rivalry Inside the Family and Beyond* (New York: William Morrow & Company, Inc., 1979), p. 116.

masturbating. It became a solitary pleasure more than anything else at that point—by myself. It seemed inconceivable to me that my mother would enjoy such things because I thought of it as something a little scandalous and improper. I don't think I wanted to think about it, and I know I felt guilty and knew that I didn't want my parents catching me masturbating or reading any of that material or playing games with my sister. &

Older sisters can also take a protective stance towards their younger sisters and help them gain parental acceptance of sexual behaviors. Harriet's sister, for instance, always acted as her guide and protector when it came to sexual matters in the family. When Harriet's mother sent out disapproving vibrations about Harriet's developing sexuality, her sister stood up for her against her mother's repressiveness:

&3 I remember I asked my mother how I was born, and she said the sperm met the egg. She didn't explain how. I remember the situation very clearly. It was in the car and I was very young. She never explained how. It was implied that there were inhibitions about it. My mother would answer but she wasn't very willing. When I was eight, my sister told me how conception took place. She told me people lie together, and not only for pregnancy. I was alarmed when she told me this. I was shocked, really shocked.

Afterwards, my sister and I talked about sex a lot. I don't remember exact discussions, but we discussed it one way or another. Once I touched my vagina when I was in bed, this must have been a few years later, and my mother came in and she said, "What are you doing?" And my sister got angry at her. "Why do you ask her and make her feel guilty about it?" She wasn't very old; she must have been around twelve years old, and she got furious for me. My sister and I always talked. I remember once we found a rubber in the street, and I didn't know what it was. We were with a group of children, and my sister said it was to prevent pregnancy when people have sex. I remember another time I was reading a story and I asked her a word and I read it wrong, saying, "What is a lesabean?" and she made fun of me. She said, "It's not a lesabean. It's not a lima bean. It's not a bean. It is a lesbian." But she told me what it was. When I had my first intercourse I told her about it. She told me about her sexual affairs before then. She didn't get into details, but she gave me the feeling that things were open, that it was a legitimate subject. ⮥

As sisters become older they may start to rehearse sexual behaviors with each other that they are unsure about, so they will feel more confident with boys. When dating starts, a girl not infrequently will demonstrate to her sister just what her boyfriend did or tried to do with her. Sheila, now in her thirties, reminisced on how her older sister gave her a French kiss and the amusing parallels this had with her daughter many years later:

⮥ When my sister was dating this guy Rob, she used to try out on me whatever he did to her. Or so I assumed. Valerie didn't talk much about what went on with her and Rob, but the day after she had a date, she would pull some new stunt on me. Like one day she came from behind me and started to fondle my as yet nonexistent breasts. The worst was one day when she asked me, "Do you know what a French kiss is?" And when I said "No," she promptly came and stuck her tongue into my mouth. Was I ever disgusted! I couldn't imagine why Rob would want to do that to her, or why she would let him. I don't think she liked it either at first because I had the feeling she was just trying to make me go through it too. I don't remember ever thinking about that incident much, but years later one day my daughter came to me—she must have been in the fourth or fifth grade at the time—and she asked me, "Mom, do you know what a French kiss is?" I was absolutely stunned, but before I could answer her, she came over to me and gave me a kiss on each cheek. What a relief that was! It reminded me of the old French saying I learned in school, which is part of the Order of the Garter: *Honi soi qui mal y pense*, which means, "Evil to him who evil thinks." ⮥

The point at which an older sister starts dating can significantly affect the dating pattern of the younger sister. As younger sisters usually copy the firstborn sister, their dating doesn't start until hers does. Because of this tendency, if a firstborn sister does not date for one reason or another, the younger sister may be delayed in her own dating behavior, waiting for the older sister to start. Sometimes the younger sister may be prematurely rushed into dating if her need to keep up with the older sister is very strong.

When sisters who are close begin the dating process, they usually share a lot. They borrow each other's clothing, experiment with each other's makeup, and exchange information about their respective dates and sexual experiences. As we saw with Alicia Travers, she not only had tête-à-têtes with her mother about her dating experiences but with her sister as well, with all three women comparing notes. Conversations about sex run the whole gamut of experiences, from how to use a tampon and what kinds of contraceptives are best, to what to do if a boy wants oral sex. About the only thing that sisters tend not to share with each other, or at least not willingly, are their boyfriends. Even if one sister has discarded a boyfriend, there is usually resentment if the other sister should take up with him. Some sisters, but it would seem relatively few, do not have such feelings of possessiveness about ex-boyfriends. They may be pleased to pass such boys along and feel relieved if their sister is available to salve the wounds of a fellow they have broken off with. When sisters are not close to each other, or if they live in markedly Sex Repressive homes, they usually have a girlfriend for a confidante.

Just as brothers and sisters may be drawn into sexual entanglements that go beyond the realm of play and exploration, sisters too can become involved in oversexualized relationships with each other. Again, the tendency to do so is greater when parental lack of involvement leaves an emotional gap that needs to be filled. Most parents are oblivious to erotic relationships between their daughters and only worry about sexual matters when they involve their daughters and their sons or other boys; thus, sisters who are needy usually find little restraint offered by their parents. Relatively few sisters seem to have strong sexual feelings for each other, or if they do, relatively few of them seem to feel free to talk about it. The sisters we spoke to who acknowledged such sexual feelings tended to experience them rather late, often not until they were in their twenties. It seems that many sisters have difficulty telling their sibling about their erotic feelings and usually do not do so until they have already experienced sexual intimacy with another young woman outside the home. Harriet only realized she was sexually drawn to her older sister when she reached her late teens, after she had already had a sexual relationship with a young woman as well as a young man. Harriet had difficulty telling her sister, maybe in part because of the memories of her sister making fun of her when she first found out what the word "lesbian" meant, but also because of her own guilt about having lesbian tendencies and being aroused by her own sister. When Harriet finally did tell her sister, the latter was supportive of Harriet's lesbian tendencies but angry that Harriet was sexually turned on by her:

⊷§ When I was small I played with my girlfriend. Sometimes we played with dolls and sometimes with our bodies. We played love games, like we were getting married and one of us would be the man, the other the woman. We were ashamed of these games. It was touching, hugging, and we tried to imitate intercourse, how it was performed. I didn't have strong feelings, though, till I was much older, and it was with another friend who I didn't even like very much. We were on the beach and we played the game, the man and woman, and I was the man, and I came to orgasm while I was on her. But this was only a very brief encounter. When I was away at camp as a counselor, I fell in love with this other female counselor like I loved my boyfriend. The same attraction, the same looking for her, the same yearning, and we finally made love. I was lured by her. It was after that that I knew I really would like to make love to my sister, but I was afraid to tell her. But one day I did. I told my sister how I felt about women and I suspected I was a lesbian, and that I was

209

alarmed by the idea that I was born this way and doomed to be a lesbian. And that it was torturing me. My sister said she understood me and there was nothing wrong with my feelings. She told me she had been attracted to a fellow student. I don't remember exactly what she said, but I remember a clear message of her attraction to another girl. And then I told her that I had those feelings for her, that I wanted to touch her, and she became very angry with me. "You're sick," she said. "What's the matter with you? I refuse to talk to you about this any more!" ह्ल

The longings of Harriet for her sister have never been mentioned again, and the two sisters have not regained their former intimacy. Harriet feels the reason her sister became so angry was because her sister has the same kind of feelings for her but does not want to face them. Whether or not that is so, sisters, like other family members, usually try not to trespass on each other's space or cross the boundaries between sororal love and sexual intrusion.

BROTHERS AND BROTHERS

Just as fathers and sons have a competitive thing going with each other, so do brothers. Their sex play and information-swapping sessions often have more the aura of one-upmanship than of sharing and mutual learning. Brothers vie with one another in a Rambo-like fashion to see who is more of a man. Don, who is one of four brothers, put it this way:

ह्ल There was a lot of sex play with my brothers. There was a lot of that. There was a lot of measuring of genitalia, and we had games to see who could jerk off the fastest. When we were younger we used to see who could pee the farthest, and once we began to ejaculate we used to see who could ejaculate the farthest—nice, competitive children. ह्ल

When brothers talk to each other about sexual matters, it is usually not to discuss feelings but to let a sibling know that they have scored. Glen, who has two brothers, one older and one younger, described their interaction:

◆§ There was no talk among us. My older brother kind of liked to keep a separation: his friends were his friends and my friends were my friends. When he got older and was in high school, he would relate his experiences, and I hadn't had any yet. He would talk about when he went on such and such a trip and how they had petted and things like that. He wasn't really talking about how he felt about it, or how the girl's reaction made him feel. What got related were stories, and you never knew if they were true. And that's how you learned about it. I remember when I was a sophomore and I was thinking, "I'm almost sixteen and I haven't had sex yet." It was not with such-and-such a person, but the act of having it itself became the point of focus. No one ever talked about romance, except in books or movies, and I think there was a real division between love and sex. I don't remember my brother ever talking about it. He never even said he liked the girl. It is just a sexual liking. That is what a crush is all about. So a lot of instances where it was talked about were just happenings, but nothing about feelings. §◆

Julius Fast had similar experiences with his brothers, who seemed to be able to talk to each other about sex only in a jocular, slightly superior, way:

◆§ I'm the youngest of three. Sex was never discussed with my father—occasionally jokingly with my brothers, but never seriously. The only good part about it was that masturbation was treated as a joke. If you were caught masturbating, it was just a big funny thing. My brothers almost never caught me. The occasional times when they did, or they were caught, it was a joke. There was a lot of joking about masturbation as a kid, and a number of phrases for it, like "beating your meat," or "whacking the bishop." This was not only in the family but among friends, and kids would joke about it all the time—that if you jerk off you get hair on the palm of your hands, and the first thing every kid does is look at the palms of his hands and everybody else goes, "Ha ha ha." Big joke. That kind of stuff. Or "You go crazy if you do it," and someone would always go, "Blub blub blub blub."

By the time I was sixteen I began to have sexual affairs and I think my older brother started at the same time. My older brother was about six years older. I knew that he went out with women, and I knew that he was sleeping with them, from jokes, from kidding around, from hints that were dropped. There was a lot of joking back and forth about sex in the house. When I was about fifteen, my older brother got me a job in the public library and then he had his first sex talk with me. I found out that he had been screwing a number of the librarians, and he gave me advice like, "Don't fool around with Miss X, forget about Miss So-and-so," and "Never shit on your own doorstep." That was the extent of his sexual advice. He wanted to say, "This is the librarian you shouldn't sleep with, don't fool around with librarians at your branch if you can help it," that kind of thing, and that was it. But as far as talking about sex or love, never. Certainly never about birth control or prophylactics or anything like that. It was assumed from a very early age that I knew. I don't know why that assumption was made. Maybe I was too sophisticated a kid to accept any advice from my brothers, and I thought I knew it all. ❧

Sometimes the competitive feelings get out of hand, as they did with Ralph, a twenty-two-year-old water sports coordinator at a resort. Arnie, Ralph's older brother, had no qualms about "making out," almost boastfully, in front of Ralph, and Ralph was not averse to trying to make out with his brother's girlfriend:

❧ My brother used to take his girls down underneath the boardwalk at the beach, and if he had to take care of me, he'd take me along too. I can remember one time that really stuck out in my head—I saw him French this girl and they passed gum from each other's mouth. That's one of the first things I remember. Another time he took a blanket down, and they stripped off their clothes and just explored. He told me to take a walk then, but I hid and watched. I'd see him and then I'd know what to do. If I didn't know something, he'd set me straight. Like, for a long time I didn't know about coming. I always thought that you pissed in the girl. And then he explained it to me, and that made sense 'cause that's how she gets pregnant. One time, when I was about thirteen, my brother and me were alone in the house and his girlfriend came by just when he was going to take a shower. He told her to hang around and he'd be out soon. When he was in the shower, his girlfriend stayed downstairs with me and she started tonguing me while he was in the bathroom. She just started French kissing me and I just got into it a little bit, and then the second she heard the shower stop, she stopped. That was pretty funny. And then, maybe a week later, he said, "Hey, did you do anything while I was in the shower, 'cause why were you both on the couch when I came out?" It was pretty funny. ৯৯

Very few men speak spontaneously about sexual play or sexual feelings between themselves and their brothers. When we have brought it up, most told us that they did not "fool around" with their brothers. Of those who did, quite a few have vivid memories of being caught by their fathers, who were quick to nip the sex play in the bud. Eddie's stepfather, as we saw before, sent his stepbrother to live with a married sister, and Roy's father took less drastic measures but still frightened Roy by screaming at him. Other men who acknowledged having sex play with their brothers described such play as brief, one-shot experiments, almost as if they felt too overwhelmed to try it again. Joe, a sign letterer who has two brothers and a sister, told us:

৯৯ I remember once, maybe I was eight or ten and my older brother was three and a half years older, and I was dressing up as a girl in my sister's clothing. And I remember he was playing with himself and he asked me to put it between my legs. This is the only sexual experience I had with my brother. Or with any of them. ৯৯

213

Judging from the people we know and have interviewed, mothers are less upset about sons being involved in exploratory sex play with each other than are fathers, perhaps because they are less threatened by the idea of homosexuality. Jeanette, for example, said that she turned her head the other way when her boys were involved in sex play, although it did cross her mind that the younger one might have homosexual tendencies:

◦§ When they were younger they took baths together, and they were always touching each other very much, especially the younger one, who was always touching his brother. But it was all very normal. They very soon didn't want me coming into the bathroom. I don't know what they were doing there exactly. They went through that, but nothing more than that. With the younger one I worried a little bit about homosexuality. It is not one single thing, but he is more quiet and he needs more loving and he needs a male figure more now that his father isn't living here. But I'm not sure. I don't really think so. He is having a big thing now with girls and is very cool with them. I really don't know. §◦

Most of the men who told us about having sex play with their brothers were not aware of having sexual feelings towards their brothers. The way they described their experiences, it seemed as if they wanted to experiment sexually and their brothers just happened to be around. A few men did, however, tell us that they also had sexual feelings towards their brothers. Clifford, a young man studying for the ministry, said:

◦§ I felt it. I was attached to my younger brother. I was young, but I felt physically attached to him and he was really cute, and if he was sleeping I would go to him and kiss him on the cheek or something like that. But sex never was part of it. I felt a lot of it was physical, but I didn't think of having sex. I didn't know about it then or that there was pleasure in orgasm. I felt a lot of attachment to my younger brother. We were only fourteen months apart in age. I was very close to him physically and that was the only close physical feeling I had. ❦

The other men who talked about having sexual feelings towards their brothers happen to be gay. They told us that they did have sex play of varying intensity with their brothers, short of penetration, but felt guilty about it as they became more sexually aware and worried about their sexual orientation.

It is difficult to know whether or not sexual attraction between brothers is a rare occurrence, which seems unlikely, or whether males do not like to talk about it because of homophobia. Sexual experimentation between brothers is a double whammy, to be condemned not only because of its incestuous overtones but also because of its homosexual overtones. Most of the early sex play reported to us by men that took place with other boys was more in the nature of parallel play than of interactive play. For example, they would masturbate in each other's presence but not masturbate each other. While exploratory sex play between brothers is no more peculiar in and of itself than play between sister and sister, it would seem to be less acceptable to most parents, and hence to their children.

As with brother and sister, the most problematic aspect of brother-brother experimentation is when it involves two boys of disparate age. Documented cases of brother-brother incest invariably involve a much older brother and a very young brother and tend to be physically violent as well. The trauma for the younger brother is, under these circumstances, quite severe and usually results in serious damage to his sense of self-worth.

Even though our language provides us with the expression "brotherly love," it is clear from the interviews that it is difficult for boys, as it is for men, to express their affectionate feelings to their brothers. The different attitudes that parents hold towards brothers as compared to sisters foster competitive feelings rather than compassionate feelings and hinder sons in their ability to form close bonds with one another. In addition to toughening up brothers so that they can make it in Little League, parents might do well to "tenderize" their sons for the big league—the adult world of interrelationships where they tend to flounder. The contemporary complaint about many men—that they are not able to commit themselves in a relationship—is just another manifestation of the relatively encased emotional life that men experience as young brothers.

It is difficult for boys to integrate their sexual feelings for their brothers or sisters into their lives because sex, as so many other aspects of life, becomes for them an avenue of domination rather than of sharing. Even homosexuality, which is feared so much by parents, becomes acceptable in some social strata if it involves a very stereotyped masculine youth "doing it" to a very effeminate one. According to Steve Ashkinazy, clinical director of the Institute for Gay and Lesbian Youth (we will hear more from Steve later), the promiscuity of gay men is related to their view of sexual partners as objects to exploit and conquer:

◄§ There are a lot of differences in socialization of boys and girls in terms of their relationships. Boys are taught to be more sexual, to be more exploitative in their view of sexual partners, to make sex objects of people they relate to, and to think of sex as a conquest. Where you have two males, each socialized to exploit, you very frequently have two men neither one of whom is interested in having sex but just doing what is expected of them—coming on to someone and making advances. Many homosexuals wind up in bed with each other because there was no way to stop it. Each was programmed to come on. §►

If parents want their children to get the most benefit from sibling relationships, each child, brother and sister alike, needs to be helped to grow as a separate and valued individual. Creating differential sex roles and hierarchies within homes such as Colleen's and Harriet's provides children with a model of relationships based on power and domination instead of mutuality. Given a sharing and loving environment, such as the one Gloria and James Jones cre-

216

ated, children can engage in the exploratory sexual activities that are a natural part of development without becoming overly dependent on or exploitative of a sibling. Sibling relationships can then serve as a medium for the growth and socialization of the sexuality of brothers and sisters and help them develop the self-confidence necessary to meet later sex partners from a secure vantage point.

EIGHT

COMING OF AGE IN THE FAMILY:
PARENTS FACE
TEENAGE SEXUALITY

Family passions usually reach new levels of intensity as children enter adolescence and start dating. Parents can no longer pretend that their offspring are sexually neuter when they see their daughters' developing bosoms and their son's developing musculature, outward changes that signal the heightening of inner urges. Like it or not, parents are faced with the fact that their teens are sexual beings with sex appeal and sexual appetites. The reality of a child's sexual development also forces parents into an awareness of their own sexual feelings towards their offspring just at the time that they must begin to deal with the sexual interests their children have in other people. For many families, the onset of dating is a time of revelation, a time when the parents' true feelings about sex, as opposed to their intellectually articulated feelings, come to the surface.

When teenagers begin to branch out towards others, parents and siblings have to adapt to one of their own becoming involved with somebody else and no longer looking to the family as the primary source of emotional support. Parents also have to be ready to relax their controls by turning over to their teens responsibility for their own behavior. This generates conflict in many homes as parents often are afraid that teenagers are not mature enough to set their own limits, and teenagers are often angry that their parents do not grant them the freedom they feel is commensurate with their age and with the tenor of the times. Unable to deal with these family conflicts, many teenagers resort to secrecy, cutting themselves off not only from criticism but also from the possibility of constructive input.

Parents' feelings about their children's sexual maturity are almost always ambivalent. Although many parents have a part of them that wants their children to grow up, to date, and to be popular, another part of them does not want their children to become sexually active, because of a basic fear of sex or concern about health issues, or because of jealousy aroused by a child's first significant involvements outside the family. Parents themselves are often confused as to how much their attitude is motivated by good judgment and how much by personal need, so it is not surprising that teenagers are just as hard put to evaluate and accept their parents' views at this critical time in their lives.

Teenagers are not always as gung ho to date and to experiment sexually as their parents fear they are. Each adolescent has his or her own fears about sexual involvement and its consequences. If they do not worry as much as their parents would like them to about the possibility of pregnancy or AIDS, they worry more than their parents realize about what their peers will think of them. Dating is a time of anxiety and self-consciousness, only made more difficult by the knowledge that what one is doing is disapproved of by one's parents. Adolescents are afraid to go to their parents for the reassurance and guidance they need at this formative stage in their life. Instead, they look for direction from peers who are as uncertain as they.

The parents' overall mode of dealing with sex has, of course, an important influence on how the parents and children deal with dating behavior. Sex Repressive parents come into strong conflict with their teenagers at this time and become even harsher as the sexuality of their children continues to unfold before them. These children, as statistics show, cannot abide by their parents' unreasonable strictures and become sexually active behind their parents' back. Children whose parents believe sex is bad are significantly more likely to have intercourse and significantly less likely to use birth control when they do have sex than children of parents who feel positively about sex. Because of the strong parental disapproval, these teens are guilty about sex as well as uninformed about using birth control. The result is not only that they more often end up pregnant than other teens but also that they enjoy sex less. Unfortunately for these teenagers, their parents' attitudes create more problems than they solve.

The children of Sex Obsessive parents may be propelled

into sexual relationships earlier than they are emotionally ready for as they try to meet the sexual standards and expectations which they think their parents hold for them. Some become sexual athletes who find no prizes are awarded for entering the sexual marathon; others rebel against their parents' sexual mores if they feel that these are too far out and might alienate them from their peers. These teens sometimes even become moralistic in their own relationships, to compensate for what they consider deviant behavior on the part of their parents.

Sex Avoidant parents find that they can no longer avoid sex as the reality of their children's blooming sexuality is thrust under their noses. Some, however, feel enjoined from interfering with their child's sexual behavior and may inadvertently encourage him or her to became sexually involved because the child interprets the parents' "hands-off" attitude as an unwillingness to be involved and therefore hesitates to seek parental advice or support. Other parents try to provide guidance, only to find that their offspring are unwilling to talk to them because the lines of communication regarding sex have never been opened.

Children from Sex Expressive homes have by far the best time of it. Their parents are accepting of their sexuality and have prepared them to relate sexually in a responsible way, as we have illustrated in various examples. Because their parents have already established a communication system with them, these teenagers are receptive to parental guidance and less likely to suffer harmful consequences from sex.

THE POPULARITY CONTEST

Although Sex Repressive and Sex Avoidant parents do not want their teens to have sexual relationships, they do want them to have social relationships with the opposite sex, and the more the better. Parents are often overly invested in who and how often their children date because they perceive dating as a measure of their child's social acceptance. Such parents urge their children to have boyfriends or girlfriends, and teenagers in these homes may find themselves forming sexual liaisons as a way of proving their popularity and pleasing their parents. Even Sex Repressive and Sex Avoidant parents can unconsciously push their teens into sex because the teen feels pressured to date, whatever the cost. Too often parents fret when their teenage daughter has only girlfriends or their teenage son has only boyfriends, and unwittingly make sex an issue in their children's lives even though they do not want their children thinking about sex. Parents are usually more concerned about their daughter's popularity than their son's, and at the same time more concerned about her virginity, a combination of worries that does not bode well for daughters, who are then caught in the bind of needing to attract boys while keeping themselves unavailable to them.

Helen, an aerobics instructor now in her twenties, was badgered by such conflicting pressures from her mother, who wanted her to have a lot of boyfriends but "not get involved." Helen's mother not only dreaded that her daughter might be a wallflower, but she also felt that going steady with only one boyfriend was more likely to lead to sex than multiple relationships would:

◄§ Mother constantly urged me to go out with a wide variety of boys. She used herself as a model. She would tell me about how she liked going out with lots of different boys and was always uncomfortable when a boy started to get serious when she was growing up, and she had a lot of anecdotes about boys who would try to kiss her and want to be serious with her and how she would rebuff them and try to be friends with them rather than getting too serious. I think it must have been assumed that she disapproved of the sensual-sexual feelings that accompany getting serious, liking to be with one person, spending a lot of time together, wanting to kiss and touch. If you barely know someone, you're not as likely to want to be physical with that person, and I realize in saying this, that must have had a very strong influence on how I related to men as I grew older, because I have almost always been friends with a man before I became romantically involved. It always came as kind of a surprise—first off friends, and then the sexual attraction. I have tended not to be swept off my feet in love at first sight, and that seems to relate back to what was encouraged by my mother. It all comes back to the sexual base: play the field, get as broad experience as you can—not sexual experience, but emotional, intellectual experience—concentrate on your schoolwork. All that is more important than sexual life. It would not have been acceptable to be a wallflower in my home, and I was supposed to have a lot of boyfriends and not get involved. ❧

If a young girl cannot attract a stable of admirers, as Helen was able to do, she may easily become sexual to fulfill her parents' overriding need for her to be popular with boys. Claudia, like Helen, also grew up in a home where it was expected that she would remain virginal until she married. Yet when Claudia was in her late teens and not "popular" with boys, her mother went so far as to suggest sex as a way to attract them:

❧ My parents always felt that you should be a virgin when you got married— that is, if you were a girl. With my brother, they expected him to be sexually active and sow his wild oats. But all that changed when I was in my senior year at high school and I didn't have a boyfriend, and mostly hung out with a few girlfriends who also didn't have steady boyfriends or date very much. My mother kept asking me how would I go to the prom, and wasn't there some boy I liked that I could get friendly with. And then she tried to promote my having sexual contacts. She offered to put me on the birth control pill. She was promoting sexual contact. I think she wanted me to feel that I was attractive to boys and that if I became sexually available I would have more dates and see myself as more a belle of the ball. In the early years it was "you should be a virgin when you get married," but as I started to become a late teenager it was—well, my mother brought it up about birth control pills, so she was obviously eager for me to get involved. ❧

223

Statistics bear out that many teenage girls have sex without real desire because they want to establish relationships.* While boys tend to have sex for sex's sake and are often less concerned about the partner than the act, girls tend to have sex for the relationship's sake. Not only do girls make themselves sexually available as a way of solidifying a relationship, but once sex has been initiated they often find themselves acquiescing in behaviors that they do not enjoy in order to keep the relationship going. The *Rolling Stone* survey of teenagers revealed that one-third of the girls continued to have sex even though they found it painful, and approximately one-fourth continued even though they did not experience orgasm. Further, the girls reported that they often provide oral sex for their boyfriends, even though they do not like it, because they feel obligated to do so. (Boys, on the other hand, tend not to provide oral sex when they do not like it, or as the survey authors put it, "teens do not find oral sex an equal-opportunity employer.")** Although many parents would be horrified to learn that their daughter is engaged in oral sex, reluctantly or otherwise, they do not always appreciate how their need to have a "popular" daughter increases her sexual vulnerability. While the pressures on boys to date as a sign of popularity are not as great, they too may feel the need to "score" in order to please their parents.

WHOSE DATE IS IT ANYWAY?

Parents may be emotionally unprepared for a child's popularity once it is achieved. These boy-girl relationships often become the focus of a teen's life, and attention is not only turned away from studies but from other family members as well. Parents may resent the secondary role to which the family is relegated and become critical of the interloper. Dating can unleash a host of passions in the parent, especially because teenagers come into their own sexually just when their parents are starting to decline. It is not uncom-

* Coles and Stokes, *Sex and the American Teenager*, p. 62.
** Ibid.

mon for mothers to feel envious of a daughter's attractiveness, of her freedom to explore new relationships, or even of her suitors. It is also not uncommon for mothers to resent a son's interest in young women or for fathers to become jealous of their son's virility and easy way with girls. Fathers may also feel pangs of jealousy as their daughters find comfort in younger and less flabby arms, and may become competitive with the young gentlemen callers. For the most part parents seem to be oblivious to the way in which they are personally affected by their children's romantic involvement, but for their offspring this can be a source of great irritation and annoyance.

Virginia's mother Eunice, although basically Sex Avoidant as we saw before, allowed Virginia much freedom in her dating and even let her boyfriends sleep over in her room while pretending that nothing out of the ordinary was going on. Apparently, this behavior served Eunice's needs as well as Virginia's by enabling Eunice to see Virginia's boyfriends as guests of the house instead of as her teenage daughter's sexual partners. According to Virginia:

◈ My mother was tremendously interested in my boyfriends. They always thought she was great and a real modern mom. She would talk to them a lot about what they were doing and their plans, and when she knew they were coming over she would be sure to make their favorite foods for dinner. I thought she was just great about it too, and one day I remember having a big discussion, or should I say an argument, with my boyfriend Arthur. He insisted that my mother was doing me a disservice by being so involved in him. He felt she was trying to horn in on our relationship by making herself important to him. I thought that was Arthur's own self-importance talking. But it wasn't so long after that that my mother one day said to me, "Your boyfriends have always loved coming to the house. I think they fall as much in love with the house as they do with you." I felt terrible when she said that. Arthur was right. What bothered me so much was not that my boyfriends might not like me—I knew they really did—but that my mother wanted it to be so. She really wanted my boyfriends to care more for her than they did for me. She said they loved the house, but she really meant that they came to see her, not me. ò℈

Helen reported very similar experiences with her Sex Repressive mother, who maintained relationships with boyfriends long after Helen broke off with them:

℈ All through my dating years, while I cannot recall any instance of her being flirtatious with my boyfriends, she somehow encouraged their interest and loyalty. I remember coming home on a Sunday afternoon date and finding my mother with a former boyfriend, having coffee. And that didn't just happen with one boy, but with several. My mother was never approving of any boyfriend the first time, and there were times she and my boyfriend Tony would discuss me in front of me as if I were their child, not Tony's girlfriend. She was furious when we separated, but she became friendly with him after and continued to see him for quite some time. I don't recall ever being conscious of her wanting to have any particular relationship with any of the boys I dated, but at the same time I observed her having some ongoing connection with the boys I dated. It's only in retrospect that I became aware of some volition on her part in seeing my boyfriends. At that point I was probably annoyed with the boy rather than my mother. I had a great stake in feeling comfortable with my mother. I don't think I felt I could afford to alienate her or have negative feelings about her. ò℈

Fathers may find themselves unwittingly playing a similar competitive game with their sons. Sometimes a son's dating so arouses a father's need to feel that he is attractive to younger women that his flirtatiousness can even extend beyond his son's dates to his daughter's girlfriends. When Miles graduated high school, he began to commute to the residential college located in his hometown. That gave his father ample opportunity to meet Miles's dates as Miles would often bring friends home on the weekend to give them a chance to sample his mother's cooking instead of the usual dorm fare. Miles reported how these visits changed his father from a basically Sex Avoidant parent into a Sex Obsessive one:

◆§ In my sophomore year I was really involved with this freshman girl I met through a classmate. I guess you can say I fell in love. I would have liked to spend the weekends with her at school, but she had this tiny little room she shared with another girl and there wasn't much chance to be alone. So I used to bring Audrey home with me, either for the day on Saturday, or when the weather was especially nice, she would stay over for the whole weekend. Audrey loved to have the peace and quiet of a room to herself and to be able to rummage in the fridge whenever she wanted, and she also loved my mother's cooking. Mom was very solicitous of her too. But Dad, forget it. At first he acted normal, but then he started acting really jerky whenever Audrey was there. My mother noticed it first. He used to get dressed up special, not in a suit or anything, but he would put on his best Izod shirt, and shave with his regular razor and use his after-shave lotion. And then he would start coming on to Audrey. Not in too obvious a way at first. He would just act like a bigshot and try to impress her, and start bragging about where he had traveled, and his Navy experiences, and about all the restaurants he knew. But then he started becoming very attentive to Audrey and would make cracks about how well she looked, and he would start making these double entendre type remarks. My mother got furious and Audrey was awfully uncomfortable, and I just was embarrassed. I know my parents had some big fights about it, but my father just denied it all. But it wasn't too long after that that he started an affair with this girl at his office. Nobody knew about it right away. Audrey and me, we found out first because we met him at the football game. He was sitting there with this secretary, with his arm around her, and they both had this one blanket wrapped around them and he would lean close and get all smoochy with her. He didn't see us at first and I was glad he didn't notice us, but the stadium was packed and we couldn't change seats. He did see us after a while, and at first I pretended like I didn't notice him, but he made a big thing out of it. He called out our names, and he waved. He actually wanted us to know he was making out with her. ໄ✑

While Miles's father represents a rather extreme case (he ultimately divorced his wife and married a woman almost as young as his son), the feelings churned up in him are not so unique.

Parents are not the only family members who can have difficulty dealing with the dating behavior and sexual involvement of teenagers. Siblings do too. Many different emotions come into play when one's sister or brother becomes involved with an outsider, as we began to see in the last chapter.

When a sibling starts to date, it means sharing someone very close with another person and sometimes finding out that that other person is, if only temporarily, more important to the sibling than you are. Many sisters and brothers have become upset when they felt that their place had been usurped by someone else who became a sibling's favored companion and confidante. Another consequence of seeing a sibling date is that it arouses thoughts about one's own dating behavior: Am I also lovable? Will I be able to find a suitable partner? Because younger siblings usually look to their older sibling as a model, their dating behavior is influenced by that of the older sibling. For example, it is not unusual for a younger sibling to rush into dating, or to delay dating, because of the pattern established by the older brother or sister. The specific details of what the older sibling does and does not do when out on a date are of immense interest to the younger sibling. Brothers tend to brag to each other about their conquests, although they do not reveal too much about their feelings. Sisters, on the other hand, tend to share details and look to each other for information and support. Sisters, like brothers, can also become competitive with each other, and both sexes, at the extreme, may commit the ultimate no-no of vying with each other for the same date. Because of the sex difference, there is no direct competition between brothers and sisters for a specific person, but competition can exist nonetheless for who gets the most desirable dates or approval from the parents.

As we pointed out before, a brother's dating can evoke much resentment in a sister if the parents allow the brother privileges denied to his sister because of her sex. Sisters, like mothers, also sometimes feel jealous of a brother's girlfriend, but younger sisters sometimes idolize their brother's girlfriend, seeing her as the embodiment of everything a teen should be. Brothers are apt to develop possessive feelings towards their sisters when the latter start dating, much like their fathers do. Because it is difficult for some teenage boys to handle their own sexual feelings towards a sister, they can become very jealous of her involvement with another young man and competitive with him. This feeling often masks itself as fraternal protectiveness, as is evident with Duncan, who according to his mother was even more anxious about his sister's dating than his father was. Duncan's mother, Debra, told us:

◄§ He is very protective towards her and affectionate to her. When he was a freshman at college, his roommate had a girlfriend who was the same age as his sister and at a boarding school. The roommate would go up and visit her for the weekend and take his condoms, and he told Duncan explicitly that he was sleeping with her, and so on, and Duncan was very upset. It made him see red, because, he said, "She is exactly the same age as my sister and he is taking advantage of a young girl to fill his needs." Duncan felt this was a travesty. He was very angry and very upset and could not see his sister in a sexual role at that age. She really didn't start to date until she was about seventeen. He gave her a very hard time. She went out with this boy for about three months and they had a very intense relationship, and then he just walked away from her. Duncan was not living at home at the time, and only knew what she told him of the event, and Duncan said if he ever saw this kid again he would just sock him right in the nose.

He was furious: "Just don't horse around with my sister." She has not had that many relationships or boyfriends she has been interested in, but Duncan has never tried to fix her up with a date. She has never fixed him up with anybody. That's interesting. Neither of them have done that at this point. ટે

GROAN AND BEAR IT

A growing body of parents seems to be getting used to the idea that their teenage children are probably going to become sexually active and that there is little, if anything, that can be done about it. While their hearts are not in it, they feel they have no alternative but to go along and hope they may influence their sons and daughters to curb their activity ever so slightly. With luck, their daughters will not become pregnant and their sons will not contract a dread disease. Teenagers experience this unarticulated attitude as a sense that they are doing something illicit but at the same time something they know they can get away with. Parental disapproval does not stop them from becoming sexually involved; it merely makes them uncomfortable and guilty when they do become involved. Josh, who is the oldest of four brothers and now in his twenties, described how his Sex Avoidant parents tolerated his first sexual experience but made him feel guilty about it at the same time:

ટે I think the first time we had sex we had gone up to watch TV in one of the upstairs rooms at my house, and it was very quick and over very quickly. I think it was my father who said something later when I came down like, "Don't keep the door closed like that," or "Don't go up there like that." Not a direct reference to what went on, but indirect, and very short. No one came upstairs or anything like that. My father just said something about going up there alone. I knew what he meant. I think my physical desire really overrode everything. The feelings came in after the sex was over, and when the physical desire was abating, that's when the guilt was building up. Nothing specific that Mom said this or that. My parents ruled by general disapproval, and

I'm still feeling that in terms of general expectations, and that was always there. In terms of sexuality, I don't know. Maybe the fact that I didn't have anything to go on made any action wrong. Even a more normal boyfriend-girlfriend relationship may have been full of guilt. My heart was just pounding with the physical nature of it, waiting for something to happen that you had been holding your breath for. ɜ✷

The precise message parents put out varies according to the sex of the teenager. And the concerns of teenagers' fathers are not the same as the concerns of teenagers' mothers. The first issue a mother addresses—although not her deepest concern—is pregnancy. Many mothers reported they made sure to advise their daughters on the importance of birth control as the latter entered adolescence. While mothers do worry that bringing up the issue of birth control might suggest approval of sex, they also feel that it is better to prepare their daughters than to have them become sexually involved without such motherly advice.

Perhaps just as important to mothers is that their daughters are selective about whom they have sex with. Mothers are concerned that their daughters not be promiscuous and that they limit their sexual encounters to a special boyfriend. Colleen, who has tried to create a Sex Expressive atmosphere in her home, started discussions with her daughter after her daughter began dating:

✷ɜ I remember we talked about sex, and telling her my feelings at the time. This is when she was in high school and started to hang out with boys. I told her I didn't expect her to stay a virgin unless she wanted to, but that if she didn't want to be a virgin and wanted to have sex that she should get birth control and she should come to me and we should talk about it. It was very important for me to let her know that and I probably put all sorts of pressure on the poor kid, but I wanted her to be sure to have birth control. And I remember talking about how it was not good to have sex with just anybody. It was just something to do with a very special boyfriend. ɜ✷

231

Debra, although basically Sex Avoidant, had similar discussions with her daughter as Ruth entered late adolescence, giving her a mixed message of approval and disapproval:

◄§ I had told her all about birth control and venereal disease and that girls had to be careful, and one day she asked to go see a gynecologist. I went with her and the gynecologist gave her the pill, and Ruth and I talked about her taking the pill. I said to be very sure that she knew why she was taking it and to be sure about her feelings towards the other person and that person's feelings towards her. She's gotten herself into two relationships with guys and they have become very intimate, and the boys weren't able to handle the relationship and walked away. The first guy she never told me about, the second one she did. She wanted to clarify with me why the relationship fell apart, and after their sexual intimacy it really did fall apart. §►

Daughters who sense a mother's disapproval underneath her grudging acceptance usually do not feel free to talk to her about sex. The mother is at a loss to understand why, as she feels she is going along with the new sexual mores. Colleen, for example, expressed surprise that her daughter is secretive about her boyfriends while her sons are able to talk to her about their girlfriends:

◄§ Interestingly enough, even after I told Kathy that I didn't expect that she would necessarily remain a virgin, she didn't talk to me at all. In fact, she never mentioned to me that she was having an affair. I only found out when it just sort of dropped out—not in direct conversation. I think she has a lot of issues about that. §►

Once mothers become used to the idea that their daughters are sexually active, they sometimes worry about the quality of the sexual aspect of these relationships. Just as mothers are concerned lest their daughters be sexually used by a young man, they also worry that their daughters may be sexually misused and not get any physical pleasure from the relationship. For example, we saw before, in our discussion of mother-daughter relationships, how Tracy talks to her daughter about becoming comfortable with her body and learning what gives her pleasure.

Fathers have a harder time than mothers accepting the reality of a daughter's sexual activity. While mothers try to get used to the idea before the fact, fathers tend to get used to it only after the fact. Intellectually they will acknowledge that it is probably OK for their daughter to have sex when she is mature enough for it, but emotionally fathers usually find that no matter when it happens, they feel their daughter is not yet ready for it. Vincent, the advertising executive whose daughter from his second marriage is now sixteen years old, takes comfort in the fact that she does not date yet, and finds it hard to imagine her being mature enough to have a sexual relationship:

◅ Dating today is not the same as it was even ten or fifteen years ago. They don't date in the same way. You're just together and you come over or go out, but it's not like it was when I was younger and you took someone out on a date. She doesn't have a boyfriend but she's with boys. She sees guys on the school bus, but so far as I know, and I think I would know, she's just never had a date. She goes to dances, but she goes with girls. I think that sex would be an expected and normal thing for her when she becomes more mature. I don't think she's an adult in her mind yet. She's still childish, and I don't think a sexual relationship of any kind is for kids. My older daughter, I guess she started having intercourse when she was away in college. When she got married, it was to the guy she was going with at college. I felt uneasy about the relationship because I was worried that she might get hurt, if she committed herself to a guy who threw her over. It wasn't so bad when she brought him home because by then I pretty well knew that he was it. ▻

Even Derrick, the Sex Obsessive father, knows he will have a hard time reconciling himself to his daughter's becoming sexually active. She is still prepubescent, but he is already

questioning whether she will be ready for a sexual relationship later on:

❧ I'm very permissive, but I know, and I've said it in a
joking manner, when it comes to my daughter I'm very
strict. I've said, "I'll cut the nuts off the first guy who tries to
get into her." I would like to believe that I'm not a hypocrite,
but I don't know. At nine years old of course she's too
young, but I'll probably feel the same way when she's
thirteen. I became sexually active when I was eleven. I also
feel, however, that I was never eleven. I grew up fast. But
she is still a kid. You're old enough when you have the
ability to make your own decisions and to have a rational
basis behind it. You're old enough when you acknowledge
the importance of consent and are willing to be responsible
for the consent, and she's not old enough for that yet. She
doesn't accept yet that it's her own responsibility—that she
is responsible for everything that happens in her life. The
age of consent is sixteen in this state, but it doesn't have to
do with chronological age but with mental age and what I
feel is acceptance of responsibility for whatever you do. I
don't blame anybody if anything happens to me, but she
does, and I don't think she's old enough on that basis. I
guess it's a fiction I've created for my own way of judging,
but the way I view it is that until that point when I see there
is responsibility, I'm going to have a strong, controlling
hand. Oh, I'd let her fall, but I'll limit the areas in which she
can fall. Let her learn her lesson, but without the harshness
of the lesson. Sex puts you in a position of vulnerability and
you have to be prepared for that. ❧

Parental concerns about sons' sexual involvements are of
quite a different order. Mothers, as we saw before, worry
that their sons might not be responsible enough. Some
identify with the girl their son is dating and do not want to
see her being used sexually. For instance, although Jeanette
is very proud of her two sons and appreciative of their
sexuality, she also worries that they might be inconsiderate
to a date in their eagerness to test out their own masculinity:

◄§ Very often I say to my sons, "You have to be nice and sweet, not brutal." And I say, "Girls will not want to be next to you when you are so brutal. You have to be nice and sweet." But I am a mother. I do not want them to look on women as an object but to take them more for what's inside. Not that I want them to take up with somebody really ugly, but then they do not have to look for someone from the cover of *Vogue* magazine either. Maybe I want to protect them a little bit, because I want to give them a feeling that you don't take your pleasure and it's bye-bye. Maybe they would get involved with a girl who is more serious, who will take care of children and be a mother too. And when they do get married, not to go from one bed to another. ໖►

Other mothers are afraid that their sons may be entrapped by their dates. They fear that the girl might become pregnant, not because of identification with her but because it would put burdens on their sons. Maria, whom we met earlier when she described her strong sexual attraction to her brother Peter, has cautioned her teenage son against having sex too readily:

◄§ I told him, I said, "Don't have sex with a girl if she suggests it to you. Girls are aggressive enough to get what they want, and you have to be careful. Girls try to catch boys by becoming pregnant, and you don't want that to happen to you." ໖►

A mother's concerns about her son's dates may also reflect possessiveness and jealousy. She may unduly criticize a son's girlfriend not only because she finds it hard to tolerate sexual activity but also because on some level she wants to keep her son for herself. Glen, the drama student, recalled how vehemently his mother criticized his first important girlfriend:

◄§ I remember bringing home a girl when I was young. My mother got very angry and called her a slut and was very against her. She got upset because of the way the girl dressed. She was very voluptuous and wore clothes that were attractive. She looked radiant. My mother disapproved. There was no direct talk about it except to call her a slut. She always considered herself a liberal and keeping that sort of attitude wouldn't have fit into her beliefs. After that first relationship there was never any problem, because I had learned my lesson. ❧

Fathers are less apt to worry about what might happen when their sons have sex than to worry that their sons might never have sex at all. It is reassuring for fathers to know that their sons have "scored," as they feel it attests to the masculine virility of both father and son. A "notch in the crotch" is still a male status symbol. If a son cannot make out, fathers worry that there is something wrong and that their son might possibly be harboring latent homosexual tendencies. While fathers may caution their sons about the dangers of pregnancy, the basic message usually is, as Reggie's father said, "Go out there and get yourself laid." Although not a very common practice anymore, some fathers still see to it that their sons are initiated into sex, by hiring the services of a prostitute. Wendell's father "treated" him to a prostitute when they were on vacation:

❧ My first experience with sex was in Las Vegas when I was sixteen. My whole family was there—my mother and sister and me and Dad. Dad took me aside one day and said he would give me the money to go see a prostitute and he knew where to go so she would be healthy and the place would be nice. I was very excited about it, but at the same time it was the last thing in the world I wanted to do. Dad wanted to make a man of me, as he used to say, but he made me feel like a little boy instead. I was afraid to tell him no, and I was also afraid of what the prostitute would be like and how I would manage. He walked me over to the whorehouse, stuffed money into my pocket, gave me a big wink, and said, "Have fun, son." It was all over so fast, and it was a big relief to get out of there. When I got back to the hotel, he asked me how I liked it and I said, "It was OK." He was disappointed that I didn't say any more or rave about the experience, but I had all I could do not to tell him how bad I felt. ☞

THE BOTTOM LINE

While many parents are resigned to their teens becoming sexually active or, in the case of boys, actually want them to be sexually initiated, they are still disapproving of sex. Such typically ambivalent parents may countenance sexual activity outside the home, but not within it: even otherwise Sex Expressive parents cannot easily adapt to the thought that their sons or daughters might bring a lover into the house and have sex under their roof. For example, according to a recent survey conducted by *People* magazine, seventy-seven percent of the parents surveyed thought it was appropriate to discuss birth control with their teens, but seventy-six percent said they would forbid a twenty-one-year-old child to share a bedroom at home with a person of the opposite sex.* Although most teens do have their first intercourse at home (either at their own or their partner's house), it usually happens without their parents' knowledge.** When parents find out about it, they tend to have a strong negative reaction although they cannot explain why. Teens see this as hypocritical, and this issue can develop into a major source of tension. In some homes the teenager can get grudging approval, but in most others sex at home is just not tolerated.

For example, although Duncan's mother, Debra, approved of his being sexually involved with his girlfriends, she assumed that the sexual part of his relationships would evaporate once he crossed the family threshold:

⊷ His girlfriends have slept over when he comes home from school, but in different rooms. I don't know if he's had sexual relationships with them or not. With one young woman he must have had a sexual relationship, and when she came here she shared the bedroom with Duncan's sister. I didn't offer them anyplace else to sleep. She spent two days

* "What's Gone Wrong with Teen Sex," *People*, April 13, 1987, pp. 111–21.
** Coles and Stokes, *Sex and the American Teenager*.

here and slept in Ruth's room. I don't know how long they had been seeing each other or if their relationship was going strong. If he wanted to sleep with her, he would have to say to me, "Mom, we're living together." That's one thing. But she's coming here as a guest in my house and they are not living together. ह⋙

Loretta and her husband, who like Duncan's mother are basically Sex Avoidant, think sex in the home is "disrespectful." They are reconciled to their daughters having sexual relationships with their boyfriends, but not at home:

⋘ When their boyfriends are home, I don't want them to sleep in the same room, and my husband agrees with me. When their boyfriends come to visit, I just feel uncomfortable and he does too, because he has this big thing about respect, and we've established that. They can stay over, but there are separate sleeping arrangements. I'm not certain why he feels that way. I guess it is a double message. If they said, "Dad, why do we need to when you know we sleep together elsewhere," I think he would just say, "It's a matter of respect." I don't want it either. I just don't think parents should give such a message to kids. Sex is OK, but I still think they should give a message that there is appropriate behavior. You sleep together elsewhere, fine, but there is no reason why you have to sleep together when you're here. I don't know why it bothers me but it does, and I've never really delved into why. I'm just not comfortable with it, and they shouldn't foist their beliefs upon me. ह⋙

Teenagers are impatient with their parents' hypocrisy. Many go along with it, because they feel their parents have the right to set the rules in the home, but some teens bring this issue to a head with their parents, occasionally winning them over. A few parents become impatient with their own conflicts on this issue and then let their teens have sex in the house. Barbara, a free-lance writer and divorced mother of three, despite her own discomfort, eventually recognized that it was appropriate for her daughter Pamela to bring her boyfriend home to sleep over with her:

❧ I sort of wrestled for a long time with whether or not her boyfriend should sleep over, especially with younger kids in the house, but at a certain point it sort of came up when she was going with this guy in Cambridge and would stay over there, so there was no big deal on a rational level if they shared a room here. I wrestled with it the first time it came up, whether she could stay over there. When she started going out with him and he lived in Cambridge, it was a big issue, because how was she going to get home at two o'clock in the morning alone on the subway. So I preferred she stay over there, and then it became, could he stay over? I remember having trouble with it, but Pamela has a wonderful facility to argue in a rational way and it is very hard not to go along with her. And I don't think it's ever been an issue for my other kids. There has been awareness, but it's not an issue. ❧

Sherry even capitulated to her daughter without an argument:

❧ If you ask me how I feel about children having sex before they are married, I'd say fine. But I didn't with my own daughter. She had it before she was even living with the guy, and then she was even living in the house with us. I wasn't happy about it, but I thought this is the way it is, and I didn't have the feeling it was a promiscuous thing. She wasn't bringing home different people to have sex with. Unlike other people, I didn't say, "Yes, you could do it somewhere else but you can't in my house," because I thought that was just absolutely hypocritical. So when she came home with this young man from college, whom she was living with but didn't eventually marry, I didn't make a to-do about it. ❧

Our friend Doris, one of whose sons offered to educate her about sex, let all three of them have their girlfriends sleep over without a single comment about it, even though she didn't really want them to bring girls home. Doris did, however, get flak from many of her friends who thought she was betraying the parents of her sons' girlfriends: "Letting my boys sleep at home with their girlfriends was a big bone of contention with my friends. They felt it was my obligation to the girl's parents to say no. They all were sure, even without knowing who the girl was or who the parents were, that the parents wouldn't want her having sex."

RIGHTS OF PASSAGE

Parents who are Sex Expressive feel it is perfectly natural for their children to have sex at home. As few teenagers have the means to go off together to some enchanted island, what better place for sex than in the comfort and privacy of their own room? Maud, a homemaker and mother of two daughters just entering their twenties, is impatient with parents who accept the fact that their children are sexually active yet deny them a suitable place to have sex:

≈§ When my daughters became sexually active, they took it for granted that they could have their boyfriends sleep over if they wanted to. Why not? I can't stand these mothers who say, "I don't want you doing that in *my* house." I always thought it was *our* house and that the girls should be free to live in the house with the same freedom that my husband and I enjoy. If they're not bothering anybody else, let them live their own lives. Of course, if you think they shouldn't have sex, that is different, but then they shouldn't have it anywhere. This ridiculous distinction between sex in the back seat of a car is OK but sex in your own bed is out of the question just does not make any sense to me. I think when parents outlaw sex at home they force their kids into making sex something unpleasant. Why should they have to do it in doorways or hallways or in other places, always being scared someone is going to see them? They have enough to worry about at their age without worrying about being caught in the act. How can you enjoy sex and feel good about yourself when you have to sneak around to do it? ξ≈

Throughout these pages, we have been meeting Sex Expressive parents who view sex as an inseparable part of human existence and accept its place in the lives of their children. When their offspring reach the dating age, they are ready for it and fully expect that their teens will have healthy sexual appetites and desires. They prepare their children for sexual experience as they would for any other important experience in life, discussing the joys and the dangers, and provide a foundation for informed choices by allowing an open avenue for communication. Earlier we saw how Larry, the psychologist and father of five children, discussed with his daughter her choices in contraception and the consequences of different patterns of sexual behavior, and how Mary Travers helped her daughters understand the flood of emotions they and their boyfriends might experience in early sexual encounters and the importance of respect for the other person's feelings. When dating starts, Sex Expressive parents put their energies into trying to help their children have rewarding experiences rather than trying to stop them from having sex, and hope that it will be a joyful moment for their kids. Alice told us that when her son, Reggie, started his first sexual relationship she was relieved to know that it went well for him:

◄§ He started sleeping with someone when he was fifteen. He had had girlfriends before then. His friend Wendy was sleeping over but they hadn't done anything yet, but he was getting ready. He told me something was going to happen. And then she had a need for a second mother and was always giving me the poetry and notebooks she wrote, so she gave me a notebook, and there was one thing she wrote in it: "Last night was wonderful. I hoped it would happen," something like that. And I said, "Oh, is this true?" And she said, "Yes." And I said, "Is this what I think it means?" And she said, "Yes," and she left the room. I said, "Reggie, come here. I see you and Wendy slept together," and he said, "Yeah." And I said, "Reggie, did you enjoy it?" And he said, "Yeah." And I said, "Reggie, are you going to do it again?" And he said, "Yeah." And I said, "Reggie, I was worried you might have a traumatic experience or something. Why didn't you tell me that you liked it and everything is fine?" It's not always cool the first time. There's a lot of pressure put on a boy the first time, much more than what is put on a girl. ॐ

In a similar view, Gloria Jones told us about her son's first sexual experience and her hopes that both her son, Jamie, and daughter, Kaylie, will have meaningful and satisfying sexual relationships:

ॐ At the time there were about eight children hanging out at my house and staying, including two nephews, Kaylie, her boyfriend, Jamie. They all had their rooms. I wasn't having room checks. One day I found a girl in bed with Jamie. . . . This kid was living there and I didn't know it! There were so many kids living there I didn't know it, and there she was in bed with my Jamie. And I was sort of proud and perplexed. I just said, "Excuse me." . . . I just realized he was a sexual young man. He is still very reticent. That's the way he is. . . . Kaylie lived with a boy in college, but everybody does that. . . . I think she always enjoyed sex, I always sensed that she did. She certainly always had a lover since she's been sixteen. . . . She had the first one, then a wonderful one that she writes about. When you write about it you don't have to tell your mother. It's in the book. And then she had this one. . . . I would like [my kids] to have a lover and enjoy it and treat each other as equals and get the most out of the relationship without exploitation . . . they should have a companion that they love and cherish and enjoy. ॐ

HOMOSEXUAL HEARTACHES

Despite recent shifts in attitudes about homosexuality, it is still a life-style that meets with strong disapproval, especially in conservative parts of the country. Homosexual teens are likely to be faced with rejection by their parents and siblings, as well as by their peers, and at the extreme may even be physically abused. The families of homosexual teens often suffer as well, experiencing guilt about their child and shame in front of the community.

Parents may think otherwise, but homosexual teens do not choose to be homosexual. Rather, it is a way of being that they experience as compelling. To some extent their situation is analogous to that of left-handed children. Not so many years ago, it was considered somewhat "sinister" (meaning, literally, on the left hand) for children to be left-handed and stringent measures were taken to ensure that they would learn how to use the right hand instead. Today it is recognized that some children have a natural proclivity towards left-handedness rather than right-handedness, and they are allowed to develop in their own way, happily for all. Society, though, does not allow children with homosexual tendencies to follow their sexual inclinations. As a result, such children grow up feeling stigmatized by and ashamed of their sexual orientation. Many try to deny their feelings, creating a confusion about their sexual identity and place in society which may last for the rest of their lives.

Homosexual teens naturally seek the company of other teens like themselves. Here is where more problems set in, particularly for boys. Homosexual teens do not have that much in common with straights, they do not want to associate with "queens," and it is difficult for them to find other young people who are unobtrusively gay. As a result they either remain socially isolated or gravitate towards bars and clubs, where they meet older gays and leave themselves open for exploitation which sometimes leads to getting involved in prostitution and the drug scene. Environments such as these further erode their sense of self-esteem, leaving them even more vulnerable.

The fear of parental disapproval is so great among many homosexual teenagers that they hide their sexuality. Their problems are much more pressing than are those of other teens, but ironically, they feel they cannot discuss their problems with their parents. Many parents remain in the dark about their teens' sexual orientation until the latter leave home and are freer to declare themselves. Bob, whom we met before, is fairly typical in this regard. He said nary a word about his sexual proclivities to his parents until he was an adult living away from home, because he feared their rejection, which, when it came at age thirty, he was better prepared for:

◆§ I think I was probably sexually aware from the time I was about four. In my early years I found a very strong sexual fascination with men and men's bodies, but no sexual interest in women and their bodies, and that characterization of my awareness has progressed through different stages over my life. As I got older, in my teens, I started to have sexual relations with friends of mine that were clearly erotic in nature and clearly understood by both of us to be illegal, and we knew if we did those things we better not get caught. It is clear to me that that was the early emergence of a very strong sexual pattern, and what I was doing then was an early version of what I like to do now, except that I don't feel guilty about it now. It went from that stage to a teenage phase in which I kept feeling like there was going to come a point when somehow my psychological makeup or body chemistry would mature and I would get over wanting to do that and would want to have sexual relations with a woman.

I never told my parents. What kept me from telling them at first was a feeling that it was an issue I felt would solve itself in time. My view when I was ten or twelve was that the sexual relationships I was having with boys were certainly not going to be taken up with my parents because they wouldn't have allowed it and it was something I wanted to do. I didn't view anything in my sexual evolution to be a problem yet. It didn't dawn on me till later that there was something wrong, and I had a clear intuitive feeling that they would have disapproved if they had known and I was basically embarrassed about it. To admit that I was a homosexual would have been a terrible admission. I was afraid of my status as a child within the family and I was afraid for my own self-worth. Their view was that fairies were hairdressers, and my view was pretty much my parents' view. I learned in the process of coming out and telling them that actually all my apprehensions of the way they would react were accurate. In fact, they reacted in a much more negative way than I ever feared. §◆

244

Some teens hide their homosexuality from their parents not only to protect themselves from parental rejection but also to protect their parents from having to deal with such an unwelcome piece of news. Keith, who is now in his twenties and still lives at home, hides his homosexuality from his mother because he knows that she is not ready to deal with it:

≈§ At seventeen I had my first homosexual experience. This older man seduced me. I had a girlfriend after that, and we were very physical up until the point that we would take our clothes off, and I just did not enjoy that and I had all sorts of reasons for why we shouldn't go all the way. I always talked with my mom about all my problems and the communication was pretty open, but I knew she would be grossed out by my homosexuality so I didn't bring that up. When I met Eliot at summer camp and I brought him home to meet my mother, there was never anything actually said. He wasn't a homosexual and he actually had a girlfriend at that time, but he was a ballet dancer and would do ballet exercises in the room and it made me very uncomfortable 'cause I knew what my mother was thinking. She did everything to discourage the friendship. She has little ways of letting you know she did not approve. She never said "homosexual," always "pansy, weird, sissy."

One night I was in my room, and I have a phone there and someone I didn't know called me up and wanted to have a date because he must have heard I was gay, but I didn't know him so I brushed him off. And my mother had picked up the phone downstairs, and when I hung up she came charging up the stairs and accused me of being weird and said, "Is that one of your boyfriends?" I told her no, but if it was I would have lied. I was aware of her power to be rejecting and cold. She could ostracize me and she could isolate herself. I've seen her do that when she was mad at my sister.

Last Christmas we went to visit some friends and they had other friends there who were gay. My mother asked if they were gay, and I said, "Yes," because it was so obvious. Then she said she still liked them as people and she asked me about some of my friends and if they were gay, and then she got very fuzzy and started to talk about AIDS. And I told her pretty truthfully that at the moment I was not homosexual. In therapy I am working on intimacy and how difficult it is for me to get deeply involved, so I could tell her pretty truthfully that I was pretty asexual. I think she feels that as long as a sexual relationship doesn't happen to me, she'll be OK. She sees her life as a failure as a mother and as a wife, and I always feel like I'm kind of her last chance. I think my mother tells herself that I'm gay, but if I don't tell her she doesn't have to deal with it. 8~

From the parents' point of view, their adolescent is drifting and behaving in unacceptable ways. Not infrequently, a teenager will be uncertain of his or her sexual identity but will form strong attachments to people of the same sex. The parents in such situations often become worried at what they see as their child's developing proclivities but deny their real concerns, and instead attack their teen's companions. Felicity, now in her thirties and an avowed lesbian, did not think of herself as homosexual until her parents started to complain about her attachments to other young women and her lack of boyfriends:

~§ When I was in high school, I had a case of hero worship with this teacher of mine. I thought she was the greatest, and she was the first teacher I had who I felt really thought well of me. I used to hang around after school to see her, first about homework and after that I would just hang around to talk to her. She would talk to me about what I was doing and whether I wanted to go on to college or work when I graduated, and she told me things about herself. I was thrilled that she talked to me, almost like I was her friend, and I felt that I was somebody special. And then she started to invite me over to her house. She lived in the downstairs apartment of a two-family house and had the garden, and when it was nice weather, she would ask me over after school for tea in the garden and we would talk and talk. Those were some of the best moments of my life.

My mother started getting upset that I would visit so

often, and we had lots of fights about it. After a while she and my father told me that I just was not allowed to visit Miss Sands at her house anymore and that if I had homework to discuss to do it at school. It was impossible to talk to them. I decided I would just not tell them and make up some story about where I had been. My mother caught me the first time. She parked her car a block away from Miss Sands's house and waited to see if I would come out, and saw me when I did. That night my mother told me if I didn't stop she would call Miss Sands up and tell her not to invite me anymore, and tell the principal too, so I stopped seeing her except in class. I was too embarrassed to tell her what was going on and avoided her. She stopped me after class one day, but I told her I didn't have time and ran off.

After that, my parents started nagging me about going out with boys. My mother invited a lot of her friends over who had sons my age, and they would all come for lunch on Sundays and it was so embarrassing. I told her not to fix me up and she denied that she was doing it, but she kept after me to date. I became very friendly with a girl in the drama club and we started to hang out a lot together, and my mother didn't like the girl at all. She was always criticizing how Karen spoke, how she dressed, her manners, just everything about her. She never did that to her face, but Karen knew my mother didn't like her and wouldn't come over to my house. We stayed friendly, but we weren't really close after that, but the next semester I met Sasha and we hit it off right away. We were like a pair of Siamese twins. I told Sasha about my parents and Miss Sands, and she told me that my parents were afraid Miss Sands was a lesbian and was going to seduce me. That really shocked me because it had never occurred to me. Miss Sands never did anything to me or suggested anything to me, but Sasha said maybe I was the one who was interested in Miss Sands. And as soon as she said that, I knew it was true, and I knew I felt that way about her too. Sasha made it easy for me, and all these feelings came out that I didn't know I had. ❧

Other parents find themselves faced with teen behaviors related to homosexuality that may be more disturbing than the homosexual attraction. Their teenager stays out till all hours of the night, becomes truant, and seems to be more and more isolated from the usual activities of his or her peers. Parents become fed up with the total behavior pattern, and find it easier to focus on the truancy and the late-night hours than on the possibility that their child is homosexual—denial is just as strong in parents as it is in homosexual youngsters.

Many parents find the gay life-style abhorrent. They do not want to imagine their child engaged in homosexual acts, yet much to their discomfort find themselves conjuring up such scenes. Daphne, who did not want to acknowledge that her son was homosexual, found that when she could no longer deny it, this knowledge not only disturbed her romantic image of her son but that it also got in the way of her having satisfying sex with her husband:

৵ When I think of the physical sex act between males, I'm revolted. While I've never admitted this to my husband, for a while I think it actually influenced my own sex life. I think it probably affected both our sex lives to some degree. I never discussed this with my husband, but sometimes when we've had sex, for some reason my mind would go to what might be happening to my son and another male and I just got revolted at that whole idea, even though the way we practice sex is quite different from the way homosexuals practice sex. I think objectively there is no reason to think that one kind of sex is more unacceptable than another, but I do find when I think about anal sex or oral sex, but particularly anal sex, I just find it very, very unpleasant.

I think that over time my son is also becoming less the attractive masculine figure that I had envisioned before, and taking on more female mannerisms, not just the dress but the motion of his head and his hands, and so much of his life is turned into his own sex role and whether he's going to find a young man that he enjoys. It seems to me he's lost sight of what's important. Now he runs out to get flowers and he'll fuss around with flowers. He's become narcissistic, and he gets very angry when I say this to him. I have said it to him because some fellow he liked a great deal had rejected him and he said he was heartbroken, and then I said to him, "Well, there have been several. Isn't that sort of your way of life?"And he said, "That's your perception of it. Not all homosexuals live that way. If I went from one woman to another you wouldn't feel that way." As for my sex life, I think that the overtures from my husband have been fewer. I think both of us have lost the complete happiness and freedom, the feeling that everything's OK and wonderful. ❧

As soon as parents start to acknowledge a child's homosexuality they also start looking for causes, and generally blame themselves for being inadequate parents. They initially might try to dismiss the homosexuality as an act of hostility on the part of their child ("You are doing this to hurt me") or blame it on somebody else ("Someone has done this to you, someone seduced you"). In a society such as ours that blames the parents if a youngster becomes homosexual, this need to find someone else to point the finger at is not difficult to understand. Such a perspective makes the revelation that your child is gay tantamount to an accusation that you are a bad parent. Fathers tend to be more upset than mothers by homosexuality in a son. Men in general are more insecure about their masculinity than women are about their femininity, and when a father discovers that his son is gay, he experiences it as a blow to his male image. These fathers may then feel inadequate about themselves as role models, and apprehensive about what other people will think of them as well as their sons. Fathers do have a marked impact on the development of a son's masculinity. As we have already seen, the lack of a warm and nurturing father can interfere with a son's development of a strong masculine identity, and paternal overemphasis on macho behavior can create feelings of inadequacy in a son who feels he cannot live up to the role demands. Such boys often feel alienated from other boys as well as from their fathers and starved for male affection, but this does not turn them into homosexuals. Research to date suggests that some children are born with a genetic or prenatal predisposition to homosexuality and that this makes them more receptive to environmental factors that encourage homosexuality. Parents may unwittingly encourage effeminate behavior but they are not to blame for a child's predisposition to homosexuality.

Some parents manage to deny a child's homosexuality until the teen "comes out." When that happens, they often try to close their ears to what they are being told: "I don't want to hear about it," "It's just a phase you're going through," "Would you please pass the salt?" But when reality can no longer be denied, the feelings come pouring out: anger, shame, guilt, and grief. Trudy, who has a son and daughter, described the mixed emotions experienced by herself and her husband about her teenage son's recent declaration:

⊷ My husband says he sees homosexuality as something that was always there, and he even admits that maybe it's something biological. So I tell him, "If you admit that, you have to accept the whole thing and that he has no choice and you just have to say that's the way he is." The fact that my husband responds with such negativity and the fact that he also gets a heart attack if he witnesses our son with another male suggests to me that there must be some kind of feeling operating, but I'm not absolutely sure what it is. My husband doesn't acknowledge anything. I don't know why I have these guilt feelings, because even as I look at the situation now, I don't know what I would have done differently. I really don't know. Maybe I should have talked more about males and females, and shown him pictures of girls. There must be some kind of role model that operates if it is not completely physically determined. My husband isn't the kind of man who goes around talking about women or "that great chick over there," and I don't know if that represents some kind of role model that some men pass on to their children. I don't know what would have happened if he were the kind of man who talked about other women, which I would not have enjoyed, or if he talked more to our son about the pleasure of sex, or if he had a lover. I just don't know. ⊶

After a teen comes out, many parents feel that the child they knew no longer exists and they go through a period of mourning for their child and the dreams that can no longer materialize. Steve Ashkinazy, the clinical director of the Institute for Gay and Lesbian Youth whom we mentioned before, compares the process that parents undergo at this time to that described by Elisabeth Kubler-Ross on death and dying. First is a period of denial of the homosexuality, followed by anger, and then by a long period of grief and mourning during which parents eventually realize that everything they hoped would be possible for this child is no longer possible. The dancing at the wedding, the grandchildren, and all the other things they imagined have to be given up and reality accepted.

For some parents, these emotions are so overpowering that they lash out at their children in angry and destructive ways. Steve described typical differential reactions to boys and girls:

⊷ With boys there is often hitting, screaming, or threatening to throw him out of the house. . . . The parents get upset and start calling him names and get him so upset that he starts calling them names back, and they start making threats to each other and then the kid is out the door and nobody can say they threw him out, because he ran away. A boy coming out is at much greater risk than a girl of being thrown out of the house. With a girl, a typical bad reaction is that she becomes a prisoner in the house. The parents don't let her open her mail; if she has to go to school somebody will drop her off and pick her up; and she is not allowed out for many weekends. Possibly she might run away. About twenty percent of the population we serve are kids who are not living at home because their parents will not tolerate their homosexuality. About thirty percent have been physically abused by the parents. ⊶

Teens who are considering coming out to their parents should consider very carefully their motivations in doing so. Before coming out, a teen should be sure of his or her sexual orientation and not use an announcement either as a way of getting the parents to approve of one's gay life-style or as a way of hurting them. A teenager also has to consider how the parents may react and whether he or she is ready to handle all the possible scenarios that might ensue: What if your parents throw you out of the house? What if your parents take you to a shrink? What if they decide to put you in a different school, or not let any of your friends visit you, or not let you receive any phone calls? Once all the possible bad consequences are reviewed, the process of coming out can begin, and it is a process rather than an isolated act. Steve Ashkinazy counsels homosexual teens to tell their parents "through a loving act." He advises them to "set up a time, tell them there is something you want to talk about," and make it clear to the parents that "I'm telling you this because I feel there's something that's been separating us, because I have been hiding something that is making me feel distant from you and I want to get rid of that." That kind of introduction establishes a situation where there will be communication and honest discussion. Steve also cautions teens that parents may become unexpectedly irrational. Children are used to their parents knowing better, but in this particular situation the child is the one who knows better. He or she has already explored the issues for a while and perhaps has spoken with a counselor or done some reading, and the parents are the ones with the stereotypes and unexplored emotional attitudes. In a sense the child has been through the problem and has to help the parents get through it.

The parents of homosexual teens often find counseling helpful too. Parents should try not to blame themselves because their child is gay or to blame their son or daughter for being different. Parents who are accepting of a child's homosexuality should avoid urging him or her to come out before the teen is ready. It is important for the youngster to make this discovery on his or her own and to be prepared to take responsibility for that decision. Most teenagers go through a period of confusion about their sexual orientation and need time to find out if they are gay or not. It is always a threatening admission for sons and daughters to make to parents, even when parents encourage them to do so, because children fear that parents might withdraw their love. Acknowledging homosexuality to oneself is also threatening because it involves giving up conventional goals and establishing a whole new identity.

Once parents accept the reality of their child's homosexuality and come to terms with their feelings of hurt and disappointment, they can return their focus to their child and the problems that she or he has to face. The new openness between them can even make it possible for parent and teen to have a better relationship and to express their love for each other in more supportive ways than before. Some parents find that they are no longer angry at their child, but rather at the society that forces their child to live in an atmosphere of hostility and prejudice. They learn to accept their teen's homosexual partner as they would a heterosexual partner and to say to their child, "I love you as you are."

NINE

FALLING IN LOVE AGAIN

Close to fifty percent of all marriages end up in divorce, and the vast majority of divorced men and women remarry within three years of the dissolution of the first marriage. This means that love and marriage are still in style but that there is a frequent "restructuring" of families. Less than a third of the households in this country now are comprised of nuclear families, and most children no longer grow up with both Mom and Dad. Almost half of today's children live with only one parent, who may or may not have a mate staying at the house, and another sizable group of children live with a stepparent and/or stepsiblings and, if those families break up, even with step-step families. Under these circumstances, sexual issues take on new dimensions that did not exist in the family of yesteryear.

When children have to adapt to the absence of one of their biological parents and readapt to the remaining parent taking on a new mate, they tend to develop a heightened awareness of sex, and to feel less secure about love relationships. These children also have to make adjustments to the sexuality of the stepparent and, as is often the case, to that of their new stepsiblings. Of course, relationships in stepfamilies are demanding of the parents too. Remarried parents have to establish new sexual relationships with each other, and to learn, as well, to make accommodations to the sexuality of their new offspring.

In restructured families, sexual feelings tend to be intensified because relationships have not been tempered by years of familiarity, as is the case in nuclear families, and because there is an erosion of the incest taboo. How will a new stepfather feel when his teenage stepdaughter walks around the house, as she always used to do, in her underwear? What does an adolescent stepsister do when she gets a crush on her stepbrother? How does a boy, who is inclined to be possessive of his mother, feel when he knows that his new stepfather, a comparative stranger, is in bed with her? Along with the weakening of safeguards against acting on sexual feelings that exist in biological families, the seemingly endless variety of sexual life-styles that are now possible makes it even more difficult for all involved to integrate their sexuality into postnuclear families. These new patterns raise new questions: How do the children feel if every so often their divorced father changes his live-in companion? And how do they feel when a divorced mother brings her lover home and that lover is a woman? In this chapter we will explore some of the new problem situations that arise today when families break up and reshuffle, and how family members try to cope with them. First we will explore how the family is affected when single parents date and then look at the way sexual feelings impact on relationships in stepfamilies.

SEX AND THE SINGLE PARENT

Single parents go through a dating process that resembles their teenagers', but with the tables turned: this time around it is the parents who are being monitored by the children and the parent's sexuality is at issue. At this juncture in their lives, many parents find their own sexual attitudes coming home to roost. Sex Expressive parents have the easiest time of it. Their children expect and welcome new parental sexual involvements as a sign that their mothers and fathers are once again enjoying a full life. Sex Repressive and Sex Avoidant parents will probably find that their children do not take kindly to seeing them becoming sexually involved, and their dating can become a potentially disruptive force at home. Children who have been raised to feel that sex should be kept out of the family resent their parents becoming overtly sexual and, when that happens, children can also become resentful of what they consider the hypocritical attitude that sex is OK for the parent but not for them.

Children of newly single parents can feel threatened by a parent's date when he or she is seen as trying to horn in on the family. After a marital breakup, children usually become more dependent on the parent they live with and fearful of losing that parent too. Thus they tend to be jealously protective of that parent and suspicious of newcomers who might threaten the delicate family balance by making demands on the parent's attention. Sexual intimacy between a parent and a newcomer is doubly disturbing because the exclusivity of the sexual relationship reinforces the offspring's worst fears. Moments that a parent shares with a lover can make the child feel like an unwanted interloper.

Establishing a new sexual relationship after a marital breakup is an unequal opportunity situation for mothers and fathers. For one, it is generally the mother who retains custody of the children and the father who sets up a new residence; when dating, mothers not only have to make baby-sitting arrangements for young children and account for their time to older children, but they also have to be more cautious because of the impact dating can have on their offspring. A common pattern among mothers is to date only when the children are away, visiting the father for example, or when they themselves are away, as on a trip. This way the lover is kept from the children until the relationship looks like it might be a permanent one. Mothers who follow this course see it as a way of protecting the children from having to endure additional separations if the relationships end.

Another difference in dating behavior between mothers and fathers stems from the traditional double standard, most prevalent in Sex Repressive homes. Mothers, and their offspring as well, tend to be much less accepting of a mother's sexual flings than they are of a father's. Mothers, therefore, are likely to approach the dating-remating game with more hesitation than their ex-spouses and to hide their love life from their children. Those single fathers who live with their children tend to have many of the concerns that single mothers do about their children feeling displaced or jealous of the lover, but with one major difference: they are not generally perturbed about the sexual aspects of the relationship. Fathers take it for granted that it is all right for them to have sexual liaisons and they expect their children to live with this idea. According to Roger, who has custody of his nine-year-old son, David:

≈§ When I'm dating a woman and she is compatible, I try to bring her home as much as possible so that I don't leave David alone too much. Most of my friends go out more—to restaurants, to the movies—but they don't have a kid living with them like I do. I sometimes make dinner at home and rent a movie for the VCR and have a home-date so I don't have to leave David with the housekeeper. More than one woman has slept over and David knows that. I don't think it is necessary to hide that. He has asked me about it, like do we just sleep together or do we do things together, and I have told him we have sex. He was a little excited about whether that meant he would be having a kid brother, but we got that squared away. I think it's good for him to grow up knowing what life is like. As far as when he visits his mother, what she does is up to her. I'm pretty sure she has guys sleep over, and if she wants them to stay when David is visiting, that's OK by me. I have no problem with that. From what David has told me, they are always alone together, but maybe she wants it that way because they do not see each other often. ે≈

Fathers' assumption that it is acceptable for them to have a sex life is, indeed, correct, because people in general and their children in particular do not react as critically to single fathers as to single mothers having relationships. When children do become critical about a single father's sexual relationship, they are as apt to react negatively to their father's female friend as to their father. Negative feelings towards the father usually center on his absence from the family rather than on his sexual behavior per se. Frank's teenage daughters resent his departure from home but see his live-in companion, Diana, as the sexual villain. According to Diana, when Frank's daughters come for the weekend they are accepting of their father but condemnatory of her. What's sauce for the gander is hot water for the goose:

≈§ When Frank and I first met we were both married. His marriage was not a good one when we met. We dated for a while and then my marriage was annulled and he had a divorce, but I am looked on as the one who broke up his marriage. His children had no real idea. He was invested in letting them believe that he and their mother had a wonderful relationship and that everything was la-di-da. I don't think he ever let on that when he didn't come home at night, it wasn't because he was working so hard. It never occurred to them at any point until I came on the scene that he had a very bad marriage. They were totally unaware of the fact that he had other lovers before we met, and I am still the woman who broke up the marriage. The girls reacted very negatively to me—that goes without saying—extremely negative. There is still this constant wall of hostility between us. Innuendos all the time and nasty cracks. Recently Frank was talking to the girls about relationships because he believes the girls should be informed, and they were talking about the difference between fucking and making love and I heard them, and when he got up to answer the telephone they started to whisper and giggle and get hostile. They spoke in stage whispers and said, "I wonder if Diana was fucking or making love." They whisper like that all the time. Not so long ago, on a weekend when they were here, they had all gone to the movies in the afternoon and Frank and I were upstairs, and they came in and didn't see us and they yelled, "Is anybody home?" and Frank yelled down, "We're here." And then Angelica said, "Where are you? What's doing? Come on down!" And Frank said, "No, we're in the bathtub together," and then she yelled up, "Diana, what kind of woman are you?" It could have been just a cute comment, but I think it was a double-edged sort, and I yelled down, "I'm the worst kind around," and her father added, "That's why I love her." ॐ

Mothers, like their children and ex-husbands, also take it for granted that divorced fathers have sexual liaisons, but they still tend to feel that what is all right for men is not all right for women. They hide their sex life from their children and do not let their lovers sleep over, in order to protect the children, but part of what they are protecting them from is that fact that their mother is sexual.

At heart, many mothers, because of their own Sex Repressive or Sex Avoidant upbringing, feel guilty about having postmarital sex and, although this does not stop them, they keep their "transgression" from the children. These parents tend to rationalize their behavior on the basis that they, being adults, can handle temporary sexual liaisons, while their children are too immature to deal with these situations and should not be given any such examples to follow. Vanessa, a single mother of a teenage boy and a preteen daughter, has sexual relationships even though she feels that it is wrong and wants to shield her children from seeing her doing the things she cautions them against:

◆§ I have sex, but it doesn't please me because I still believe it is wrong to have sex without being married. I try to avoid it, but you can't always and I like it tremendously. I like it very, very much, and most of my life I'm trying not to. A lot of my girlfriends say, "Get married and that will solve your problem," but I don't feel that I could put up with a man just to be married. I do have a lot of moral standards and I do believe in God. Sometimes I just say it must be very sweet to be able to just want to be with somebody and do it—just not to think about it, but enjoy it. But I start to have problems. I don't have sex that often and I don't do it around the children. I don't want to set a bad example and I don't want them to be upset. My son was very upset when his father left. Then he was upset that his sister's father left, because he thought of him as a father. It has caused a lot of problems, but there is nothing I can do about it now except not to make it worse. My daughter knows that my present boyfriend will come by some time and we sit and talk for a while before we go out, but that's all she knows. My son knows a bit more and sometimes acts like a spy. §◆

More often, mothers' conflict about sexuality is that they *think* it is OK to have sex, but they don't *feel* it's OK to have sex. In other words, they have a Sex Expressive head and a Sex Avoidant heart. These mothers also are not likely to bring their lovers home for sleep-overs, but they are hard pressed to make a logical case for their hesitation. Ann

Marie, who tries to be Sex Expressive, was open about her sexual relationships when her children were younger, but is reticent about her sexuality now that she has her teenage son living at home with her:

❧ I wanted to be different from the way my parents were and I wanted my kids to feel comfortable and free about their sexuality. But I think if I had to do it over again as a single woman, I would be more careful in that I probably wouldn't have exposed as much as I did about the men I was sexually involved with. I slept with several people at home. I wouldn't sleep with anyone in the house unless it was somebody I was involved with, but when I look back, I think it was too many men. Maybe the kids would say that is the way they live and it is OK. The man I'm sleeping with doesn't stay over in my house overnight, because my son is sleeping here. When my kids were little I did it, but I think if I had to do it over again, I wouldn't do it. I'm so aware now of how aware children are of their parents' sexuality when they are in a situation like I'm in, and that because they didn't ask questions or didn't seem that interested I just assumed that they weren't affected by what I was doing. But now I think they were affected by it very much.

I'm continuing doing what I'm doing—being sexual—but I don't have to do it right here. I'm not putting it on them and I don't think I'm projecting because I'm comfortable with my own sexuality, but when it comes to the kids, now I'm protective of them. If they want to see me as a sexual person, they have the opportunity to do so because they've seen my life-style. But maybe I'm not supposed to be sexual to them at this point. They are supposed to be sexual, but not Mommy. It has something to do with my self-image as a mother and keeping that separate. It does have to do with them being more grown-up now. ❧

Jeanette is another otherwise Sex Expressive mother who is torn between her natural desires to have sexual relationships and her resistance to acknowledging this need to her two sons:

✒ They see men come, but not the men I sleep with, never here. I do not want them to know I have a sexual relationship. Absolutely not! There is a difference between their father and me. They see women there with him, but it is not necessary here. If it is not a serious relationship, there is no reason that I start to bring men here. It hasn't happened yet that it has been serious. It is different with their father. He is more free, more relaxed, it is more accepted. I see men when the boys are away. I don't worry about whether they are uncomfortable about it. It is *I* who is not comfortable. It is not necessary. For two months I am by myself every year. I don't think it's because I don't want them to see I have a man, but it hasn't happened that I have had a serious affair. That is just my personality and I do not feel comfortable to do something like that. ✒

For many women, the conflict is exacerbated if they have sons. Mothers can more easily acknowledge their sexuality to their daughters than they can to their sons because they sense daughters are more in tune with their basic feelings about sex. They fear their sons' disapproval not only because of sexual possessiveness but because sons tend to equate their mother's sexual activity with her being used as a sexual object.

Acknowledging her sexuality by having a lover can classify a mother as "that kind of woman" in the eyes of her sons, and perhaps also in the eyes of his peers. A few mothers who have live-in companions told us that their sons were taunted at school by friends who called their mothers "whores" or the like. For this reason, mothers who are comfortable about having an ongoing relationship often do not want their sons to see them involved with men on a casual basis. Even some Sex Expressive mothers shy away from acknowledging that they have casual lovers. Faith, for instance, who has no qualms about semipermanent affairs, has kept her other affairs private:

✒ I was very aware that I didn't want transient men walking through this house for Joey to see. I had alternate weekends with his father, so there was plenty of time for me to make arrangements for relationships, but it wasn't going to be on weekends that Joey was here. The feeling was—some of it was ego on my part—I didn't want him to think badly about me, and yet I had needs I wanted taken care of. I just thought, let me give him the foundation and then when he's old enough he can work out his own relationships. There was no way I could say to a four-year-old, "I need to have men in my life, I need to be in bed with them, deal with it!" And I knew that it would not be a major inconvenience with the alternating weekends and that I could do it. As soon as I thought a relationship was developing into something comfortable, I didn't feel as if I had to hide it or quickly jump out of bed in the morning before he was up. There's been some name-calling, and he'll say to me that "So-and-so called you a whore," or something like that. And I asked him, "Well, how do you feel about it?" And he says, "A lot of parents are divorced, but I don't think you are a whore." And I said, "If you have a problem with it, we'll talk about it." That was a few years ago. I don't know if he knew what the word meant when he said it. ஒ

When parents do not observe boundaries and involve their children too directly in their sexual affairs, it can have disastrous consequences. Not infrequently, parents who were Sex Repressive or Sex Avoidant while married become Sex Obsessive when they divorce. They may want to "make up for lost time" or show up the ex-spouse, but they often end up hurting their children, who are totally unprepared for this sudden reversal. In Rebecca's situation, both her mother and her father became Sex Obsessive, but Rebecca and her sister, Francine, were more affected by their mother's behavior. Not only was she, as a female, their role model, but her behavior was more out of line with the sexist attitudes with which they had been raised and with what had previously taken place in their home. Following their parents' example, Rebecca and Francine also got sexually involved, but over their heads. It affected Francine so badly that she required psychiatric hospitalization, and Rebecca came to us for psychotherapy because of her own intense feelings and fear that she might go over the edge too. Their parents' sexuality was seemingly nonexistent during the marriage, but it hit the girls with a vengeance after the divorce. When Francine and Rebecca visited their father in his new apartment, he would have his women friends there and be blatantly sexual. Their mother had her own flings at home with a series of lovers. Both sisters had a hard time seeing their parents behaving in ways that they had come to regard as unacceptable. They also took away from this the notion that one's worth as a woman is measured by the number of sexual liaisons one has. Francine let herself be swept into sexual adventures she was not ready for, and Rebecca, though not as vulnerable in her sexual encounters, nevertheless felt compromised by her mother's behavior and lost her self-respect. Rebecca is only now beginning to look at the role that her father has played in her negative feelings about herself and her sexuality. Here is the situation as summed up by Rebecca:

◄§ After Dad moved out, my mother started dating right away. She made no bones about it and brought her boy-friends home to sleep with her. Usually she would act very nonchalant about it. They would come home and sit in the living room, have a glass of wine, and she would make a big display of introducing us and trying to make it a four-way conversation and show him how interested she was with what we were doing. Often the guys would sit there with their arms around her or put their fingers through her hair. She has this long dark hair that she is very proud of. And she would smile and give them a suggestive look, and pretty soon she would say good-night to us and disappear into the bedroom. Just like that. At first Francine and I both tried to act real cool about it. We would ask in the morning how he was and my mother would tell us, and we thought it was all very grown-up. Then Francine started to have her boyfriend sleep over and my mother never said anything about it, except that she would try to be very blasé and sometimes make these sexual cracks to Francie's boyfriend that she thought were very clever. Francine accused mother of coming on to her boyfriend, and she got into a fight with her boyfriend and they broke up. Francie got very depressed after that and felt she was unattractive and that nobody else would ask her out. She also started to get very flirtatious with mother's boyfriend. This one man, Greg, was into showing off his body, and he would walk out from the bedroom into the bathroom with nothing on, and Francie would usually have to go to the bathroom just at that minute and they would meet in the hall. That got mother very jealous and she acted just like Francie, but then Greg would cool her down. Greg became a semipermanent fixture in the house and in the mornings when my mother left for work, Greg started to sleep late and Francie would stay home from school just to be with him. They never told mother about that. Pretty soon Greg and Francie started to have sex together, and I still don't know exactly what happened, but it just blew Francie's mind. I think maybe he thought she was more sexually sophisticated than she really was or that he tried to do things to her that she didn't want. She would never tell me about what happened, but she had a nervous breakdown. She couldn't go to school and was very depressed, and she started screaming at my mother, calling her "whore" and "bitch" and things like that. She went to a sanitarium for four months. When she got out, she wanted to live with Dad but mother wouldn't allow it so she came back home, but they are not on good terms. Francie blames mother for what happened to her and Greg, and I agree with her. I think mother should have exercised more self-control. She is supposed to set an example for us. Instead she set us both up. ❧

Children not only react to their parents being sexually involved but also feel strongly about whom their parents are seeing. Because they are still dependent on their parents, children are easily threatened by any vulnerability they sense in a parent and are highly critical, therefore, of any relationship in which they sense their parent is a weak partner. They need their parents to be strong both in order to protect them and to serve as role models to emulate. When a parent dates a person whom the child does not respect, the child also loses respect for the parent and becomes angry at both the parent and the partner. It is not the parent's sexuality but the parent's weakness that upsets the child. Timothy, for example, a worldly eighteen-year-old who was brought up in a Sex Expressive home and now lives with his divorced mother and sixteen-year-old brother, does not mind his mother having sexual encounters, but he is distressed by seeing her vulnerability vis-à-vis her lovers:

๛ There are certain guys that I look at and I say to myself, "You're not good enough to be with my Mom." There was one guy she saw who was kind of weird, and he was much younger than she is and that really bothered me. I thought, how could she even think of seeing this guy? I was afraid people would look at him and laugh, so how could she be attracted to him? I couldn't figure that out. Every now and then, my Mom goes on this kick and she'll say, "I just need to be loved and I need to be with somebody," but then she'll go with such weird guys. There were a couple of guys that I really would have just liked to knock their heads in, like this one who slept with my mother just because he wanted to sleep with her, just for the hell of it, and maybe so he could laugh at her. He was a real jerk and a loudmouth. Sometimes I tell myself it's OK, and it's her right, but it's just like I still have to face my friends and that is really hard for me to deal with. ๛

Timothy was upset at his mother's poor choice of companions, but we have also seen children upset by their father's unsuitable mates. Sons and daughters will complain, for example, that their father is making a fool of himself by dating some woman who is after him for his money or his connections. Fathers frequently run into criticism for dating women who are much younger than they are. Mothers usually date men who are older than themselves, which their children approve of, but fathers sometimes date women so young that they are closer in age to the children than the former wife. For daughters this may exacerbate the feelings of abandonment and for sons it may induce ambivalent feelings—arousing both envious competitiveness and contempt. In Jeanette's situation, her ex-husband's predilection for younger women not only gets him in trouble with her sons but has its repercussions on Jeanette too:

◄§ When the boys are together with him, it gets very competitive. Their father is very competitive with them. The way he dresses—all the "in" clothes the boys wear. And they compete with their father. There's something wrong there. Then they see him with his girlfriends. Always young girlfriends. The boys feel embarrassed to go out to dinner together, because the waiter thinks it is their sister or their date. I think the sex is natural and the children accept that. But when they come home from the weekend, they get annoyed with me too. They tell me how to dress, they say, "You know, you're not well dressed." They want me to dress like the fifteen-year-old girls they are going with and the girls their father goes with. So they criticize me and tell me I'm old-fashioned. So it is sexual that they don't like me the way I am. They get that from their father because he sees much younger women and is very much involved with them. So the boys compare. I think they feel if I were more female and made myself more beautiful, maybe their father would come back. §►

When children have been brought up in a Sex Expressive home and a parent dates someone whom the children see as suitable, they more often than not welcome the partner as a source of happiness for the parent. Monica, now in her twenties and engaged, reflected with pleasure on her mother's first male companion after the end of a stormy marriage. For Monica, her mother's dating was an important indicator that a relationship can bring joy as well as turmoil:

◄§ Before my parents divorced, it was awful at home. My mother and father were constantly fighting. My sisters and I swore we would never get married and had these fantasies about how when we grew up we would all buy a house together and have each other and not need anybody else. My mom used to tell us we would change our minds and marry, but we told her, "Never."

After a while Mom met this man called Norman, who owned a stationery store where she used to stop at lunchtime. They got very friendly and he asked her out. Mom wasn't sure at first what to do. She wanted to go with him, but she was worried about how we would feel. . . . They went to the movies a couple of times, and then she invited him home to dinner for us to meet. It was funny seeing Mom with him, like she was on a date. Norman was very nice to her, a real gentleman. They dated for quite a while, and he even used to sleep over sometimes on the weekend. He didn't stay too long at our house because he had two young sons at home and didn't like to leave them too much. He had his mother living with him to take care of the boys, but he still felt that he should be around. . . . He wanted to marry Mom, but she didn't want to. She didn't want to get involved with taking care of young boys and wasn't sure how things would work out with Norman's mother. She said he was a nice companion and she loved to be with him, but she wasn't ready to get married again, and at any rate not to Norman. We were kind of sad that she didn't marry him, because he took such good care of her and really loved her. ঌ

In Leslie's situation, too, the fact that a divorced parent is having a sexual relationship (in this case her ex-husband) is helpful rather than harmful to the children. Leslie ended her marriage seven years ago because of many differences with her husband, only one of which was his sexist attitudes, which are in sharp contrast to her own Sex Expressive sentiments. The children (four teenagers, two girls and two boys) visit their father on occasion and find it more pleasant to be with him when he is with his companion than when he is by himself. They accept both parents' sexuality, and their only complaint is that their father is hypocritical in his sexual standards:

ঌ I don't think their father's sexual relationship is much of an issue for the kids, and I was relieved that he was involved with someone so he would leave me alone. I think on some level he was very lonely because I had the kids, so I found it reassuring that he was occupied with her and didn't bother us. She's nice to the kids, and they like her. He's talked about marrying her but then he says he won't, but I don't think they see anything wrong with it at all. The only time it has bothered the kids is when he preaches to the girls about morality. Jennifer has gotten very angry with him when he accused her of being immoral because he thought she was having sex with her boyfriend. When she asked him about his living with a woman to whom he is not married, he answered her that when he goes to her parents' house they sleep in different rooms, and that you have to go with society's rules. He's also told her it's OK if men are sexually involved but girls shouldn't be. They are very fed up with his inconsistency. The kids are after me to date and go out more, but I've told them I haven't found the right guy yet. They've threatened that if I don't find somebody soon, they are going to fix me up themselves. &

WHEN PARENTS COME OUT OF THE CLOSET

Realignments in family relationships after marital break-ups are not easy for children under any circumstances, but they become particularly difficult when the breakup occurs because one of the parents wants to pursue a homosexual life-style. Depending on how the parents handle the separation, the children either have to adjust to the departing parent's homosexuality or learn to live with the remaining parent's homosexuality.

Although homosexuality is often seen as antithetical to family life, it is not that unusual for homosexuals to marry and have children. Studies show that approximately twenty percent of the acknowledged gay population and about half of the lesbian population have been married at least once, and these figures are thought to be underestimates because not all homosexuals are open about their sexual orientation.*

---

* Alan P. Bell and Martin S. Weinberg, *Homosexualities: A Study of Diversity Among Men and Women* (New York: Touchstone Book, Simon & Schuster, 1978).

About fifty percent of married homosexuals have children, meaning that there are many children who have homosexual parents. Most homosexuals marry for the same reasons that heterosexuals do—because they love their spouse, they want to have children and build a family—but some marry to conceal their sexual orientation or to test their heterosexual responsiveness. A good number of homosexuals, especially women, do not even consider themselves to be homosexual at the time they marry. These marriages tend to be very unhappy and short-lived, usually ending up in divorce and reshuffling of the family. Most typically, a father may leave the family to set up housekeeping with another man instead of another woman, or a mother might bring home a life partner who is a woman.

As we saw before, many people grow up not sure of their sexual orientation. In spite of a pull towards a homosexual life-style, there is also a pull towards traditional family life. If people of uncertain sexual identity marry and are open with their spouse, when they feel confirmed in their homosexuality both partners are better able to deal with that reality and ease the impact of the impending breakup for the children. This is what happened with Gary, a lawyer now in his thirties. Gary experienced a strong homosexual pull from early on but hoped it would resolve itself when he became older. When he was in his teens, he had sexual experiences with boys but also dated girls. Gary spent several years in therapy trying to "get over" his homosexuality and then, with his therapist's encouragement, started living with a woman he had been dating since college. She was aware of his homosexual leaning but willing to accept it, and the two married after knowing each other for several years. During the marriage Gary had affairs with other men, which his wife vaguely knew about, but he continued to have sexual relations with her as well, although he had to drink heavily in order to be able to do so. They had a daughter, whom both adore, but Joanna's presence in and of itself could not alter Gary's homosexuality, and he and his wife eventually decided to divorce. They gave careful consideration to how they would present this information to Joanna, and tried to be as honest as possible with her in explaining the reasons

270

for the separation and the reasons for her father's change in life-style. Gary told us:

◆§ Something very fundamental which my ex-wife and I discussed in great detail when we decided to break up was how we ought to explain why we were breaking up and, after that, my homosexuality. Joanna was two at the time so it was not an immediate concern, but it seemed to us that what we ought to tell her should be part of the decision. What we decided was that if she asked why we broke up we should tell her why: because Daddy loves Mommy very much, but Daddy came to realize he was gay, which means that he would be happier partnered with a man than a woman and sometimes you don't figure that out before you get married but afterwards. And even though both partners care for each other, they frequently elect to dissolve the partnership in pursuit of another one. The second question which ensues from that is how much should Joanna see about my sexuality, and how should that be handled. It was very important to me that my wife and I come to a consensus so that whatever information reached Joanna would be consistent. Again what we decided was that the truth is always the simplest and best route. Joanna is a very bright, perceptive kid, and it seemed clear to us that if we tried to keep anything from her or if she felt that there was anything about my sexuality that I was afraid to have her know or wanted to keep from her, when the eventual moment came when she had to make up her mind about her own view of me, which might happen on its own or because some kid at school said, "Your Daddy is a faggot," or she started dating a guy who found out that I was gay, or wherever that would come from in life—if she felt that there was something about me that I felt ashamed about or not at ease enough about to share with her, then she would in turn feel ashamed of it. If she felt that I was proud to be the way I was and at ease with it, and there was nothing that needed to be hidden, then the odds were that she would have a much better time accepting it on her own. §◆

Not all families work out the problems of a parent's homosexual orientation as well as Gary's family. More often the straight parent will accidentally discover that his or her spouse is homosexual, and the latter may deny the homosexuality even if confronted with the evidence. But according to Stu Gross, founder of the Gay Fathers Forum and himself a gay father, not infrequently the homosexual spouse acts out in such an extreme manner that the denial can no longer work. Once the cat is out of the bag, the straight spouse usually tries to get a promise from the gay spouse not to be sexually active, but such promises are rarely kept. The homosexual spouse is torn between the desire to maintain the marriage and the family and the desire to live the life that feels natural to him or her. And so the cycle repeats itself. The straight spouse discovers that the gay spouse is sexually active again, and is no longer able to ignore what is going on. The anger towards the gay spouse, which has usually built up to a very strong pitch at this point, is not so much based on feelings of rejection on the part of the straight spouse as on the break of trust and being "tricked."

When there is animosity between the parents because of the homosexuality, it does not bode well for the children, just as any parental dissension impacts negatively on them. The straight spouse may heap verbal abuse upon the homosexual parent in front of the children or may dump the entire burden of dealing with this issue on the homosexual parent. Homosexual parents often have great difficulty discussing their homosexuality with their children. Some, with the spouse's connivance, make believe that other factors are responsible for the marital breakup, hoping that the children will not learn the truth or that the truth can be dealt with when the children are older and in a better position to understand what has happened. Such delays are usually a mistake, as the older a child is, the more rather than less difficult it becomes to accept a parent's homosexuality. As children grow up they become focused on their own emergence as full sexual beings, with all that entails, and are less motivated to deal with their parents' problems in this realm. Adolescents who are forming their own sexual identity may also feel very threatened if a parent chooses to come out at that time, as any doubts or fears they might have about their own sexual adequacy can be exacerbated by any deviation from the social norm on the part of their parents. Teenagers also are particularly vulnerable to peer attitudes and worry that their parent's homosexuality will hold them as well as the parent up to ridicule. A bigger problem with withholding information about a parent's homosexuality from a child, however, is the issue of trust, the same issue that creates so much discord between the parents. Children who "find out" later feel betrayed by the parent for not trusting them, and these feelings create a barrier that is hard to overcome.

The dominant fear for the homosexual parent is rejection by the children once they know. Because of this fear, Hal, a homosexual father of two children—a daughter and son now in their twenties—did not come out until after his divorce, and did not tell either of his children about his homosexuality until they brought it up. The first to confront him was his son, who was living with his father and whose suspicions were confirmed when he came home from college for the weekend earlier than expected. This is the way Hal described their encounter:

◄§ I was afraid to tell the kids because I was afraid they would reject me. That was my biggest fear. My son became aware of my homosexuality when he was away at school. I never told him. He sort of deduced it. He turned up at the apartment one morning, and I was seeing someone and my friend was taking a shower. I had actually been thinking about telling my son, so when he showed up early and we sat down, I said to him, "Do you ever wonder what my life is like?" And he said, "Yeah, sometimes I think you are a homosexual." And I said, "You're right. It's true." And in questioning him a little further, I asked him, "Why did you think I was homosexual?" And he said that the wheels started turning when this other friend of mine came to call for me once who was obviously gay. §►

Although Hal's son did not reject him as Hal feared, he was very upset at the news, which came to him at the wrong time in his life, as he was going through crises of his own. As Hal continued:

◆§ It was a very difficult time for him because he was having his own personal kind of turmoil in relation to school and work, and when he became aware of my homosexuality it just threw him for a loop. He said something to me about what kind of role model am I. And he said something about having his own homosexual feelings. He was afraid that he was going to be a homosexual, and he was so distressed, that I didn't know what to do and I handled it wrong and said to him, "Look, if I'm an embarrassment to you and you want me to drop out, I'll just drop out. If you just want to be finished and done with me, that's that. I'll just have to live with that." Apparently it hurt him a great deal when I said that, because he told me that later. ◆∾

Hal's concern about rejection made him too quick to offer to withdraw from his son's life, further threatening the boy's need for close attachment to his father. By the time Hal's daughter confronted him he was better able to deal with it, and she did not appear to be at all troubled by it:

◆§ My daughter was living with my ex-wife, who had remarried, and because there was a man on the scene in that household, I felt afraid I would lose her to him. I didn't tell my daughter, but she figured it out on her own. I was away for the weekend and she had come to stay at my apartment with my son and she asked him point-blank if he knew that I was homosexual, and he said yes. She was asking for information but obviously suspected it because it was a long time that she hadn't seen me with women. She didn't see me with men either, but she didn't see me with women. So he said yes. It happened that I called home to speak to my son and she answered the phone, and she said over the phone, "Dad, I know that you're a homosexual. I know about your homosexuality." And I asked her, "Oh, how do you know that?" And she said she had talked to her brother and she said, "I still love you, you're my father, and the only thing I'm concerned about is why you didn't tell me." I explained to her that I didn't want to add to her own problems, and she seemed to understand.

After we hung up, I was ruminating about the whole situation and what was going on in her mind and how she was feeling about me and if she was going to finally reject me. To tell me I was still the same man and she loved me anyway was a very nice and good thing, but with time passing, I thought maybe she would see things differently, but it turned out that was not the case. But I felt very insecure. I should have known better. She does not seem to have had any problem with it. It is amazing. Occasionally we got out to dinner with a friend of mine and she'll ask me later if it's anybody special in my life, but it has never been the case. It's just been a friend of mine we were going out to dinner with, but she is interested in getting me paired off. ?~

The support Hal received from his daughter is not unusual. Most children continue to love their parent when they find out he or she is gay, but things do not go too smoothly when the other parent is very angry and hostile. These feelings usually communicate themselves to the children, and the homosexual parent's worst fears then may come true. Yolanda's situation is a case in point. Yolanda, who has two children, a son of fifteen and a daughter of seventeen, had been married almost twenty years when it became clear to her that one of the reasons she was so unhappy in her marriage was that she could not find fulfillment with her husband and was drawn to women. This discovery came about through her relationship to a younger woman, Norma, whom she met at a consciousness-raising group. Yolanda told her husband that she wanted a divorce, but she did not tell him about her relationship with Norma, fearing that he would use that information against her to retain custody of the children; she also rationalized that this relationship was irrelevant to her desire to end the marriage, which with or without Norma was no longer viable for her. After the divorce the children stayed with Yolanda, and Norma soon came to live with the family. The children were a bit put off at first at having another person in the house. Yolanda was not explicit about the fact that the two of them were having a sexual relationship, even though they slept in the same bed, and the children did not seem to want to acknowledge that either. Nobody did until Norma made an issue of it, feeling that the children were treating her like a guest who was overstaying her welcome rather than as Yolanda's life partner, which is the way she saw herself. With this announcement, according to Yolanda, things flew apart fast:

ᵉ§ The kids were very upset and started calling me names. "You're just a dyke. My own mother, a butch!" Dreadful things like that. It was impossible to carry on a sensible discussion with them. I told them that this is the way I was and the way I felt and that I expected them to treat me with respect as their mother and as a human being, but they both said they thought it was disgusting and how could they go to school and face their friends after that. They called up their father that night and he asked me to get on the phone. He told me off too, that I was a disgusting bitch, that I had ruined the marriage and had lied to him, even though he suspected me all along because I was always queer, and now I was ruining the kids' lives as well and he would not have them living under the same roof with me anymore. The kids, after he got through with them, didn't want to stay with us, and they packed their overnight bags and left that evening. I figured there was no point in trying to make them stay, and that it would be better for all concerned if they left. They came back sometime the next day while Norma and I were at work and took the rest of their things. I called them after that but they didn't want to talk to me, but I insisted that I wanted to have some report at least once a week, so I arranged with their father that I would call on Sunday, but he would just tell me if everything was OK. This went on for about three months, but one day my daughter called me up and said she wanted to move back in, and I said, "Sure, come whenever you want. I'll be glad to see you and so will Norma." She moved back on that weekend and I waited for her to say something but she didn't, so I decided to leave well enough alone. I didn't ask her any questions and she never brought it up, and we have left it there. I think she just got fed up living with her father. He was never very tuned in to the children and their needs, and she needs more support right now for school and her college applications and she can get that from us. She treats Norma with polite distance, and Norma keeps her cool and doesn't try to get too close, but she is always there to help if asked. Norma thinks she'll get over it one of these days. But as for my son, I don't know. I think his father has poisoned him against me, and it's part of his male thing. The idea that I am in love with Norma threatens him and his sense of his masculinity. He can't understand it has nothing to do with him. It has to do with who I am and what I need. ह़

While the homosexual parent fears rejection, other family members, including the spouse and often the grandparents, may fear that the homosexual parent will somehow corrupt his or her children. One concern is that a homosexual parent will be sexually abusive of the children, but this is not borne out by the facts; sexual abuse of children is largely a heterosexual phenomenon. Another concern is that a homosexual parent will in some way influence the children to become homosexual. Again this is not borne out by statistics. On the contrary, because of their own difficult experiences in growing up as homosexuals, many homosexual parents would prefer that their children be straight. When Hal's son voiced his fears about possible latent homosexuality, Hal said, "I wrote that off to his being upset. That is just something that happens with teenage boys. I didn't tell him anything like that, but that is what I ascribed it to because he is very different than I am. In his early adolescent days he was much more aggressive sexually with women than I ever was. I just knew it was a phase he was going through." It is clear that Hal does not want to entertain the thought that his son might be homosexual. Another gay father, Alan, told us:

ह़ If my son would turn out to be homosexual, I would be sorry about it, but I certainly would accept it. I would be sorry about it because it is just not an easy life. I think that, given the choice, it is better not to be homosexual. Being a homosexual is not easy. I've talked to other homosexuals about it, and they say that given the choice they would prefer to be just what they are, but I hope my son is not gay. &

Because of their own struggle with social nonacceptance, homosexual parents tend to be much more protective of their children's need to express themselves sexually in their own way. As Stu Gross pointed out:

&§ One of the advantages of being gay, I think, is to know that you have to create your own world, and I think that's true for everyone, no matter what your sexuality. You have to create what works for you and what works for your partner. We may be the catalyst for the rest of society to wake up to their own needs. . . . One of the advantages for kids whose parents are gay is that whatever way they are different, they have support. Gay parents are concerned that the kids be themselves and that they be able to be whatever they are capable of. The truth is that if the kids are gay, they can say, "At least my father survived this, so maybe I will too." &

Homosexual parents tend to be sensitive to the impact their own life-style may have on their children and take pains to help them build a healthy identity. Gary, for instance, does not want his homosexuality to undermine his daughter Joanna's feelings about herself as a female who is attractive to the opposite sex. He is careful to let her know that his preference for a male partner in no way lessens his respect for women:

&§ The principal concern I have is that in the time she spends with me, she lives in a gay environment. I have a summer house in the gay community which I share with another gay man who is not a lover but a housemate, and she spends every other weekend out there all summer. I don't hide anything about my sexuality from her. Her resulting view of sexuality, to the extent that I can understand it from what she says, is that adults tend to live in pairs but gender is not a condition of the parent—it can be a man or a woman, or it can be two women. Beyond that she probably understands as much about sexuality as any seven-year-old would. I have concerns about sexuality with respect to her and the gay environment. I want to be certain that she sees enough women during those stretches of time she is with me and sees me relating to enough women so she does not develop apprehension over whether I like women as people and whether I like her because she is a woman or will come to recognize herself as a woman. I make no pretense about having any sexual interest in women. She knows I am gay, and she knows that means I like to be with men as partners, in whatever sense she understands that. She hasn't asked me about the mechanics of sex or anything specific about it. My hunch is that if she were going to ask those questions, she would probably be more likely to ask her mother than me. If she were to ask me, I would explain to her that I like to relate sexually to men, that I find them attractive, and that we share the same kinds of physical processes of hugging and kissing that men and women, and sometimes women and women, do together. ∂∾

PASSIONS IN THE STEPFAMILY

When parents remarry and form stepfamilies, the sexual aspects of their relationship become less of an issue in the permissible context of marriage. Sexual feelings between the stepparents are only part of the package, however, and may be overshadowed by feelings that are aroused between stepparent and stepchildren or between the new stepsiblings.

The same dynamics that exist between fathers and daughters, mothers and sons, sisters and brothers, can hit with a new vengeance when they erupt between stepfather and stepdaughter, stepmother and stepson, stepsister and stepbrother. Fears about incest, and the disgust that many people harbor at their own tendency to become sexually aroused by a person in the family, can be intensified in stepfamilies. Although much of the incest taboo is carried over, in stepfamilies it has more to work against. Sexual feelings may be inflamed by the newness of the attractions, the lack of a common history, and the heightened awareness of sexuality that exists in the family as a result of the new sexual relationship of the stepparents. When the sexual orientation of the parents allows family members to acknowledge their feelings, as in Sex Expressive homes, tensions are dissipated and children do not feel isolated from the family but instead get support from the parents. When the various members of the stepfamily are frightened by their sexual feelings and too guilty about having them, as may happen in Sex Obsessive, Sex Repressive, and Sex Avoidant homes, they often react with defensive hostility or withdrawal. The extreme antagonisms sometimes seen in stepfamilies of one steprelative towards another often mask strong sexual attractions which the new family members may wish to hide from others as well as from themselves.

Not infrequently, problems arise because of a mutual attraction between stepfather and stepdaughter, as was the situation with Robin and her stepfather, Curtis. After Robin's father died, his business associate Curtis took Robin, who was then sixteen, and her mother under his wing. Curtis became a regular visitor at their house, helping out with the paperwork connected with the estate and performing such husbandly functions as hanging up the storm windows. When Curtis and Robin's mother married a year later, he gave up his place and moved in, much to Robin's delight as she had developed a crush on him. It was only afterwards that Robin realized that the sexual chemistry between her and her stepfather was too much for her to handle, and she asked to go to boarding school to escape. This is the way Robin described her predicament:

◄§ I met Curtis when my father was still alive. He would occasionally come to the house or I would see him at my father's office, and I found him glamorous. He is very good-looking and tall, and he always dresses well and has an elegant and very gracious air. After my father died, he was around a lot and very supportive. He also would take us out to dinner and it was always in his Cadillac convertible. He would come with flowers for my mother and candy for me, and he used to talk to me and treat me like a woman, even getting up when I entered the room. I was so pleased that my mother and Curtis were going to get married and thought it was going to be wonderful to have Curtis there all the time. And it was for a while. I don't know exactly what happened, but it just got to be too much after a while. I was always vaguely romantically attracted to Curtis, and it made me feel good, but at some point I realized that I was sexually attracted to him and that he was attracted to me. Nothing ever really happened and nothing ever was said, but it was all there. Sometimes when Curtis knew I was off from school for the day, he would invite me down to his office for lunch. We would go to an elegant restaurant and talk about my school plans and things like that. When we walked to the car he would keep his arm around me to guide me. Always very proper, but at the same time I think we both knew that it wasn't really. He never invited me in my mother's hearing, and we both acted as if it was a very casual thing, when we knew it wasn't. I never told my mother about our meetings, and I knew it would be totally unacceptable to her. It scared me and I really didn't know how to handle it. It scared me because I knew that I couldn't continue to play these games with him and put him off after a certain point, and I was afraid we would become sexually involved. I was also very upset because of my mother, because she did not know and I knew we were both doing something that was betraying her. It really scared me, and I started going out with this boy at school just to be busy and have an excuse to stay away, but I would feel uncomfortable when I got home again. I just wanted out and decided that it would be a good idea to go to boarding school, and that is what happened.

Essentially since then I have not lived at home, because I went to college after boarding school and managed to spend most of my summer vacations away someplace. I don't know what my mother ever thought about it, because it was something we just did not discuss, not me, not Curtis, not my mother. I just could never tell my mother. I think she would be too hurt. She and Curtis seem to get along just fine, and I don't think that he has been involved with anyone else. It was just a fluke with me, I suppose. But I have really become very angry with Curtis about what happened. At the beginning I was just so taken with him, so flattered by his interest, that I never dealt with the fact that he acted in a really abominable way. ॐ

Robin's situation makes it very clear that when the sexual feelings between a stepchild and stepparent are hard to contain, they have the potential for disturbing other relationships in the family as well: Robin was put in the position of lying to her mother in order not to jeopardize her mother's relationship with the stepfather. If the climate in the family was such that these sexual feelings were accepted as natural, they could have been openly acknowledged without threatening anyone. Robin would have been reassured to know that it is not unusual to be attracted to one's stepfather and not a betrayal of one's mother to experience that pull.

Roy, the systems analyst who had problems with his sexually intrusive mother, also had problems with his stepdaughter and wife. When Roy married, he went to live with his wife and Margot, her eight-year-old learning-disabled daughter from a previous marriage. Margot had no recollection of her natural father, who had left the scene when she was less than two, and she was very excited at finally having a daddy in the house. Roy's wife was overprotective of Margot because of her disability, and Roy, with his background as systems analyst, undertook his own highly structured tutorial program for Margot, spending lots of time with her. As she entered puberty, Margot's strong attachment to her stepfather become eroticized and Roy felt that her mother, out of misguided concern for Margot, actually fostered those feelings. Roy was conscious of his own attraction to his stepdaughter, but he had no problem maintaining the boundaries. After his divorce from Margot's mother when Margot was in her late teens, he and Margot kept up a close relationship, and it is still necessary for him to exercise the controls that Margot is not capable of enforcing, in order to protect her:

◄§ I think at certain times I had feelings of arousal towards Margot. And even now when I see her at certain times, those feelings will come up. She has those feelings for me because she sometimes likes to get real close and she'll put her hand on my leg and she gets coy. I think sometimes there's an interest on her part sexually, and she talks about it every once in a while. She told me that she said to her counselor that she and her stepfather are very close and immediately her counselor said, "HOW CLOSE?" And Margot said, "Oh no, no, not that close! I wouldn't let him do anything to me." And my feeling is that she's talking about it and half wishing. That's my interpretation, and I feel that at other times too from bits of conversation. When I was married to her mother, I think at one point her mother decided that Margot would never have any sexual experience, and since she was not too interested sexually, why didn't I transfer my affections to Margot? She felt Margot would be deprived of absolutely everything, including sex, and she wanted me to provide that. That wasn't my imagination. I felt she specifically said I should have sex with Margot. I objected to the whole thing because I didn't think that was right, for one thing, and I wasn't interested in Margot but her mother. I was a little interested in Margot but not in following it up. Maybe her mother noticed and that's why she made the proposal. But it seems to me that although Margot might be attractive, there is no question that there is such a possibility. I wouldn't want to inflict that on her when she was young, and even now when she's twenty-four it's just not right. ◊►

Fortunately for Margot, Roy was able to face up to his own sexual attraction for her, which made it easier to keep those feelings under control. Unfortunately for Roy and his wife, her repressive attitudes towards her own sexuality made her withdraw from her husband and unconsciously encourage her daughter to fill the marital role. These sexual undercurrents eventually led to the breakup of the family.

Turning to stepmother-stepson relationships, we can see the same patterns of disturbing interaction when sexual feelings are aroused, as happened in Evan's situation. When he was seventeen, his parents divorced and he went to live with his father while his two sisters stayed with his mother. Initially, Evan was not upset by the divorce. On the contrary, he was looking forward to the change and setting up housekeeping with his Dad in their own bachelor apartment. Or so he thought. Evan was unaware that his father was involved with a young woman, Valerie, whom he was going to marry as soon as things quieted down. The first time Evan saw Valerie he was totally unprepared. When his father announced he was bringing a girlfriend home, Evan expected to see someone who looked vaguely like his mother. Instead, he saw a young woman not much older than himself who quite took his breath away. After Valerie took up residence as the new stepmother, Evan's immediate attraction faded into hostility towards Valerie and his father, and evoked a great deal of self-doubt in Evan:

◄§ While Dad was still dating Valerie, before they got married, I couldn't help daydream about them being together and his kissing her and things like that, and sometimes I would even imagine him unbuttoning her blouse, but they never went further than that. In my head, anyway. Dad brought her to the house but she never stayed over. He always took her home at night, and he came back home and spent the night at home. I don't know why he didn't stay at her place then or let her stay at our place, but maybe he didn't want Mom to know and have something to make a fuss about. I always liked Valerie a lot, and she went out of her way to be nice to me, and would always ask me about school, and once she offered to help me write an essay I was having trouble with for a social science class on third world nations because she said she was an expert on that from one of her MBA classes. . . . Once they got married it wasn't the same anymore. She was still nice to me, but having her in the house was different. Dad and she acted just like newlyweds and they would go off to bed early. I felt like I was in the way and I didn't want to be there. Especially when they were in the bedroom. I couldn't help but hear them, and they made me feel like I was a Peeping Tom, but I heard them even if I didn't want to. I used to blare the stereo just to drown them out. That didn't work too well, because even though I wouldn't hear them anymore, I just couldn't stop imagining them having sex, and then I'd imagine me having sex with Valerie and I'd masturbate, but I would feel awful afterwards, like I was really screwing around with my father's wife. I got really annoyed too, like he was showing off in front of me and didn't think I had any feelings about it, like I wasn't really enough of a man for it to matter. And Valerie was the same way. She was nice to me, but she ignored me as a person who was somebody with feelings and she treated me like I was only a kid. It was sort of like they were saying sex is fun and sex is great, but you can't have any. 8∾

Evan was too guilty to talk to his father about his feelings and his father was too insensitive to realize that Evan was disturbed about the family situation. The result was that the three continued to live together in an increasingly hostile and distant way.

Forming a stepfamily can lead to troubled feelings between the original family members as well as between the steprelatives. Because the stepparent may be seen as interfering with the special closeness that often develops between a child and the natural parent after a divorce, the child may react with hostility to both the unwanted interloper and the natural parent for breaking up this intimate attachment. Mary Lou lived alone with her teenage son, Wally, for seven years before she remarried. When she did, Wally became nasty to her and to his stepfather, Ralph. Both Ralph and Mary Lou were very upset by Wally's behavior, and the family came to us for therapy to work out this troubling situation. It helped Wally that his mother and stepfather joined him for the therapy sessions and accepted it as a family problem rather than as his problem. Ralph easily realized that Wally's hostility came from his feelings of displacement rather than from personal animosity, and Wally learned how these feelings were being fueled by his jealousy and unmet sexual needs. This is how Mary Lou described the conflicting emotions that were aroused, and their resolution:

❧ My relationship with Wally became very intense, with a lot of anger, and I always thought there was an Oedipal component there. When Ralph moved in after we were married, Wally would start drinking, and then he'd go to his room and it was apparent he was really angry at what had happened. He became a real pain in the neck and was disruptive of our lives, and Ralph became very upset by it all. I told Wally he could see if he could arrange to live with his father if he wanted, or we would try to find another arrangement and I would help him pay the rent, but it became clear that he just couldn't leave me. He started hanging out with a lot of girls, and when he first had sex, he made sure that I knew. He would say things like, "Now I know all about women," "It's so extra special being with Heidi," "I'm having a complete relationship." Cracks like that all the time. It's funny, I did have pangs when he told me that. I remember feeling jealous and sad that I was no longer the woman in his life. I really felt it for a while. And it helped me be more patient with Wally because I felt more what he was going through. Having Heidi helped Wally a lot, but so did therapy. He came to me and told me that talking about how he was acting around the house in therapy made him recognize that he was being selfish and he didn't want to share me with Ralph, and he was sorry for the way he was acting and he wanted me to have a good marriage. ❧

Although Wally initially felt threatened when Ralph arrived on the scene, the strong bond he had with his mother helped him overcome his feelings of displacement. When children do not have the security of a parent's love to fall back on, the arrival of a new stepparent can throw a child into a panic if he or she comes to feel that now it will never be possible to win that love. This is what happened to Claudia. Her mother died when she was young, and her father was not available to her as much as she needed him to be. She felt betrayed when he remarried, and became alienated from him. As she entered adolescence, her heightened longings for a closer relationship with him were frustrated and she found her father showering his attentions on his new wife instead. Though Claudia grew close to her stepmother, who tried to compensate for Claudia's lonely years without mothering, this was not enough to fill the emotional gap left by her father's distancing of himself. As a result, Claudia began to experience deep feelings of rejection:

◄§ Before my mother died, I saw about as much of my father as other kids do. He would come home from work in the evenings and be around part of the weekends. When my mother got sick, he wasn't home very much. He spent a lot of time at the hospital to be with her. She was in the hospital almost a year. Most of the time I was home with this woman who took care of me. Over the summer vacation I went to stay with my grandmother, and my mother died while I was at her house. We drove back home for the funeral and I thought my father and I would stay together at home, but he told me that night he needed to go away for a while and take a vacation too, and that I could finish my vacation at my grandmother's. I felt terribly hurt and deserted, but my grandmother tried to explain how rough things had been for my father and how he needed to rest up and have a change of pace. That summer vacation turned into three years. My father got himself transferred to his company's L.A. office, and he sublet our house and I stayed with my grandmother. When he did come back, he came back to be married and to get me and to start up family life again. I was so happy that we would be together again and I would be back in my own room and see all my old friends again. Dad and Gina moved in first to fix up the house, and I joined them when school was over. That turned into a disaster. Gina had redecorated the house and it was not like I remembered it at all, and when I said they should have left my room alone, Dad yelled at me for being ungrateful when Gina had spent so much time to fix it up for me. He was always afraid I was not polite enough to her or that I did not help her out enough in the house and that I was old enough to take on more responsi- bility if I was old enough to start high school. In the evenings after dinner, he'd always be busy with Gina or they'd go to the movies together or he'd take her visiting to meet old friends. He was so wrapped up in Gina, he made me feel like Cinderella, except that my stepmother was nicer to me than my own father. When we did spend time together, I used to feel like two's company, three's a crowd. After a while it really started to get to me. ঌ

Claudia began losing control over her feelings and started to act out the role of the unwanted daughter she felt herself to be. She became depressed, withdrawn, and even though slender, very concerned about what she saw as her flabbiness. With this came a refusal to eat the meals her stepmother prepared and a self-imposed diet. When Claudia's weight loss became serious, her stepmother and father tried to coax her with specially made dishes, but to no avail. Claudia's eating habits and appearance became the main concern of the family. They took her to the family physician, who warned that Claudia was developing anorexia and referred her to us for psychotherapy. Claudia has painfully come to recognize her rage at being rejected and how she was taking out these feelings on her body. She could see that using her dieting as a way of making herself more appealing to her father and of forcing him to pay attention to her was only doing her physical injury and not healing her hurt feelings.

Sexual undercurrents exist between stepsiblings as well as between stepchildren and stepparents. Often, these attractions come closer to expression because the children involved are not pitted against a parent or encroaching on an existing parental relationship. Siblings in that sense are more available to each other, and the only guilt involved derives from the incest taboo. When the taboo is strong, sexual feelings for stepsiblings are masked, often by horseplay that provides a legitimate avenue for physical expression. Sometimes, though, especially if stepsiblings meet when they are already in their teens, they do not experience each other as siblings and do not feel bound by the incest taboo. This is the situation with Adrienne and her stepbrother Cameron. Adrienne's father and Cameron's mother recently married and moved to a new house to accommodate the combined families, which also include Adrienne's two younger brothers and Cameron's younger sister. Adrienne, who is sixteen, met her stepmother several times when her father was dating, and likes her very much. Similarly, Cameron, who is seventeen, met his stepfather before the wedding and he too was pleased with his new stepparent. The first time all the stepsiblings met was at the wedding and the party that followed it. When Adrienne and Cameron saw each other, there was an immediate attraction between the two. They hit it off exceptionally well, dancing and talking together the whole evening. Two weeks later, after the honeymoon, both families moved in together, and Adrienne and Cameron could hardly wait for this to happen. It was clear to both of them that they had fallen for each other and they wanted to spend all their time together, just like any other adolescents in love. Cameron and Adrienne were initially amused by their situation, and thought it auspicious that they were following in their parents' footsteps, but their parents are dead set against it. Adrienne's stepmother is more outspoken in her objections. The course of events is still unresolved, with feelings running high on both sides. This is the way Adrienne described the family conflict:

⋅§ I think our parents are being narrow-minded about it. They both tell us it has nothing to do with the fact that we are brother and sister, but because we live together. But it doesn't make sense to me, and I think what really bothers them is that they think we are brother and sister. That's not fair to us. We're not blood relatives or anything like that and we never saw each other before in our lives. If we met each other some other way and started dating, it would be perfectly all right, but just because our parents met first they don't want us to have anything to do with each other. My stepmother says that there are lots of guys around and I don't have to go out with Cameron, and the same for him. But she says it's mostly to protect me, because I haven't dated before and I've had no experience so I don't know what I'm getting into. She keeps saying, "Now you think you love each other, but what if your feelings change?" She says that if we got involved with each other and then don't want to be so close to each other or want to see other people, it would be difficult to break it off because we have to live in the same house together. She says, "What if Cameron decides he wants to date someone else and brings a girlfriend home and you get jealous?" She says it could happen the other way around too, but that girls get more upset than boys about these things. She says when you're living together under the same roof you just can't go out together, and that at our age we'll be falling in and out of love and shouldn't complicate our lives. I can see her point, but I think she's making too much of a thing out of it. We could get our feelings hurt if we broke off with other people too. And if you're going steady with somebody at school, you keep bumping into them too, and you see them with their new girlfriends, so what's the difference? My father says it can be hard on the family if we get involved with each other, because then if anything happens he will take my side and my stepmother will take Cameron's side, but I told him then they would be acting immature! I think it bothers them that we are related now, and they think it's like incest. My stepmother has talked about sending Cameron away to boarding school, but he told her he wants to graduate from his school with his class, and besides, when he comes home on vacation it's going to be the same thing and he'll feel the same way about me that he does now. So far Cameron and I haven't done anything so that anybody else outside the family knows how we feel about each other, and we're waiting for our parents to calm down a bit and get used to the idea. &

Adrienne and Cameron's attraction to one another highlights the way sexual feelings can threaten family stability. Both parents are worried, with good reason, that a romantic relationship between their children can create tension and divisiveness in the family which they have just formed. The parents are also right that Cameron and Adrienne could be letting themselves in for future woes by getting involved. But by asking the children to ignore their feelings, they are

290

creating family disharmony rather than family unity. It speaks well of the pre-existing relationships between the parents and their respective children that Adrienne and Cameron have been able to talk about their feelings and desires openly, and it would be helpful for the family if the children are not forced to go underground. If their attraction remains so strong in the face of all the warnings, perhaps the best course is to allow them to go out with each other and be prepared to help them with the heartaches that may ensue.

Another area of potential conflict in the stepfamily is any change in attitudes towards the children's sexual behavior outside the home. If parents remarry when their respective children are quite young, life for the stepfamily is much easier as the new family can start pretty much from scratch. The children grow up as with any other parents, absorbing the family attitudes and adapting to the parental standards. For these children, their relationship with the parent with whom they do not live, and with that parent's new spouse or children, may be more of a complication. Older children may have a more difficult time adapting to stepfamilies than younger siblings, particularly if they have grown up under parental rules and family habits that are quite different from those of the new family, or if they have strong loyalties to the absent parent. When there is a conflict, it is usually better for the stepparent to defer to the natural parent in setting behavioral standards for the children, especially if the stepparent is the stricter of the two. Enforcing new and more restrictive rules for one's stepchildren is not only a difficult task but one bound to create tension in the relationship between stepparent and stepchild. Sometimes, though, it is an unavoidable job. After a divorce and remarriage, it can often happen that children take out their anger about the separation on the custodial parent and behave in rebellious ways, especially sexually. The natural parent, in these circumstances, may feel too guilty to set appropriate limits for the children and needs the stepparent to take the initiative.

So far we have been talking about the bad news for stepfamilies. Now for the good news. In some families, where there is openness about sexual feelings, it is possible for the stepparent to enter the family circle not as a disruptive element but, rather, as an enhancing element. When acknowledgment of feelings and tactful communications are a given, stepfamilies can avoid the disruptive phases and concentrate on enjoying each other. For a good many people, a stepfamily is not second-best but a preferred way of life. Stepchildren are considered an extra benefit rather than an impediment. Childless people who marry a spouse with children may welcome the opportunity to have a family without having to deal with the anxiety about reproduction and genetic accidents, go through the hassle of caring for infants, or disrupt a career. Divorced parents who have lost custody of their own children often prefer to marry into a ready-made family to help ease the pain of separation from their own progeny. And some people, who love having an extended family and lots of children around, relish the idea of having more relatives with whom to share life. Children who have been living with a single parent often look forward to the addition of a new parent or siblings to the house. When sexual feelings between stepparents, stepchildren, or stepsiblings surface in these homes, they are more easily understood as an expression of the full appreciation of each other and usually can be talked about in a nonthreatening way.

When Elsa married, she became stepmother to three children, the oldest being a fourteen-year-old boy named Lenny. She was looking forward to becoming a mother and had read up on stepparenting and talked with friends who were stepparents to help prepare for her new role. When all was not peaches and cream, Elsa took it in stride, realizing that many of the arguments were the result of typical strains and stresses of adjusting to stepfamily life rather than of any shortcomings in her stepmothering. Lenny remained fairly aloof and acted a bit strange at times, but Elsa assumed that it was par for the adolescent course and that he would become more friendly with the passage of time. She did not know until Lenny left a note on her dresser, declaring his passionate feelings for her, that his aloofness was masking a heavy crush. That took Elsa off guard but she did some quick consulting with her friends and source books, and then handled the situation in a very thoughtful way:

⊷ I knew that things like that could happen, but when it happened to me.it did throw me off at first. I wanted to talk it over with my husband, but I had a sense that I should develop my own strategy and not involve him unnecessarily. After all, it was a note to me and why blow it up right away? I called my more experienced friends for advice and the general consensus was "Ignore it and it will go away," although one suggested a direct confrontation and a "cut this stuff out" approach. One friend suggested saying something like "Oh, isn't it nice that we all love each other so much," as if the feelings were asexual. None of that sat well with me because I felt that Lenny was trying to be honest and adult and that I should respond in kind. I didn't want it to be a putdown of him. Then I asked myself, "How do you really feel about this, forgetting about how you feel the perfect stepmother should act?" My real feelings were I was a little embarrassed, like when anybody has strong feelings for you that you have not suspected, but also I was flattered that I could evoke those feelings in Lenny. I do think of myself as attractive, and being attractive to a younger person somehow made me feel very good about myself. I also knew that I had no feelings like that for Lenny, although I did feel a lot better that he liked me and that he wasn't being cool out of dislike. I asked him that night if we could take a walk, and we talked along the way. I told him that I was very flattered that he felt that way about me, and very pleased that he liked me, because I wasn't sure about that before. I told him I liked him a lot too and that I had the same kind of feelings he had for me for his father. Feelings like that are very volatile and can change, and that was one reason his father and mother split up and that was also the reason that I had been married before too. Fortunately we could meet new people and have those feelings all over again. And I told him that I was sure he would find somebody, too, where they hit it off together. We gave each other a hug and walked back home. . . . Lenny was a bit embarrassed about the whole thing, but it helped bring us closer together. He asked me whether I told his father. I told him not yet, that I wanted to talk to him first, but I was sure his father would understand how he felt. ह~

Elsa wanted to acknowledge the feelings and accept them as natural and not lay a guilt trip on Lenny. Once out in the open, his very positive feelings for his stepmother no longer were a source of shame and made it possible for the family to relate in a warmer, guilt-free way.

Tammy is a Sex Expressive mother who has been divorced since her son, Shane, was two years old. She has had a series of relationships and has never attempted to hide the fact that she was sexually involved with her partners, some of whom lived with her and Shane for a while. Tammy is now planning to marry her companion, Russel, much to Shane's delight. He has grown up accepting the role of sexuality in his mother's life, and in his own, and it is not a disturbing issue for him. Instead, he can focus on the benefits that pending family life will bring. Tammy told us:

✑ Shane has never had any problems with the men who lived here. Not as long as they include him and love him. He'll go through this whole thing with me. He's said to me, "All right. I feel jealous sometimes because I want you all the time, but I also know you need time with grown-ups." He's also told me, "I like being a kid and I like being a family." He loves to use the word family. When Shane and I and Russel went to Mexico for two weeks, we were a family to him. He thought it was fun to introduce Russel as his dad. He calls him Russel, but when he introduces him he'll say, "This is my dad." He loves very much to have that family feeling because it includes him. He's dying to have a brother or a sister. He is very excited that that can all really happen now. ह~

As for Russel, he is just as excited, if not more so, about his upcoming family:

✑ When I first met Tammy I wasn't thinking about kids one way or the other. I was into finding the right woman and I like kids so it was never a problem for me that she had one. As it turned out, I think I fell in love with Shane as much as his mother. He's a real super kid, and Tammy did a great job bringing him up. I think part of the reason I am looking forward to having one of our own kids when we get married is so we can make another one as nice as Shane. He has come on vacation with us a couple of times and I get a real charge out of it when people think I am his dad. You never know with kids if they are going to resent you because you are not their father, but we get along real well. My family is not so keen on me marrying a woman with a child from another man, but even my mother has to admit that Shane is a winner. 8

Stepsiblings also frequently find their lives enriched by their relationship, and the warmth of their feelings enables them to appreciate the other's sexuality without being intrusive. Sybil has a stepbrother, Jerry, who is eight years older than she. Their parents were married when Sybil was around five. At first, their relationship was characterized by his protectiveness, but during puberty he became very rough with Sybil, which she nonetheless enjoyed. Now that they are older, the roughhousing has stopped, but Sybil is aware of the strong sexual attraction between them. They both know it is there, but they do not let it get in their way. They consider themselves lucky to have each other and do not want anything to disturb that closeness:

When I was five or six, I was still considered the baby in the house. Jerry could walk into the bathroom when I was in the tub, and I couldn't care less. I would swim with just bottoms, no tops. Everybody in the family knew what my body looked like. I was the baby. I had nothing to show. I used to sleep with my stepbrother all the time. I wouldn't dare go to my sister's room at night because she liked her sleep. I was scared a lot, and I would rather be in Jerry's bed than go to my parents and disturb them. There were times when I woke them up and they took me into their bed, but there was no discussion about me sleeping in Jerry's bed. I've always loved my brother. . . . My brother wasn't physically affectionate; he would torture me. He would rough-house to the point where I was surprised I was not scared. It was an experiment for him. He'd swing me very hard, dangle me, tie my tights at the bottom. He was affectionate in one sense, but he enjoyed torturing me. But I definitely loved it! There wasn't a lot of sitting on the couch and cuddling up.

He's twenty-six now and an executive, and I still adore him to death. We feel that we're one hundred percent related, not stepbrother and stepsister. When I was little he was rough, but now that he's a grown person he's more physically affectionate. He has his own apartment but he comes over to visit me. Sometimes we lie in my bed together and watch TV. He has a girlfriend, but we have never discussed that other than, "How is she?" "She's fine." I've been more open with my brother about my boyfriends than he has with me. I could definitely go for someone like Jerry because he has a great sense of humor, very intelligent, smart, and he's good-looking, like my stepfather. My mother thinks Jerry and I should get married, and I'm not sure if she's joking or not, but I could never do that because I do feel that he's my brother and I do feel that would be incest. Even though he's not related to me, mentally he is. I think of him as my brother, I grew up with him. Someone like him, sure, but not with Jerry. It would be like sleeping with my brother. I could never conceive of myself thinking about a sexual relationship with anyone related to me. It just doesn't seem right, I guess, because society says it's wrong. &

We prefaced this chapter with a few words about the difficulties families face when they are reconstituted in new ways, and then illustrated that point with troublesome situations drawn from a variety of families. Our purpose, of course, is not to dissuade people from regrouping but to alert them to typical problems that may have to be faced along the way. Tensions and conflict are an unavoidable part of life, and our growth as individuals comes not from avoiding difficult situations but in finding ways of responding to changing demands.

That said, how do we go about meeting the new challenges of stepfamilies and beyond? Perhaps the most important caveat to bear in mind is that children are capable of more understanding and mature behavior than we usually give them credit for. They want to know what is going on, they want to be able to express their feelings and have them respected, and they want to be able to share in both the fun and the problems of the family. Your children, and your partner's children, will respond in kind to the way you treat them. When parents remarry, they are not just choosing a spouse but entering a new family constellation. Children are asked to make accommodations to a choice of father and mother that may not be their choice, and parents have to live with children who may not be their choice. The family comes with the territory, however, and will survive best as a family when each individual, adult and child, is respected and given room to grow.

An important part of that growth is the flowering of one's sexuality, which needs as much light and room in a stepfamily as in a natural family. It is helpful for stepfamilies to keep reminding themselves that sexual feelings are a natural part of life and an unavoidable aspect of living together. The more these sexual feelings are accepted and the more everyone in the family can look these feelings in the face and talk about them without shame, the less problematic they will become and the happier the family will be together.

TEN

SEX EDUCATION FOR PARENTS

Through the voices of mothers, fathers, sisters, and brothers, we have seen that sexual feelings are an essential part of all family relationships. Parents set the tone about sexuality at home, but most of them do not find it easy to integrate sexuality into day-to-day family life. When sexual feelings are accepted it makes for warm, spontaneous interactions among family members. When these feelings are denied or shoved aside, it creates a tense atmosphere that leads to antagonism rather than harmony. The way sexual issues are handled at home affects more than the quality of family life; it also affects children's sexual behavior outside the family. Learning how to make a place for sexual feelings in the family is therefore vital, and the crux of what sex education for parents is about.

Since we began work on this book, the issue of sex has moved from an occasional story inside the newspapers to the front pages. Practically every day brings an article on AIDS, abortion, contraception, homosexuality, or teenage pregnancy. Cover stories on sex education and on AIDS have appeared in *Time* and *Newsweek*, as well as in other magazines. The media treatment of sex recognizes it as a public health issue as well as a moral issue. Parents are frightened for their children, and with good reason. Sexual activity no longer ruins one's reputation, but it can ruin one's life. Everyone agrees that the time has come to do something, but there is little agreement on what, exactly, to do.

Part of the difficulty is that sex is generally perceived to be a problem that occurs outside the home and one that has little relationship with the family. As a result we look outside the family for solutions, primarily to sex education programs for children. Sex education has a place in the schools, if only as a safety net for children who have no information or else misinformation on the subject. Particularly with the danger of AIDS and other sexually transmitted diseases, it is important to help young people protect themselves. But people are so caught up in how sex ed should be taught at school that they forget that children's attitudes to sexuality have been set before they even get to school; as far as attitudes are concerned, such courses tend to come too late to do much good. The sex education offered by schools does no more than supplement the powerful sexual value system which is unconsciously transmitted by the family from birth. These basic familial sentiments determine how—and whether—the information conveyed to children in sex ed courses is assimilated. Studies have shown that sex ed courses alone have little effect on views about premarital sex or contraceptive use; attitude and behavior changes occur only when parents are involved.*

When we sat in on sex education courses, we found a lot of embarrassed tittering and whispered asides among the younger children. They come into class already having learned at home that sex is really not something to talk about, and they are therefore not disposed to absorb what they are being told. At the high school level there is a similar embarrassment. The students are unwilling to ask questions or betray too much concern. Boys especially are apt to act in a bored, smart-alecky way, as if they already know everything that's being said, although they are generally less well-informed than the girls in class. Because the impetus in these sex ed classes is the need for prevention and protection, they give sex a bad name. Students are taught that sex is a high-anxiety activity that is associated with unwanted pregnancy or disease, and that they should not place too much trust in their sexual partners. Sometimes teenagers develop so many fears that they deny them altogether; they take the attitude that somebody else is going to get pregnant or get AIDS, but that it isn't going to happen to them and they do not have to take the precautions they are being taught.

Every child needs to be given a realistic assessment of

* Analysis by Mathtech, Inc., of nine sex ed programs around the U.S. studied over a seven-year period, as reported in *Time*, November 24, 1986, p. 56.

what sex involves, but this has to include the positive aspects of sex as well as the dangers. Most sex ed courses do not take this into account. Even when they try, the sense that sex is a loving activity that brings fulfillment cannot be instilled by the sex ed teacher; it is a feeling that can only be generated by the family. This is why it is so important for parents not to shut the subject of sex out of the house and to share pleasure in their children's development as sexual beings. Whether they are aware of it or not, all families have a built-in curriculum for sex ed. We believe that what parents teach can be divided into the four basic programs described in this book: Sex Repressive, Sex Avoidant, Sex Obsessive, and Sex Expressive. As with any other education programs, the way to evaluate their worth is by how well the children master the material and how well they are able to use what they have learned outside the classroom. By this yardstick, there is only one home sex education program that works, namely Sex Expressive. The others need a major overhaul. The way to improve these in-home sex education courses for children is to improve the sex education techniques of parents.

Think of your home as the primary classroom for sex education. The following section may help you evaluate the effectiveness of your family's teaching program.

Sex Repressive Families

1) Educational goals—To teach children that sex is immoral and keep them from becoming sexually active until they marry.

2) Instructional method—Parents hide their sex life; they offer little sex information in the belief that it stimulates experimentation. Instead, children are given cautionary lectures on the evils of sexual activity.

3) Home classroom climate—Children are too intimidated to ask questions; they feel their parents' disapproval if they show curiosity.

4) Effectiveness of educational program—Poor. Children become rebellious, sexually active, often promiscuous, and

have a high rate of teenage pregnancies. Girls do not particularly enjoy sex even though they tend to be more active than many of their peers.

Sex Avoidant Families

1) Educational goals—To teach children that sex is a healthy part of life.

2) Instructional method—Parents hide their sex life. Some parents provide technical information on reproduction as part of the instructional program, but others provide information only on request. Children are taught by example to blush when talking about sex and to change the topic if it comes up.

3) Home classroom climate—Children feel inhibited about asking questions because they sense that sex is a topic to be avoided.

4) Effectiveness of educational program—Poor. Children become resentful, sexually active but guilty about it, and dependent on friends and outside authorities for advice.

Sex Obsessive Families

1) Educational goals—To teach children that sex is an appetite that should be cultivated and satisfied.

2) Instructional method—Parents give their own sexual activity prominence in the family and frequently push sex as a topic of conversation.

3) Home classroom climate—Children feel impelled to follow the parents' behavior and are somewhat frightened.

4) Effectiveness of educational program—Poor. Children became sexually active before they feel comfortable about what they are doing and sometimes are sexually exploited.

Sex Expressive Families

1) Educational goals—To teach children that sex is an enhancing part of life that needs to be responsibly nurtured.

2) Instructional method—Parents are open about their sexuality and discuss the emotional as well as physical aspects of sex.

3) Home classroom climate—Children feel free to raise

questions with parents and comfortable about having sexual interests.

4) Effectiveness of educational program—Good. Children express their sexuality in ways that are comfortable for them. They become aware of the consequences, emotional and otherwise, of what they are doing, and are responsible in their sexual activity.

When we describe Sex Expressive atmospheres that acknowledge the role of sexual feelings in the family, parents are often apprehensive at first: "How are you going to protect children if you teach them it is OK to be sexual?" This is a sentiment we often hear. This anxiety comes from the tendency to equate *being* sexual with *acting* sexual. It's important to stress the distinction: by accepting their children's sexuality, as well as their own, parents who are naturally Sex Expressive, or who learn to be, are able to teach their children how to cherish this part of themselves and treat it in a respectful, responsible manner. A Sex Expressive home atmosphere does not encourage sexual irresponsibility and promiscuity—just the opposite. By keeping the communication lines about sex open, accepting children's sexual needs, and providing a living example of the place sex has in a loving relationship, Sex Expressive parents help their children develop self-regulating attitudes and standards of behavior that include consideration for one's partner as well as for oneself.

To understand how a Sex Expressive home atmosphere accomplishes these ends, a useful parallel can be drawn between attitudes to sex and attitudes to alcohol. There is a movement underway to raise the minimum legal age for drinking so as to reduce accidents caused by teenagers' drunken driving. As the minimum age has been increased from eighteen to twenty-one, highway fatalities have, indeed, decreased among those eighteen to twenty but the rate of fatalities among twenty-one-year-olds has gone up. The restrictive legislation obviously did not teach teenagers not to drink but seems to have postponed their drinking-driving behavior. The way to stop irresponsible drinking is the same way to stop irresponsible sex—by helping young people develop self-regulating attitudes based on self-respect.

When children learn that the sexual part of themselves is good, they respect themselves. When they learn that their sexual feelings are bad, they cannot hold themselves in high esteem or act in a responsible way. Promiscuity and pregnancy often have less to do with the lack of information than with the lack of self-respect. When children are told they are bad because they have sexual feelings, they do not feel good enough about themselves to be able to say "no." Paradoxically, many children cannot say "no," because they were never taught how to say "yes" to something better. If children had a positive example of what a loving sexual relationship is like, they would aspire to that instead of settling for the painful relationships they often have, in which the girls get pregnant and the boys walk away. Parents do not want to talk about sex or make a place for it at home because it makes them uncomfortable, but the aftermath of avoidance is worse. Once a dialogue gets started at home, it clears the air and soon both parents and children feel better about themselves, about each other, and about sex. The job for most of us is overcoming the initial inertia.

It is difficult for parents to communicate an affirmative attitude about sex to their children when the parents are still having trouble accepting the role of sex in their own lives. Most parents, after all, were brought up in Sex Repressive environments themselves and consequently feel uncomfortable about sex. Uncomfortable or not, parents still want to give their children a constructive education about sex, and we would like to give you some pointers on how to go about doing it.

A SEX ED PROGRAM FOR PARENTS

If you feel awkward talking to your children about sex, the best way to psych yourself up is to practice first. By role-playing conversations with your children without them being present, you can rehearse the things you want to talk about, and the way you want to talk about them. Role-playing means going through the whole process as if your children were there, talking out loud, not just in your head. A good way to do this is with a tape recorder. Go to your room, close the door, and start talking. A tape recorder lets you listen back and see how you come across. Maybe you will find your style is too aggressive or too hesitant, or that you say things you don't really mean. If you don't have a tape recorder you can practice with your mate or a friend to get feedback. The advantage of this method is that another person can make the practice session more alive for you by role-playing your child and asking questions.

Practicing conversations out loud helps to defuse the topic of sex and your uncomfortable feelings about it. If you find it hard to talk about certain aspects of sex or to say certain words without blushing or stammering, the process of actually mouthing words and hearing yourself say them will help you feel more matter-of-fact about it. Hearing yourself talk also builds confidence by making you feel more sure of yourself and what you have to say.

General Principles:

Before you begin your conversations, let your children know that you love and accept them, sexual needs and all. They can't get rid of their sexual needs nor do you want them to, but with your help they can learn to modulate them. The more secure your children are in your love, the more receptive they will be to what you have to say, especially things they might not want to hear. Remember also to differentiate between your children's behavior and their feelings. Every child has the right to have his or her feelings respected, and these invariably include natural sexual stirrings and interests. These are not "bad" feelings but a sign that your child is growing into a healthy adult. You certainly do not want to make your child feel guilty about that.

As a parent you have the right and the responsibility to set the standards for sexual behavior, but when you talk to your children, be considerate of their point of view. They may not agree with you about everything, so part of your conversation has to be the readiness to listen. An "I don't want to hear about it" attitude on your part is going to close their ears too. If you are concerned about their behavior, don't make accusations like "What were you doing out so late last night?" Instead, let them know you are worried: "I was feeling anxious last night that you came home so late. I hope everything is OK."

Some issues of sexual behavior may be too critical for you to compromise on. Still, don't lose sight of the ultimate goal, which is to help your children develop attitudes about sex that they will be willing and able to live by. One more thing. Be careful not to become impatient with your children for asking questions—that's a sure-fire way to cut off communications. Some parents feel it is rude for children to ask questions about sex, especially personal questions, and they get angry. Children usually don't ask questions to provoke but because they want information. When parents get annoyed it is usually because they are uncomfortable with the answer, particularly when it involves a question about their own sexual life. If it's hard for you to answer, give it your best effort, and if you're not sure what to say just tell your children you'll get back to them soon when you have thought about it more.

Opening up a Dialogue with Your Children:

If sex is a topic that has been avoided in your home, the first step is to create a climate where it is OK to talk about it. Anyone would feel awkward just announcing, "All right, now we are going to talk about sex." Instead you can make sex a natural part of conversation by picking up on what comes up during the course of the day. For instance, if you are watching TV with your children you will find many instances of sexual interaction and innuendo. Day or evening soaps are chock-full of sex and therefore chock-full of discussion possibilities: "Frank is afraid to tell Jenny he loves her, so she is dating Glen but she really loves Frank. What do you think? How should people talk to each other if they'd like to date?" Or: "Look at how Shane and Kimberly make love just like that. You never see them doing anything about birth control. What would happen in real life? Would they stop to use birth control?"

Suppose you are watching a game show. There are questions to ask there too: "Look at how the contestants are dressed. How come the women are all dressed up and the men are wearing plain suits? What does that say about how men and women feel about each other?" "How come the moderators are usually men, and the assistants usually women? And how come those women usually wear miniskirts or sexy blouses?"

If you are watching the news: "There's been a lot about rape on the news lately. Why is that? What do you think of men who rape women? Why are people afraid to report it?"

You will also have lots of opportunity to initiate discussions on sexual issues when your children are talking about their friends, or when you are talking about your friends. If your kids tell you that so-and-so is going steady, you could ask, "What does it mean to go steady these days? What do kids expect of each other when they go steady? Would you like to go steady?" If you talk about your friends you might say, "Jane is getting married again but she's afraid of how her new husband's son is going to feel about their marriage. He seems to be very angry with her. What do you think is going on with him? I don't know how I'd feel in a situation like that. What about you?"

Talking about sexual issues on a day-to-day conversational basis has a lot of advantages besides announcing your accessibility. It places sex into a context that is broader than just what goes on in a boy-girl relationship. Focusing on sex as an issue rather than asking your child, "What are *you* doing sexually?" will create a less threatening atmosphere and make it easier for you and your kids to talk about sex. This situation will also give you an opportunity to voice your views without giving them a lecture, and by the same token, your child will not feel put on the carpet or feel a need to be defensive.

Answering Your Children's Questions About Sex:
Once your children know that it is not only OK, but that you want them to talk about sex, the questions will start

coming. It's a very good idea to start rehearsing before that happens.

Go into your room, preferably with your tape recorder or with a friend, and practice. Answer every question on the list that follows even if you don't think your child is likely to ask it. You can't really know in advance and, anyhow, you want to develop the confidence to answer any questions that may come up. If you don't like answering a particular question, that is the one you need to practice the most. You can also practice saying, "That's too personal and I don't feel comfortable answering it." There are limits to what you need to answer and you have the right to privacy, as does your child. Whatever your response, though, *don't get angry at your child for asking.* And if you find yourself pleading the right of privacy on too many questions, you probably are not setting the stage for a helpful exchange with your children. For example, if someone at a party asked you, "How often do you and your wife (husband) have sex?" you'd probably react indignantly, feeling the question was presumptuous. If your child asks you, it's almost certainly because it's information he or she needs to understand what the process is all about and to learn its place in his or her own life and that of the family. You may not want to answer specifically—"We do it about X times a week"—but you may want to say, "It depends on what else is going on in our life, but most people have sex . . ."

After you go through our list of questions, you may want to add any others that have already come up in your house or that you think are likely to arise:

- Do you and Daddy (Mommy) have sex? How often do you have sex? What is it like?

- How do you do it? Is your sex life good?

- Do you have orgasms when you have sex?

- How old were you when you had sex the first time? Who did you do it with?

- What was it like? Did you enjoy it? Did you tell your mother or father about it?

- What is oral sex like? Did you ever have oral sex? Do you and Daddy (Mommy) do it together? Should I do it? Can I get herpes or AIDS if I have oral sex?

- When you and Daddy (Mommy) have sex, what kind of contraceptives do you use? What kind do you like best? What kind does Daddy (Mommy) like best?

- How do I know if my penis is a good size? Is it too small? Is it true that all penises are the same size when they are hard? What if I like a girl and my penis gets hard and she sees it?

- Do I have a hymen? Will it hurt when I have intercourse? Can I break it my myself? Do boys make fun of girls if they have a hymen?

- Can I use tampons? If my friends use tampons does that mean they had sex with boys?

- Does anything bad happen to you if you masturbate? Is it good to masturbate? How do boys masturbate? What do they do? How do girls masturbate? What do they do?

- Did you masturbate before you were married? Does Daddy (Mommy) masturbate? Do you ever do it together?

Having Your Own Say:
Dialogue is a two-way street. Let your children know how you feel about sex and how those feelings relate to them. Again, it is always good to let your children know how you feel in the context of day-to-day events, but it is also important occasionally to set aside a special time for conversation with them just about sex. This lets them know that you take their sexual feelings and behavior seriously and that you are concerned about their happiness and safety in this area.

If you are uncomfortable about your upcoming conversation, you can prepare for this too by practicing beforehand. For the first go-through, it might help to prepare a list of points you want to cover. On your list you will probably want to include when you feel it is OK and when it is not OK to have a sexual relationship; the nervousness accompanying the first time; the importance of not being pressured into doing things you do not want to do; how respect for a partner means mutual responsibility for birth control, for health, and for feelings; options about birth control and your recommendations about what to use. You can check back to earlier parts of the book to get the flavor of how such a conversation goes. One of Mary Travers's conversations is described on page 59 and one of Larry's conversations appears on page 112.

Calling All Men:

We would like to add a special word for fathers and sons because they tend to be left out of the sex education process. Fathers usually leave this job to mothers, but it's a job for both parents to undertake with each child. Your children need to know that each parent, regardless of sex, accepts the role of sexuality in his or her child's life. When no words are spoken between father and son the message comes through that boys do not have to take sex seriously.

Boys want to hear what both their mothers and fathers have to say. These conversations are more important for boys because they have more discomfort talking about sex than girls do, and they are less informed about it. Even though sexually active, few of them consider contraception their problem. They see it as a girl's concern. Boys are now becoming interested in condoms because of fear of AIDS, not pregnancy. If boys are to develop more responsible and positive attitudes about sex, then fathers as well as mothers have to take a more active role in communicating them!

Learning by Immersion:

Children learn about sex the same way they learn a language. It comes about naturally through the process of living. Their concepts of what sex is and their attitudes towards their own sexuality are absorbed like vocabulary and grammar. In many homes children do not learn a language that is effective for communicating their sexuality, and therefore they don't have the means to express themselves or define limits. The program we've talked about teaches children a modern language of sex. They learn through immersion—because sexuality is a natural part of the home environment. Language immersion programs are successful because the instruction they offer is not limited to an isolated hour here or there but extends to a total living style. That is what we recommend here. If placed in a learning environment where a new language is consistently spoken, students learn very quickly. If you want to teach your children the language of Sex Expressiveness, set up a program in your home so the family can start communicating in a Sex Expressive manner from the beginning.

HOW TO INTERVIEW YOURSELF

To interview yourself you need about an hour's uninterrupted time, a tape recorder or a friend/relative who can serve as an interviewer, and the interviewing guide that follows on the next pages. The interview is divided into two parts: one section covers attitudes to sex in the family you grew up in, and the second section covers attitudes in your present family. If you want to do the interview at more than one sitting, these two sections are a convenient way to divide it. Try to go through each section as a whole so you don't interrupt the flow. The idea is to evoke memories and highlight patterns in your life that will help you analyze your sexual attitudes and feelings.

The easiest way to do the interview is to have someone ask you the questions. If you do the interview on your own, it helps to make believe you are actually having a conversation with someone and to talk out loud as if that person were really with you. Read the questions and answer them out loud. Having a tape recorder helps because it keeps reminding you to talk and it also lets you listen back to yourself later.

The questions in the interviewing guide are grouped together around particular topics. Instead of reading each question one at a time and answering it, as you would do on a questionnaire, read all the questions under a topic area first before you start talking. Taken as a whole, the questions provide an outline of a conversation around a family sexual issue and give you an idea of what that particular conversation should include. You might want to modify some of the questions to fit your own situation and add questions of your own. Similarly, encourage your interviewer to feel free to add questions as you go along. If you are doing the interview by yourself and having difficulty getting started, don't give up. Read some of the excerpts from other people's interviews that are in the book, and then come back and do your interview again.

SEXUAL ISSUES IN YOUR FAMILY OF BIRTH

Learning About Sex
- How did you first learn about sex? Whom did you learn from?
- Did you feel free to ask questions at home or did you ask outside?
- What did your mother tell you about sex?
- What did your father tell you?
- What conversations do you remember? Did you ask any questions? What were they? Who answered them, and how were they answered?
- Did your parents tell you about reproduction only or did they tell you about the sex act?
- Did they communicate that sex is for pleasure, or only for reproduction?
- What kind of a feeling did your parents give you about sex?

Parents' Sexual Life
- Were you aware of your parents as sexual partners?
- How did you become aware of that—from what they said, how they behaved, or direct observation?
- Were they open about acknowledging their sex life or did they hide it?
- Did you ever ask them anything about their sex life? How did they respond to your questions?
- Did you and your sibling(s) discuss your parents' sex life? What was said?
- What feelings did you have about your parents' sex life?

Exploratory Sex Play
- What experiences of sexual play do you remember?
- Did you play alone or with someone else? With whom?
- Was your sex play done openly or did you hide it? Why was that?
- If you got the message not to engage in exploratory play, how did you get it?
- Did your parents ever "catch" you? How did they react—what was said or done?

315

- In general, what were their attitudes about you exploring your body?

Role Differences at Home
- What did your parents communicate to you about what was suitable behavior for you as a boy or girl?
- If you had an opposite-sex sibling, were you and your sibling(s) allowed the same activities or were different restrictions put on brothers and sisters? How did they differ?
- How were the sexual roles of boys and girls defined?
- What were your feelings about the sex role behavior defined for you?

Relationships with Sibling(s)
- How would you characterize your relationships with your same-sex sibling(s) as compared to your opposite-sex sibling(s)?
- If you had both brothers and sisters, in what ways did you relate differently to them? In what ways the same?
- How open were you with each other about your bodies and sexual interests?
- Did you experiment with each other or play sexual games together?
- Did your parents worry about your play together?
- Did you sleep in the same room? Until what age?
- Did you experience sexual feelings towards your sibling(s)? Which one(s)? Did they to you?
- How were these feelings handled? Were they expressed, spoken about, denied?
- How did you feel about having those feelings?

Attitudes to the Body
- What was your family's attitude to the body? Was the body considered natural and admired, or was it considered provocative and kept hidden?
- When was it OK to be nude, and when not?
- Were there differences among your family members—Who was comfortable with nudity and who was uncomfortable with it?

- Did you know what your parents' bodies looked like? How did you come to see them?
- Did you know what your sibling(s)'s sex organs looked like? How did you come to see them?
- What were your feelings about your body as you were growing up? How did you feel about your body in situations outside the home—in the locker room, at the doctor's office?

Dating
- What was your parents' attitude to your dating? Were they encouraging, discouraging? Did they have different rules for sons and daughters? How did they differ?
- How did your parents feel about you bringing your dates home? Were they pleasant, unpleasant, accepting, nonaccepting? Did they give you privacy to be with your date at home or did they watch over you?

- What preparation did your parents provide for dating and sex?
- What information did they give you on birth control, on what sex is like, about when to have sex?
- What did they tell you about the emotional aspects of sexual relationships, about dealing with peer pressure, about the satisfactions and frustrations of sex?
- Did they prepare you adequately or were they too withholding?

- How did you feel about dating and sex? Were you eager, ambivalent, afraid, guilty?
- To what extent did you follow your parents' rules and advice, and to what extent did you go your own way?
- How did you feel about going along or not going along with them?
- How satisfying were your first sexual experiences?
- Did you discuss them with either of your parents? If not, did you go elsewhere?

- How did your sibling(s) feel about your dating?
- How did you feel about their dating?
- Did you share information, come to each other for advice?

Did you tease each other or act boastfully to each other?

- How did you and your sibling(s) feel about your respective dates? Were you jealous of their interest in another? Were they jealous that way of you?
- At any time would you have wanted to be your sibling's date, or vice versa?
- Did you ever talk about any of these feelings with your siblings?

Relationship with Mother
- How did your mother feel about you as a sexual person? Was she pleased about your sexuality, jealous, angry, seductive?
- On what do you base this? What did she say to you, how did she respond to you, how did she relate to you physically?
- How did you feel about your mother as a sexual person? Did you think she really liked sex and was comfortable with herself that way?
- Did you find your mother sensual and warm?
- Did you ever experience erotic feelings towards your mother?
- When did you notice those feelings and what effect did they have on your relationship? Did you talk about it?

Relationship with Father
- Ask yourself the same questions as above, for your father.

Parental Attitudes
- What were the helpful and unhelpful aspects of your parents' approach to sex in general and your sexuality in particular?
- How consistent were they in conveying their attitudes— did your parents practice what they preached?
- How would you sum up your parents' attitudes to sex? Were they basically accepting of sex, overly involved with sex, evasive about sex, or repressive about sex?

SEXUAL ISSUES IN YOUR FAMILY
This part of the interview covers sexuality from the time you started to make a new family of your own.

Sex and Pregnancy
- What changes were there in your sex habits after you (your wife) became pregnant? What accounts for these changes?
- How did you feel about sex during pregnancy as compared to before?

For Women:
- How did you feel about yourself during pregnancy, your attractiveness, yourself as a mother, your sexuality?

For Men:
- How did you feel about yourself during your wife's pregnancy, yourself as a father, your sexuality?
- How did you feel about your wife's sexuality during pregnancy?

Sexual Life After Children
- How did having a baby at home affect your sexual life? What changes were there in desire, habits, enjoyment?
- How is your sex life now compared to before you had children? Do you feel as free to make love as you want to or do you feel inhibited with the children home?
- How do you handle it when you want to have sex?
- What about having children makes you feel differently about your sex life?

Infancy
  For Mothers:
- Try to recapture what it was like to hold and fondle your children, and describe it. How did it make you feel?
- If you nursed your children, describe that experience. What feelings did it arouse in you? How did it make you feel about yourself sexually?
- Was it different nursing your son(s) than your daughter(s)? What made it different?
- What feelings did you have when you bathed your children: matter-of-fact, warm, protective, sexual?
- How did you feel when your boy babies had erections, when your children touched their genitals? How did you react?

- How did your husband feel about your involvement with your children, nursing them, washing them?
- How did you feel about your husband's involvement with your children?

For Fathers:
- Try to recapture what it was like to hold and fondle your children, and describe it. How did it make you feel?
- Did you participate in bathing, diapering, feeding them?
- Why did you; why didn't you?
- How was it different for you holding your son(s) than your daughter(s) in play, in caretaking?
- How did you feel when your son had an erection? How did you feel when your children touched their genitals?
- Did you have different reactions with your son(s) and daughter(s)? What did you do?
- How did you feel about your wife's handling of your children, her nursing them, fondling them?
- How did this differ for your son(s) and daughter(s)?

Exploratory Sex
- Did you ever notice your children having exploratory sex play?
- How did you feel about that?
- What has happened when you have seen them masturbating, exploring each other's bodies, playing doctor games with their friends?
- How did you react?
- What do you tell your children about these activities?
- What makes you feel that way?

Nudity at Home
- How comfortable or uncomfortable are you about your son(s) and daughter(s) seeing you nude?
- What makes you feel that way?
- Are your children curious about what your body looks like?
- Do your children feel embarrassed about seeing you in the nude or pull back from you?
- Why is that?
- Do you think they find your nudity arousing?
- Is it arousing for you if you see them or if they see you nude?

- How do you feel about seeing your children nude or in any state of undress?
- How have your attitudes changed as your children have grown older?
- How do your children feel about you seeing them nude or only partially dressed?

Sex Education at Home
- Did you introduce sex as a topic of conversation or do you wait for your children to ask questions?
- How do you answer their questions? Do you limit the information or do you give full responses? Do you try to answer all questions or do you brush some aside?
- What kind of language do you use when talking about sex and sexual organs? Do you use juvenile or adult words?
- If your children ask questions do you prefer to talk about it or give them a book to read?
- Do you talk with them about the sex act as well as the mechanics of reproduction?
- Have you discussed problematic areas of sex such as pregnancy, disease, being used by others?
- Do you talk about the gratifying aspects of sex as well as the problems?

- How aware are your children that you have sex?
- How do you feel about them knowing that you are sexual?
- Have they asked you questions about your sex life? What have you told them?
- How do you think your children see you sexually, and how did they form those attitudes?

- What attitudes have you conveyed to your children about sex—that it is bad, a necessary evil, healthy, fulfilling?
- How close do these attitudes come to how you really feel about sex?
- What do you think their attitudes about sex are?
- How are they different from yours?

Family Sexual Feelings
- Have you ever had any sexual feelings towards any of your children?
- Try to recapture those times. What happened—what was it

like? Was it a warm feeling, an uncomfortable feeling, a mixed emotion? Does it make you feel ashamed, or feel good?

- How did that affect your relationship with your child(ren)?
- How about your children—do you think they have sexual stirrings towards you?
- What makes you think that?
- How do you handle those feelings when they come up? Are you pleased, do you try to brush it aside, does it make you angry? Do you acknowledge it or talk about it?
- How about your spouse?
- Does he or she have sexual feelings towards any of your children?
- Is your spouse aware of those feelings?
- Have you talked about it together?
- Does it bother you that your spouse feels that way?
- How do you think the children react to your spouse's feelings?
- Generally speaking, is the climate in your family accepting of sexual feelings or do they tend to be concealed?

Sexual Roles
- How do your attitudes about what is appropriate and inappropriate behavior differ towards your son(s) and your daughter(s)?
- Do you have different standards and expectations for each? Do you feel more comfortable about the sexuality of your son(s) than that of your daughter(s)? What makes you feel this way?
- How do you convey those feelings to your children?

Children's Sexuality
- What are some of the ways in which you have become aware of your children's sexuality: the way they behave with you, your spouse, siblings or other children, adults of the same or opposite sex; their appearance, attitudes, questions?
- How does your children's sexuality make you feel? How pleased or displeased are you? How comfortable are you with the way they are developing sexually?

Children's Dating

- How do you feel about your children's dating? Are you proud, anxious, jealous, unconcerned?
- Do you give them privacy to see their dates at home?
- Do you know about their sexual experiences?
- Do they ask your advice about sex or questions about the sex act, birth control, disease prevention?
- What do you tell your children when they ask you?
- Do you ask them about their sexual interests and activities?
- What do you tell your children in the way of unsolicited advice?

- Do you trust your children's judgements about sex?
- If not, what do they need to become sexually responsible?
- Do you worry about unwanted pregnancy, sexually transmitted diseases, or their being used sexually?
- Are you also concerned about whether or not they can enjoy their sexual activities?
- Do you talk with them about your concerns?
- Do you expect your children to behave sexually as you did when you were growing up, or do you want them to have more freedom, less freedom?
- Do your feelings about what you do and don't want your children to do coincide with what you say your attitudes are?

For Separated and Divorced Parents:

- How do you handle your dating in front of your children?
- How open are you with them about people you see?
- Do your children know when you are having a sexual relationship?
- How do you feel about their knowing that you are sexually active? How much do you want them to know?
- How do your children react to your companions? Are they approving or disapproving of your involvements?
- Why is that?

323

ABOUT THE AUTHORS

Dr. Miriam Ehrenberg and Dr. Otto Ehrenberg are clinical psychologists and practice individual and family psychotherapy in New York City. Miriam Ehrenberg taught psychology at the City University of New York and directed the psychotherapy program at Spence-Chapin Services to Families and Children. Otto Ehrenberg taught graduate psychology at the City University of New York and was a supervisor of psychotherapy at several training institutes. The authors are married and have two grown daughters.